MW01493686

"With thorough research, er
tion to often neglected aspect
Maddock make a notable con .... Life
series. If Whitefield is best kn, ... as a celebrity preacher and, more recently, as
having tolerated slavery, he still provided many insights that lead from 'the new
birth' he so famously preached into mature, enduring Christian existence. This
book explains all that and much more."

Mark Noll, Research Professor of History, Regent College; author, *America's
Book: The Rise and Decline of a Bible Civilization, 1794–1911*

"By all accounts, George Whitefield was one of the greatest, most prolific, most persuasive preachers in evangelical church history. At the heart of his preaching was a
gospel experience that tragically became a Christian cliché and is often neglected
altogether: the necessity of a new spiritual birth to a saving relationship with Jesus
Christ. This accessible yet comprehensive introduction to Whitefield's ministry
and theology helps us to recapture the cruciality of conversion for our own spiritual experience and evangelistic ministries."

Philip Graham Ryken, President, Wheaton College

"Zealous in mission, Christ-centered in doctrine, experiential in piety, peripatetic
in ministry, and fiery in preaching, Whitefield was consumed, for his entire postconversion lifetime, with the inexhaustible riches of Jesus Christ. This masterful
portrait is at once balanced, nuanced, and thoughtful—far from hagiographical,
delightfully historical, and at times painfully human and realistic. May the flaws
and failures of this great (if somewhat complex) evangelist remind us that even
the godliest of men on this side of eternity are far from sinless, yet those flaws too
should point us to the Savior whose gospel he so freely proclaimed. Above all, may
this story of Whitefield's life and doctrine encourage us to pursue what he pursued
with passion—the glory of Christ, the presence and power of the Holy Spirit, the
satisfying smorgasbord that is the means of grace, and a life of vital, heartfelt,
experiential, and *enjoyable* piety."

Joel R. Beeke, Chancellor and Professor of Systematic Theology and
Homiletics, Puritan Reformed Theological Seminary; Pastor, Heritage
Reformed Congregation, Grand Rapids, Michigan

"George Whitefield has been called 'the apostle of the English empire' for his evangelical zeal but also 'God's erring and human instrument.' This book unpacks the
glorious gospel that Whitefield preached so fervently and successfully, yet it doesn't
shy away from the flaws in this celebrity preacher's business methods more clearly
seen from a distance (including an attempt to redeem but still use the institution
of slavery). It both inspires us to live as wholehearted Christians today and rightly
warns us of our own potential pragmatic complicity with fallen prevailing culture."

Lee Gatiss, editor, *The Sermons of George Whitefield*; author, *Living to
Please God*

"Evangelicals must rediscover their identity as evangelists. Other accounts of George Whitefield's life and ministry analyze many strengths and notable weaknesses of the preeminent evangelist of the evangelical movement. This guide offers more—an intimate picture of Whitefield, showing us how to cultivate a relationship with Jesus that can't keep quiet about the gospel."

Sean McGever, Adjunct Professor, Grand Canyon University; author, Born Again and Ownership

"Avoiding 'chronological snobbery,' Schwanda and Maddock's engaging and well-researched biography masterfully summarizes the immense legacy of George Whitefield to today's evangelical church. Whitefield, perhaps the first celebrity evangelist, had his personal flaws and struggles. Yet ultimately his commitment to God's word, his dependence on the Holy Spirit, his evangelical ecumenical mindset, and his desire that sinners like himself discover the new birth in Jesus Christ were used powerfully by God to impact countless people. Read this book and be encouraged to know that God can use you too for his purposes."

Joel Woodruff, President, C. S. Lewis Institute

"Evangelicalism has a rich, complicated, sometimes contradictory history. As one of evangelicalism's founding leaders, George Whitefield too has a rich, complicated, and sometimes contradictory legacy. His life not only is worthy of study in itself but also illuminates the larger history of the movement. To better understand evangelicalism today, one can do no better than to read this probing account of Whitefield's place in his time and ours."

Karen Swallow Prior, author, The Evangelical Imagination: How Stories, Images, and Metaphors Created a Culture in Crisis

"The 'relational glue' of the Great Awakening is how the authors of this fine book describe George Whitefield. And given the central role he played in the revivals of his transatlantic world, it follows that his vision of the Christian life was equally influential and far-reaching, both for good and for ill. What I appreciate in this fresh study of Whitefield is the attention paid not only to the good but also to the bad—specifically, the English preacher's disturbing advocacy of slavery. All in all, this is a helpful guide to Whitefield's theological convictions and key elements of evangelical thought and piety."

Michael A. G. Azad Haykin, Professor of Church History and Biblical Spirituality, The Southern Baptist Theological Seminary

"If you want to understand early American views of Christian spirituality, you would do well to spend time reading Whitefield. He emphasized intimacy with Jesus, the vital importance of evangelism, and the practical side of a distinctive Calvinistic approach to the Protestant faith. This volume nicely captures all of that and so much more. Thankfully, the authors do not romanticize the man, especially as they dive into Whitefield's complex relationship with slavery, but rather offer a nuanced and honest treatment. There is much for us to learn in this book."

Kelly M. Kapic, Professor of Theological Studies, Covenant College

"Tom Schwanda and Ian Maddock have created a lucid introduction to the Christian life—from deadness in sin to sinless perfection in glory—as lived, preached, and journaled by George Whitefield. This book is a treasure of the Christian life given as a thick description in candid illumination. Theology preached, friendships cultivated, and evangelistic sermons printed—all reveal the full humanity and large persona of this great founder of modern evangelicalism. The apt subtitle of this volume, *New Birth to Enjoy God*, reminds us that Whitefield's theology, and the best of ecumenical evangelicalism, is driven by gratitude and joy."

Scott W. Sunquist, President, Gordon-Conwell Theological Seminary

"By examining occasional writings like sermons and letters, Schwanda and Maddock distill Whitefield's understanding of the spiritual life and present to us the abiding themes of Christian experience celebrated in the midst of Whitefield's peripatetic ministry. Along with crisp prose and thoughtful structure, we encounter in this book refreshment and inspiration for our own walks with the Lord."

Rhys Bezzant, Principal, Ridley College, Melbourne

"Writing with clarity and grace, Tom Schwanda and Ian Maddock give us a fresh spiritual biography of the Great Awakening's most renowned evangelist. Without sugarcoating the problematic aspects of George Whitefield's life, they explore the many salutary aspects of his spirituality. This book is a compelling invitation to live a life marked by a new birth, a transformed heart, and sweet communion with God."

Gwenfair Walters Adams, Professor of Church History and Spiritual Formation, Gordon-Conwell Theological Seminary

"Schwanda and Maddock do a tremendous job helping us appreciate the potent spiritual message at the core of Whitefield's ministry, especially his concern for regeneration—new life in Christ. But the authors are more than just cheerleaders. They show us Whitefield in all his complexity to help us learn from his flaws as much as from his virtues."

Bruce Hindmarsh, James M. Houston Professor of Spiritual Theology and Professor of the History of Christianity, Regent College; author, *The Spirit of Early Evangelicalism*

WHITEFIELD

on the Christian Life

THEOLOGIANS ON THE CHRISTIAN LIFE

EDITED BY JUSTIN TAYLOR AND THOMAS KIDD

Grimké on the Christian Life:
Christian Vitality for the Church and World,
Drew Martin

Whitefield on the Christian Life:
New Birth to Enjoy God,
Tom Schwanda and Ian Maddock

EDITED BY STEPHEN J. NICHOLS AND JUSTIN TAYLOR

Augustine on the Christian Life:
Transformed by the Power of God,
Gerald Bray

Bavinck on the Christian Life:
Following Jesus in Faithful Service,
John Bolt

Bonhoeffer on the Christian Life:
From the Cross, for the World,
Stephen J. Nichols

Calvin on the Christian Life:
Glorifying and Enjoying God Forever,
Michael Horton

Edwards on the Christian Life:
Alive to the Beauty of God,
Dane C. Ortlund

Lewis on the Christian Life:
Becoming Truly Human in
the Presence of God,
Joe Rigney

Lloyd-Jones on the Christian Life:
Doctrine and Life as Fuel and Fire,
Jason Meyer

Luther on the Christian Life:
Cross and Freedom,
Carl R. Trueman

Newton on the Christian Life:
To Live Is Christ,
Tony Reinke

Owen on the Christian Life:
Living for the Glory of God in Christ,
Matthew Barrett and
Michael A. G. Haykin

Packer on the Christian Life:
Knowing God in Christ,
Walking by the Spirit,
Sam Storms

Schaeffer on the Christian Life:
Countercultural Spirituality,
William Edgar

Spurgeon on the Christian Life:
Alive in Christ,
Michael Reeves

Stott on the Christian Life:
Between Two Worlds,
Tim Chester

Warfield on the Christian Life:
Living in Light of the Gospel,
Fred G. Zaspel

Wesley on the Christian Life:
The Heart Renewed in Love,
Fred Sanders

WHITEFIELD

on the Christian Life

NEW BIRTH TO ENJOY GOD

TOM SCHWANDA
AND IAN MADDOCK

WHEATON, ILLINOIS

Whitefield on the Christian Life: New Birth to Enjoy God

© 2025 by Tom Schwanda and Ian Maddock

Published by Crossway
          1300 Crescent Street
          Wheaton, Illinois 60187

Cover design: Josh Dennis

Cover image: Richard Solomon Artists, Mark Summers

First printing 2025

Printed in the United States of America

Trade paperback ISBN: 978-1-4335-6604-2
ePub ISBN: 978-1-4335-6607-3
PDF ISBN: 978-1-4335-6605-9

Library of Congress Cataloging-in-Publication Data

Names: Schwanda, Tom, 1950– author. | Maddock, Ian J. (Ian Jules), 1975– author.
Title: Whitefield on the Christian life : new birth to enjoy God / Tom Schwanda and Ian Maddock.
Description: Wheaton, Illinois : Crossway, 2025. | Series: Theologians on the Christian life | Includes bibliographical references and index.
Identifiers: LCCN 2024038801 | ISBN 9781433566042 (trade paperback) | ISBN 9781433566059 (pdf) | ISBN 9781433566073 (epub)
Subjects: LCSH: Whitefield, George, 1714–1770. | Evangelists—Great Britain—Biography. | Evangelists—United States—Biography.
Classification: LCC BX9225.W4 S39 2025 | DDC 269/.2092 [B]—dc23/eng/20241207
LC record available at https://lccn.loc.gov/2024038801

Crossway is a publishing ministry of Good News Publishers.

VP   34   33   32   31   30   29   28   27   26   25
15   14   13   12   11   10   9   8   7   6   5   4   3   2   1

For Tom's children,
Rebecca and Steve,
and for Ian's,
Lachlan, Phoebe, and Silas,
all of whom know the new birth
and enjoy God

CONTENTS

SERIES PREFACE

Some might call us spoiled. We live in an era of significant and substantial resources for Christians on living the Christian life. We have ready access to books, videos, online material, seminars—all in the interest of encouraging us in our daily walk with Christ. The laity, the people in the pew, have access to more information than scholars dreamed of having in previous centuries.

Yet, for all our abundance of resources, we also lack something. We tend to lack the perspectives from the past, perspectives from a different time and place than our own. To put the matter differently, we have so many riches in our current horizon that we tend not to look to the horizons of the past.

That is unfortunate, especially when it comes to learning about and practicing discipleship. It's like owning a mansion and choosing to live in only one room. This series invites you to explore the other rooms.

As we go exploring, we will visit places and times different from our own. We will see different models, approaches, and emphases. This series does not intend for these models to be copied uncritically, and it certainly does not intend to put these figures from the past high upon a pedestal like some race of super-Christians. This series intends, however, to help us in the present listen to the past. We believe there is wisdom in the past twenty centuries of the church, wisdom for living the Christian life.

Justin Taylor and Thomas Kidd

ACKNOWLEDGMENTS

While an author may conceive the ideas for a book in isolation, its development is best shaped by interaction with a community of scholars and colleagues.

We are grateful for the support and counsel of Justin Taylor and Thomas Kidd, editors of the Theologians on the Christian Life series, as well as Steve Nichols, who originally guided this project. Our appreciation is also extended to all the staff of Crossway who assisted in the various phases of the publication and marketing process.

Various themes that eventually found their way into this book were tested at several gatherings of the Evangelical Theological Society. Thank you to all those participants who raised questions to further refine our ideas.

Additionally, we acknowledge the following colleagues, who in some ways stimulated our thinking or suggested resources to assist our writing of this book: Keith Beebe, John Coffey, Geordan Hammond, Michael A. G. Haykin, Bruce Hindmarsh, Digby James, David Ceri Jones, George Marsden, Sean McGever, Alan Morgan, Mark Noll, Mark Olson, Isabel Rivers, Steve Rockwell, John Thomas Scott, Sara Singleton, John Tyson, and Timothy Whelan.

Finally, and most importantly, we thank our wives, Grace and Pam, for their patience and encouragement.

INTRODUCTION

George Whitefield's life as a Christian was dedicated to knowing God and making him known. His transformative personal experience of the new birth in Christ undergirded and propelled a remarkable public preaching ministry that not only transcended denominations and oceans but also attracted listeners from all segments of society. For over three decades, rapt audiences flocked in the thousands to hear him deliver dramatic extemporaneous sermons. Indeed, by the age of twenty-four, as he set sail for North America and the first of many preaching tours of the American colonies, he had already become something of a transatlantic sensation: arguably the first—but by no means the last—evangelical celebrity.

Whitefield might have been relatively singular in his evangelistic focus, but he was by no means a simplistic thinker. While admittedly not a conventional systematic theologian—and this by his own design—he preached and embodied an experiential Calvinism in the Puritan mold. No armchair theologian, he had a lifelong allergic reaction to unapplied and abstract theology, decrying "letter-learned" professing Christians who wrote about the new birth but lacked a corresponding experience of these truths. And yet, at the same time, he was a surprisingly nuanced and dexterous practical theologian willing to expend significant time and energy defending cherished and nonnegotiable Calvinistic convictions in the public arena.

As a veritable "founding father" of this burgeoning movement, Whitefield always instinctively deferred to Scripture as his normative source of religious authority. He found in the pages of the Bible the way to enjoy a true and restored relationship with God by grace through faith in the justifying merits of Jesus alone. On what he understood to be the core and essentially salvific message of Scripture, he once wrote:

> The foundation of God's revealing himself thus to mankind, was our fall
> in *Adam*, and the necessity of our new birth in Christ Jesus. And if we
> search the Scriptures as we ought, we shall find the sum and substance,
> the *Alpha* and *Omega*, the beginning and the end of them, is to lead us to
> a knowledge of these two great truths.[1]

Promoting the gospel of Jesus Christ throughout an itinerant ministry that saw him preach a staggering eighteen thousand sermons—an average of nearly 530 sermons a year from 1736 to 1770—Whitefield was
relentlessly ambitious about proclaiming the gospel to those who had
never recognized their need for salvation and those who needed to mature
deeper in their relationship with Christ. However, at times this ambition
was interpreted by detractors as evidence of an insatiable appetite for self-
promotion and personal advancement, whether financial or reputational.
He cultivated many distinctive practices that continue to find expression
among professing evangelicals today. Of particular note, his evangelistic
entrepreneurialism has helped to normalize, wittingly or otherwise, evangelicalism's fondness for parachurch ministries and seemingly insatiable
receptivity to high-profile, platformed preachers.

Without a doubt, his vocation and self-identity as an evangelist were
tightly bound together. Overflowing from a heart shaped by God's grace,
Whitefield's sermons proclaimed the gospel boldly and passionately, in
that he first devoted himself to cultivating a life of communion with God.
Before calling others to follow Jesus in a life of discipleship, he first sought
to walk intimately with God through the intentional use of the means of
grace and a perennial reliance on the felt presence and experience of the
Holy Spirit. A hunger and thirst for knowing and loving Jesus Christ enabled him to delight in and enjoy God and motivated his desire to serve as
a spiritual guide. In the process, God used him to help usher others into
a deep friendship with God that so characterized his own experience of
walking with Christ.

While he had his share of fallings-out over differing theologies and
ministry philosophies, he was an evangelical ecumenist at heart. He craved
and sought reconciliation wherever possible. Indeed, the wealth of relationships he established and worked hard to maintain not only were conspicuous for their variety but also afford us a glimpse into his expansive

---

[1] Whitefield, "The Duty of Searching the Scriptures," in *Works*, 6:80 (italics in the original).

vision of the Christian life as one to be lived in relationship—not simply with God but also with fellow divine image bearers in all of their theological, demographic, racial, and socioeconomic diversity.

Just as Whitefield encouraged his eighteenth-century contemporaries to journey alongside him in his experience of the Christian life, we too invite readers to encounter George Whitefield in all his complexity. Unavoidably influenced, without being inevitably determined, by the times and places he inhabited—much as we are today—Whitefield embodied contradictions common to many first-generation evangelicals of his day. Most notably, this included his active role in advancing slavery, one of the most ubiquitous features of life in the British Empire. Initially known for his excoriating attacks upon slave masters in the American south for their physical and spiritual maltreatment of slaves, Whitefield would eventually become an enthusiastic advocate for the introduction of slavery into Georgia—and even a slave master himself. While he boldly urged slaves to experience spiritual freedom and, in the process, helped establish the emergence of Black evangelicalism, he never advocated for their physical emancipation—a failure of biblical justice and love that invites us to interrogate the clarity of our own moral vision.

All told, if Jonathan Edwards was evangelicalism's most profound and original theologian, and John Wesley its most able organizer, then Whitefield provided the evangelical community's relational glue: his seemingly ceaseless peripatetic ministry lifestyle, intricate and widespread correspondence networks, and publishing ventures were instrumental in creating a unified sense of transatlantic evangelical fellowship. It is to George Whitefield's experience of the Christian life as one to be lived in enjoyment of God that we introduce you now.

ABBREVIATIONS

Names of nearly all recipients of Whitefield's letters cited in the footnotes have been abbreviated by the editors of his *Letters* and *Works* to maintain a degree of privacy. A few also lack first initials. For consistency, we are using a long dash to indicate omitted names or portions of names.

Eighteen Sermons	George Whitefield. *Eighteen Sermons Preached by the Late Rev. George Whitefield, A.M. . . . . Taken Verbatim in Short-Hand, and Faithfully Transcribed by Joseph Gurney: Revised by Andrew Gifford, D.D.* London: Joseph Gurney, 1771.
Journals	George Whitefield. *George Whitefield's Journals.* Edinburgh: Banner of Truth, 1960.
Letters	George Whitefield. *Letters of George Whitefield for the Period 1734 to 1742.* Edinburgh: Banner of Truth, 1976.
Memoirs	John Gillies. *Memoirs of the Life of the Reverend George Whitefield.* London: Edward and Charles Dilly, 1772.
Works	George Whitefield. *The Works of the Reverend George Whitefield. M. A.* Edited by John Gillies. 7 vols. London: Edward and Charles Dilly, 1771–1772.

CHAPTER I

THE NEW BIRTH

Central to George Whitefield's life and ministry was the new birth. In 1769, one year before his death, he recounted a retrospective review of his conversion in which he narrated his struggle to find peace with God. His listeners were reminded that baptism alone does not assure anyone of entering heaven. He vulnerably rehearsed his misguided journey of excessive asceticism that almost killed him and the futility of seeking God solely by external human efforts. He joyfully credited Charles Wesley's gift of *The Life of God in the Soul of Man* by the Scottish minister and professor Henry Scougal (1650–1678), which confronted him with his need to be born again. With a tinge of delight, he then added, "Whenever I go to Oxford, I cannot help running to that place where Jesus Christ first revealed himself to me, and gave the new birth." His frequent return to this specific place illustrates how it served as an Ebenezer for him (1 Sam. 7:12) as he vividly remembered what Jesus Christ did for him, and could do for anyone else. When he concluded his sermon, Whitefield extended God's gracious invitation to the unconverted.[1]

Twenty-nine years earlier, when he had completed his first journal, he expressed the same hope that his conversion narrative would inspire and guide others to discover their same need to be born again. Some readers, he observed, might experience less intense struggles, while others might face even greater obstacles. Regardless, his "hearty prayer" was that "whoever thou art, mayst experience the like and greater blessings."[2] Because of his own experience, he never grew tired of proclaiming the same joy and liberating

---

[1] Whitefield, "All Mens Place," in *Eighteen Sermons*, 345–72, quotation at p. 360.
[2] *Journals*, 70–71, quotation at p. 71.

news of the new birth. How Whitefield discovered this freedom that became the cornerstone of his new life in Christ is the story of this chapter.

Whitefield's Early Life

Whitefield was born on December 16, 1714, in Gloucester, located about 105 miles northwest of London.[3] The youngest of seven children, he was raised in the Bell Inn, owned and operated by his parents. Gloucester's largest inn, it served as the social hub for city life. During his life, inns were the most reputable institutions for providing food, drink, and accommodations. Whitefield became fatherless when only two, and eight years later his mother remarried in what he later described as "an unhappy match."[4] It meant he had a dependable father for only the first two years of his life.

Early in his childhood, Whitefield recognized the corruption of his heart. He was addicted to vulgar language and often stole money from his mother. He recounted using this money to satisfy his "sensual appetite" by buying plays, playing cards, and romance novels. When he compared himself with the young man in the Gospel who claimed that he had kept all God's commandments (Matt. 19:20), Whitefield confessed he had broken every one of them. Starkly aware of his immorality, he also recognized the occasional movements of God's Spirit that reminded him that he was loved by God. Despite his rebellion and degeneracy, Whitefield considered becoming a minister and mimicked the way they prayed. By this time, he was convicted to give the stolen money to the poor or to purchase books of devotion. At twelve he was enrolled in St Mary de Crypt, the local grammar school, and demonstrated an aptitude for speaking and memorizing, and he was given key roles in school plays. Later he regretted, with a sense of embarrassment, being cast in plots that required him to wear girls' clothing.

Before the age of fifteen, Whitefield discontinued his education to assist his mother in managing the Bell Inn. Increasingly his thoughts turned to God, as he read the Bible nightly and composed a few sermons. When he had the unexpected opportunity to attend Oxford University to become a minister, he declared that God had called him "from drawing wine for

---

[3] In 1752 the British Parliament switched from the Julian to the Gregorian calendar, which accounts for Whitefield's later usage of December 27 as his birth date. Thomas S. Kidd, *George Whitefield: America's Spiritual Founding Father* (New Haven, CT: Yale University Press, 2014), 4.
[4] Peter Clark, *The English Alehouse: A Social History, 1200–1830* (London: Longman, 1983), 5–19. Taverns and alehouses were the other two types of institutions. Arnold A. Dallimore, *George Whitefield: The Life and Times of the Great Evangelist of the Eighteenth-Century Revival*, 2 vols. (London: Banner of Truth, 1970, 1980), 1:43; *Journals*, 39.

drunkards, to draw water out of the wells of salvation for the refreshment of His spiritual food." This passionate desire to become a minister was later deleted from his *Journals*, which he revised in 1748, though they were not republished until 1756. Following the release of his first published journal in 1738, he was attacked by critics as well as friends for his perceived immaturity and frequent spiritual glosses.[5] Statements in which he compared himself with biblical persons, including Jesus and Paul, and expressed an immodest sense of himself were eliminated. He also deleted or revised references to impressions of the Holy Spirit, ecstatic encounters with God, and battles with intense temptations from Satan. Additionally, rash judgments made against other Anglican ministers and bishops were purged.

Whitefield's spiritual life continued to oscillate between valleys of spiritual anxiety and mountain peaks of peace with God. Yet his introspective efforts to draw closer to God were soon smothered by Satan's temptations. New hope and encouragement arose when he dreamed that he would see God on Mount Sinai. When he reported this to a woman, she interpreted it as a "call from God."[6]

Social and Spiritual Context

Whitefield's inner anxiety mirrored a similar tension he observed in a society characterized by "drunkenness, debauchery, licentiousness, profanity, Sabbath-breaking, and heterodox beliefs."[7] Born into the Church of England, he was shaped early in life by worship that had lost much of its fervor and often was consumed by external forms devoid of heart engagement. Mark Noll observes that "confident religious life, persuasive preaching of the gospel and effective Christian pastoring were in relatively short supply during the first decades of the eighteenth century."[8]

While many ministers sought to provide pastoral care to their congregations, some devoted more energy to their dinner menus than to their

---

[5] *Journals*, 37–41, quotations at pp. 37, 41. Whitefield began keeping a private journal in 1735, no doubt from John Wesley's urging. While many critics accused Whitefield of self-conceit, Tyerman deemed immaturity, impulsiveness, and defective training the real culprits. Luke Tyerman, *The Life of the Rev. George Whitefield*, 2 vols. (London: Hodder and Stoughton, 1876–1877), 1:45–46.

[6] *Journals*, 41, 43–44, quotation at p. 44.

[7] For a valuable introduction to Whitefield's eighteenth-century context, see Mark A. Noll, *The Rise of Evangelicalism: The Age of Edwards, Whitefield and the Wesleys* (Downers Grove, IL: InterVarsity Press, 2003), 27–49.

[8] W. M. Jacob, "England," in *The Oxford History of Anglicanism*, vol. 2, *Establishment and Empire, 1662–1829*, ed. Jeremy Gregory (Oxford: Oxford University Press, 2017), 111; John Walsh, "Origins of the Evangelical Revival," in *Essays in Modern English Church History*, ed. G. V. Bennett and J. D. Walsh (London: Black, 1966), 139; Noll, *The Rise of Evangelicalism*, 39.

parishioners' souls.[9] For the average British churchgoer, this created a conventional faith, though some laypeople still desired deeper experiences of God.[10] This accounts for the attractiveness of Whitefield's preaching to many dissatisfied worshipers. Additionally, a hunger for devotional literature created a strong market for his *Journals* and sermons.[11] But if some congregations found themselves led by spiritually lethargic ministers, it was equally true that some Anglican clergymen serious about their spiritual duties encountered congregations indifferent to living consistent Christian lives. For example, while some ministers "frequently lectured their parishioners against sin and vice," elsewhere laypeople criticized their ministers as "incompetent" and "poor preachers," whom they "accused of intemperance in drinking."[12]

Deism and the excessive consumption of gin were two of the major challenges faced by the church during Whitefield's time. Deism denied the supernatural nature of Christianity and challenged the integrity of the Bible. It also sought "to replace traditional Christianity with a religion of mere morality and a distant God."[13] Whitefield often warned of the danger of deists in his sermons. He countered their assaults by affirming a personal God revealed by the miracle of the virgin birth and Jesus's resurrection from the dead. Furthermore, the dynamic power of the Holy Spirit—which was central to Whitefield's ministry—assisted him in refuting the limitations of deism.

The gin epidemic—usually dated between 1720 and 1751—afflicted England both socially and morally. Drinking was especially problematic in London and affected every class of people, including ministers. Samuel Johnson (1709–1784), the well-known British biographer and lexicographer, confessed, "A man is never happy in the present, unless he is drunk."[14]

When the popularity of gin subsided, it was due to the price of malt rather than to moral convictions.[15] Sexual morality was at a low ebb, and

---

9 John Walsh and Stephen Taylor, "Introduction: The Church and Anglicanism in the 'Long' Eighteenth Century," in *The Church of England, c. 1698–c. 1833: From Toleration to Tractarianism,* ed. John Walsh, Colin Haydon, and Stephen Taylor (Cambridge: Cambridge University Press, 1993), 13.

10 Jacob, "England," 112.

11 Jacob, "England," 98, 112; Walsh and Taylor, "Introduction," 25.

12 Jeremy Gregory and Jeffrey S. Chamberlain, "National and Local Perspectives on the Church of England in the Long Eighteenth Century," in *The National Church in Local Perspective: The Church of England and the Regions, 1660–1800,* ed. Jeremy Gregory and Jeffrey S. Chamberlain (Woodbridge, UK: Boydell, 2003), 23.

13 Walsh and Taylor "Introduction," 13, 21. For a helpful introduction to deism during Whitefield's time, see Henry D. Rack, *Reasonable Enthusiast: John Wesley and the Rise of Methodism,* 3rd. ed. (London: Epworth, 2002), 30–33; Dallimore, *George Whitefield,* 1:20–24; Noll, *The Rise of Evangelicalism,* 41.

14 James Boswell, *Life of Samuel Johnson,* vol. 2 (Oxford: Oxford University Press, 1817), 483.

15 Paul Langford, *A Polite and Commercial People: England, 1727–1783* (Oxford: Clarendon, 1989), 148–49.

erotic literature and "scatological satire" abounded in the press. A directory of local prostitutes provided a variety of resources for those seeking sexual pleasure.[16] During Whitefield's life, the increase of adultery and fornication disrupted family and public life, and created a greater financial burden to provide for illegitimate children.[17] Isaac Watts (1674–1748), a British minister best known today as a hymn writer, challenged laypeople regarding this immorality: "'Tis time, my friends, when religion is sunk into such universal decay in the nation, to enquire whether we have not suffered it to decay amongst us also, and whether we are not sharers in the common degeneracy."[18]

Whitefield was a keen observer of his surroundings, no doubt sharpened by his awareness of the destructive potential of alcoholic abuse from working in the Bell Inn. He grasped the power of the gospel to transform these social ills. During his initial voyage in 1738 to America, he witnessed the drinking habits of the crew, which prompted his sermon titled "The Heinous Sin of Drunkenness," based on Ephesians 5:18, "Be not drunk with wine, wherein is excess; but be filled with the Spirit." He denounced the "plague of drinking" and claimed that excessive consumption could lead to six sinful outcomes: it abuses God's "good creatures"; it is a sin against the person's own body; it robs a person of reason; it usually leads to other sins, including "horrid incest"; it separates one from the Holy Spirit, and it makes a person unfit to enjoy God in heaven.[19] Whitefield recorded with gratitude the ship captain's response, which affirmed the effectiveness of his sermon and strongly encouraged the crew to heed his warning.[20]

Morality was no better in the American colonies, which Whitefield would visit seven times. During Jonathan Edwards's time at Yale, it had already established a reputation for drinking, which prompted the professors to emphasize piety to reduce immorality. Edwards preached a sermon in 1729 declaring that both the American colonies and Britain had fallen into degeneracy displayed in debauchery and profanity. Bundling was a common New England practice during Edwards's time. It permitted young couples to sleep in the same bed partly clothed but separated by a

16 Roy Porter, *English Society in the Eighteenth Century*, rev. ed. (London: Penguin, 1990), 25, 147, 148, 261; Porter, *London: A Social History* (Cambridge, MA: Harvard University Press, 1994), 171.
17 W. R. Jacob, *Lay People and Religion in the Early Eighteenth Century* (Cambridge: Cambridge University Press, 1996), 143.
18 Isaac Watts, *Humble Attempt toward the Revival of Practical Religion among Christians* (London: E. Matthews, 1731), 288, 292–93.
19 Whitefield, "The Heinous Sin of Drunkenness," in *Works*, 6:303–16, quotations at pp. 304–5, 309.
20 *Journals*, 141–42, 149, 171.

"bundling board." The purpose was to develop relationships without sexual intercourse, though, not surprisingly, premarital sex and pregnancies escalated in New England. Further south, in Pennsylvania, Presbyterian minister Samuel Blair (1712–1751) lamented in 1744 the "dead formality" of the spiritual landscape and that the Christian life "lay a-dying, and ready to expire its last breath of life."[21] This moral landscape of the American colonies and Britain created a hunger for Whitefield's gospel preaching.

Time at Oxford

Amid these swirling social and spiritual anxieties, Whitefield entered Pembroke College at Oxford University as a "servitor" in 1732. John and Charles Wesley's father, Samuel (1662–1735), attended the university under the same provision. It marked Whitefield's humble background and required him to fulfill menial tasks for wealthy students. His training at the Bell Inn had prepared him well for this. These early student days were difficult to navigate as his serious desire to prepare for ministry collided with the corruption of fellow students, not to mention his continued struggle with "playing at cards and reading plays." This inner tension raged within Whitefield's heart until God convicted him during a period of personal fasting, which intensified his desire to pray the Psalms, fast, and receive the Lord's Supper more regularly.[22]

Influence of Anglicanism

Whitefield's spirituality leading up to his conversion was shaped by Anglicanism, Pietism, Puritanism, and the direct experience of the Holy Spirit. These continued to influence him throughout his life, though the degree of their importance varied.[23] The Anglican spirituality of his childhood was his initial formative factor. His eagerness to know God more intimately soon united him to John (1703–1791) and Charles Wesley (1707–1788) and their friends known as the Oxford Methodists. The term *Methodist* was pejorative. Whitefield surmised its origin lay in their "custom of regulating their time, and planning the business of the day every morning," and it became the "re-

---

21 George M. Marsden, *Jonathan Edwards: A Life* (New Haven, CT: Yale University Press, 2003), 102, 130, 296–97, and quoted in Tyerman, *George Whitefield*, 1:322.
22 Rack, *Reasonable Enthusiast*, 63; *Journals*, 45–46, quotation at p. 45. This reference to playing cards was removed in a 1756 journal revision.
23 This section is indebted to Bruce Hindmarsh's analysis, though revised and supplemented with our thoughts. D. Bruce Hindmarsh, *The Spirit of Early Evangelicalism: True Religion in a Modern World* (New York: Oxford University Press, 2018), 15–36.

puted mad way."[24] He soon submitted himself to this same spiritual paradigm, which included morning and evening spiritual disciplines, visiting the sick and prisoners, and providing charity to those in need each day.[25]

While he acknowledged his awareness of *A Serious Call to a Devout and Holy Life* (1728), by William Law (1686–1761), before entering Oxford, Whitefield did not have the money to purchase it until he became a student. Law's *Serious Call* had a profound effect on many evangelical leaders, including the Wesleys, John Newton (1725–1807), and Henry Venn (1725–1797).[26] Whitefield himself confessed, "God worked powerfully upon my soul" through reading *A Serious Call*, as well as Law's "other excellent treatise upon *Christian Perfection*" (1726). This devotional classic was written to awaken a person from superficial piety to a more methodical and integrated holy life through the cultivation of various disciplines, including prayer, fasting, and self-examination. Reading this treatise heightened Whitefield's efforts at praying and singing the Psalms five times a day.[27] During this period, his life resembled that of a monk. Luke Tyerman, Whitefield's prominent nineteenth century biographer, criticized Whitefield's devotional intensity for its "somewhat pharisaic tinge."[28] The expression of Anglican piety in which Whitefield was immersed in his youth knew little of the nature of grace or justification. This theological and spiritual formation eventually led him to a more discerning resistance toward Law.

Whitefield also read *The Imitation of Christ* (ca. 1427), by Thomas à Kempis (1380–1471), which he called a "great delight," before arriving at Oxford.[29] *The Imitation of Christ* ranks as one of the most popular devotional writings in church history, and one source claims 444 different editions were printed just in the seventeenth century.[30] Thomas was a German monk of the Modern Devotion, a movement dedicated to countering the dry scholasticism of his day.[31] Scholasticism was originally a medieval

---

[24] *Journals*, 48, 75.
[25] *Journals*, 47–48. For a helpful summary of the early organization, activities, and devotional practices of Oxford Methodism, see Richard P. Heitzenrater, *Mirror and Memory: Reflections on Early Methodism* (Nashville: Kingswood, 1989), 81–105.
[26] Hindmarsh, *Spirit of Early Evangelicalism*, 217.
[27] *Journals*, 45–46, quotation at p. 45. Whitefield deleted the reference to Law's influence on his soul in his 1756 revised *Journals*.
[28] Hindmarsh, *The Spirit of Early Evangelicalism*, 21, Tyerman, *George Whitefield*, 1:26.
[29] *Journals*, 41.
[30] R. W. Ward, *The Protestant Evangelical Awakening* (Cambridge: Cambridge University Press, 1993), 48. Some make a similar claim for John Bunyan's *Pilgrim's Progress*.
[31] See Arie de Reuver, *Sweet Communion: Trajectories of Spirituality from the Middle Ages through the Further Reformation*, trans. James A. De Jong (Grand Rapids, MI: Baker Academic, 2007), 62–102. We have followed de Reuver's development of à Kempis.

approach that emphasized the importance of reason and speculation in learning while often minimizing the role of experience. Consistent with refuting the nature of scholasticism, Thomas began his book with this confession: "I would rather experience repentance in my soul than know how to define it."[32] The Modern Devotion recovered Augustine's emphasis on the inner life, loving God, heavenly-mindedness, humility, self-examination, and self-denial for the laity. All of these factors became central to Whitefield's spirituality and preaching; nevertheless à Kempis's understanding of justification and sanctification was inconsistent with the theology of the Protestant Reformation, thereby marginalizing Christ's role as the mediator and further skewing Whitefield's early understanding of the gospel.[33]

Despite the assistance from Charles Wesley in suggesting these and other books, and the counsel of John Wesley, whom Whitefield would later call his "spiritual father," he continued to battle with temptations whose origin he typically attributed to Satan. In response, he turned to another Roman Catholic, Lorenzo Scupoli (ca. 1530–1610), and his popular book *Spiritual Combat* (1589), which encouraged Whitefield to overcome temptation through increased mortification of his sinful nature and isolation from the unhelpful influence of others. Careful readers might recognize that Whitefield devoted more energy at this time to reading devotional books than to reading the Bible. This approach was reinforced by the counsel of Charles Wesley, who at the height of Whitefield's spiritual turmoil urged him to read à Kempis rather than Scripture. Shortly before his conversion, Whitefield noted that he was still reading à Kempis, Castaniza's *Combat*, and his Greek Testament, while seeking to turn every reading into a prayer. These ascetic practices were once again intensified during Lent, which led to his collapse from exhaustion during Holy Week and the ensuing seven weeks of sickness. Ever optimistic in attitude—even in the face of great affliction—Whitefield gratefully reported that God used his illness to purify his soul.[34]

Influence of German Pietism

The second major influence was German Pietism, which resembled the devotional and experiential emphasis of British Puritanism. German Pietists

---

[32] Thomas à Kempis, *The Imitation of Christ*, ed. and trans. Joseph N. Tylenda (New York: Vintage Spiritual Classics, 1998), 3.
[33] De Reuver, *Sweet Communion*, 99.
[34] *Journals*, 49–57, quotations at pp. 49, 52, 56–57. The reference to seven weeks of sickness was removed in the 1756 *Journals*.

discovered the liberating message of à Kempis within the context of their scholastic formalism and what they considered to be the dead orthodoxy of their Lutheran tradition. Pietists turned to Scripture not only for doctrine but also for guidance on how to live the Christian life. Whitefield's faith was nurtured specifically by the writings of Johann Arndt (1555–1621) and August Hermann Francke (1663–1727). Charles Wesley first introduced Whitefield to Francke's *Nicodemus: or, A Treatise against the Fear of Man* (1706), to help alleviate his spiritual struggles and later encouraged his boldness in evangelistic preaching.[35] Further, Francke's *Pietas Hallensis* (*Piety of Halle*, 1705), the story of his orphanage in Halle, Germany, inspired Whitefield to establish his own orphan house in Georgia.

Arndt became the champion for revitalized Christian living. During the seventeenth and eighteenth centuries, his popularity rivaled that of even Luther, producing the proverb "Whosoever does not savor Arndt's *True Christianity* has lost his spiritual appetite." Whitefield's reading of *True Christianity* (1606) introduced him to a personal faith that was vibrant and life-giving, and the necessity of the new birth in contrast to the mere external formalities of his Anglican background, which rarely penetrated his heart. "The main scope of the whole book" was to reveal "the secret and abominable depth of original corruption cleaving to mankind," and "to set forth Jesus Christ as the sole" means of "our whole conversion to God." This shaped Arndt's agenda, which proclaimed the centrality of grace and faith of the Protestant Reformation. Justification by faith would soon transform Whitefield's life and become foundational to his evangelistic preaching. For Arndt, it was critical to grasp that "works do not justify; because we must be engrafted into Christ by faith, before ever we can do any good work; and so this justification, O man, is a gift of God, freely given before, and preventing all thy merits." Later Arndt added, "True justification is only through faith, not through works."[36]

While Arndt claimed that God's grace freely gives justification and is a gift to receive by faith, eighteenth-century Anglicanism commonly taught that justification is "conditional" and, despite the role of grace, the process needs to be supplemented by the person's own "practice of holiness and

---

[35] Carter Lindberg, introduction to *The Pietist Theologians*, ed. Carter Lindberg (Malden, MA: Blackwell, 2005), 3; Hindmarsh, *The Spirit of Early Evangelicalism*, 21–24.

[36] Cited by Lindberg, *The Pietist Theologians*, 6; Johann Arndt, *True Christianity*, pt. 1, trans. Anthony William Boehm (London: D. Brown, 1712), v, vii, xiii, liv, 44. Similar references throughout *True Christianity* assert the primacy of divine grace and faith, always reinforcing "that justification cannot be the work of man, but must be the work of Christ only." *True Christianity*, pt. 1, 390.

good works."[37] This in part clarifies Whitefield's continuing frenetic and consuming asceticism, which nearly drove him mad during his Oxford days. One writer has observed that before their conversions, Whitefield and his Oxford companions "were legalists, trying to save themselves" and "were morose ascetics rather than happy Christians."[38]

Despite having experienced the new birth in 1735, Whitefield did not come to grasp this redemptive truth of justification until sometime later in 1738. One plausible explanation is that the teaching of Peter Böhler (1712–1775)—an early Moravian influence on both Whitefield and the Wesleys—had filtered down to him and corrected his distorted understanding.[39] Whitefield's continuing embrace of the formative nature of German Pietism is validated by the response of those who perceived him as a Pietist in positive and negative ways. Those who admired Whitefield prayed that his style of preaching might create future revivals in Germany, while his detractors promptly rejected him.[40]

Influence of Puritanism

Puritanism was the third primary influence that shaped Whitefield's spirituality.[41] Like German Pietism, it stressed the importance of Scripture and the necessity of the new birth. Scougal's *The Life of God in the Soul of Man* (like *The Imitation of Christ*) was originally published anonymously and challenged Whitefield's understanding of authentic Christianity. Whitefield confessed that at his "first reading" of it, he was amazed and "wondered what the author meant by saying, '. . . some falsely placed religion in going to church, doing hurt to no one, being constant in the duties of the closet, and now and then reaching out their hands to give alms to their poor neighbors.'" Confused, he wrote, "If this be not true religion, what is?" Finally, he discovered the redeeming message: "True religion was union of the soul with God, and Christ formed within us."[42] The Pauline phrase "Christ formed within us" (Gal. 4:19) communicated that a person

---

37 Mark Smith, "The Hanoverian Parish: Towards a New Agenda," *Past & Present* 216 (August 2012): 85.

38 Tyerman, *George Whitefield*, 1:31–32. Dallimore asserts that Whitefield's spirituality at this time stressed "outward ritual" devoid "of grace as taught in the Scriptures." Dallimore, *George Whitefield*, 1:71–72.

39 Ward, *The Protestant Evangelical Awakening*, 342; *Memoirs*, 31.

40 Andrew Kloes, "German Protestants' Interpretation of George Whitefield, 1739–1857," *Wesley and Methodist Studies* 8, no. 2 (2016): 118.

41 For a partial list of the Puritan authors that inspired Whitefield, see Michael A. G. Haykin, *The Revived Puritan: The Spirituality of George Whitefield* (Dundee, ON: Joshua, 2000), 72–74.

42 *Journals*, 47; Whitefield to Mr. H—, February 20, 1735, in *Letters*, 6. For a helpful treatment of Scougal's influence on Whitefield, see Sean McGever, *Born Again: The Evangelical Theology of Conversion in John Wesley and George Whitefield* (Bellingham, WA: Lexham, 2020), 122–27.

experiences true freedom not through self-striving or human regulations but through a new life in Christ.

Whitefield soon recognized his self-deception, due in part to the preceding verse of Scripture: "But it is good to be zealously affected always in a good thing" (Gal. 4:18). No one ever questioned his zeal, but he lacked the proper perception of union with Christ and that the new birth is not attained through external practices that do not engage a person's heart. However, this enlightening discovery did not immediately produce his desired conversion. Instead, he was persuaded to engage the means of grace promoted by the Oxford Methodists with greater intensity than before. Throughout this turbulent time, he experienced steady temptations from Satan. Whitefield's retrospective journal reflections five years later acknowledged the benefit of these trials, which reduced his "self-love" and taught him "to die daily."[43] Despite Whitefield's appreciation of *The Life of God*, Scougal was clearer on the nature of the divine life than on the means of growing in it. This lack of clarity later led to Whitefield concluding his sermons with specific applications shaped by the needs and contexts of his listeners.[44]

The Puritans also gave Whitefield new eyes to read Scripture. Before attending Oxford, he declared, "Frequently I read the Bible," and he confessed his "diligence . . . in studying [his] Greek Testament." However, this reading was more academic than for personal growth. Now as he followed Scougal, Scripture took on a radically new meaning for him: "The lively Oracles of God were my soul's delight. . . . I meditated therein day and night."[45] This recalibrated his reading as he devoted two hours nightly in rigorous prayer over his "Greek Testament, and Bishop Hall's most excellent *Contemplations*."[46] Joseph Hall (1574–1656), a popular devotional writer admired by many Puritan readers, authored *Contemplations on the Historical Passages of the Old and New Testament* (1612–1662). This multivolume collection ushered readers into a careful integration of biblical instruction coupled with devotion. Hall's vivid retelling of the scriptural narratives likely stimulated Whitefield's imagination and inspired his future preaching. In response, he declared, "I began to read the holy Scriptures (upon my knees) laying aside all other books, and praying over, if possible, every

---

[43] *Journals*, 47, 51. The last reference was deleted in 1756.
[44] J. I. Packer, *Puritan Portraits* (Fearn, UK: Christian Focus, 2012), 42–43.
[45] *Journals*, 40, 44, 48.
[46] *Journals*, 48, 57.

line and word." This became his lifelong practice of meditating, in an attentive posture, on the Bible. With a combination of delight and discovery, he continued, "I got more true knowledge from reading the Book of God in one month, than I could *ever* have acquired from *all* the writings of men."[47]

Whitefield also began to read the biblical commentaries of William Burkitt (1650–1703) and Matthew Henry (1662–1714). These Puritan authors examined Scripture in a manner that included a devotional awareness rather than mere cognition and contributed to his maturing understanding of the gospel. This new method of reading proved refreshing for Whitefield and other Oxford Methodists, who at this time privileged devotional books over biblical and theological writings. Once he recognized his unbalanced habits, he challenged all readers that the Christian life must always be nurtured by both doctrine and devotion. His experience helped validate that devotional classics could deepen a person's desire for Jesus, but they must never become a substitute for Scripture. Given the choice, he would have adamantly stressed that it was more important to read Scripture to learn of Jesus than to read about Jesus in secondary sources.

The Puritans also assisted Whitefield's understanding of the nature and dynamics of the new birth. He devoured *Alarm to the Unconverted* (1671), by Joseph Alleine (1634–1668); *Call to the Unconverted* (1658), by Richard Baxter (1615–1691); and *The Holy Life of Mr. John Janeway* (1673), by James Janeway (1636–1674). These writings galvanized his understanding of the new life in Christ and began his early introduction to Calvinism, to which he had not yet been exposed at Oxford.

One Whitefield biographer observes the "spiritual bricolage" of his sources, and indeed some readers might be amazed by the breadth of Whitefield's reading of numerous Roman Catholic authors.[48] Another historian accurately observes, "The new evangelical devotion was not cut off from the Christian past; it depended upon it."[49] But evangelicals did not blindly consume Roman Catholic writings; nor did they borrow from Catholic doctrinal writings. Rather, they read with a discerning eye, through their theological sensibilities, not only Roman Catholic sources but Anglican as well. Whitefield's revision of Law's *Serious Call* in June 1748 confirms this. His lengthy title provides a commentary of why he revised this

---

[47] *Journals*, 60 (italics in the original). This phrase was deleted in the 1756 *Journals*. See *Journals*, 87, for Whitefield's continued practice of reading Scripture on his knees.
[48] Kidd, *George Whitefield*, 17, 26, 30.
[49] Hindmarsh, *The Spirit of Early Evangelicalism*, 95.

classic: *Law Gospelized; or An Address to All Christians concerning Holiness of Heart and Life: Being an Attempt to Render Mr. Law's Serious Call More Useful to the Children of God, by Excluding Whatever Is Not Truly Evangelical, and Illustrating the Subject More Fully from the Holy Scriptures.*[50] Some believe Law himself became frustrated with his moralistic teaching and eventually became a follower of Jacob Boehme (1575–1624), the controversial German Lutheran mystic whose views eventually rejected biblical orthodoxy.

Influence of the Holy Spirit

The Holy Spirit's presence and power was the fourth major stream that fashioned Whitefield's life. He recorded his early awareness before he attended Oxford, noting the Holy Spirit's role in "bringing many things to my remembrance," "movings of the blessed Spirit upon my heart," and "illuminations" of God's "foretastes of his love." This inner sensitivity to the promptings of the Spirit imparted valuable guidance but also required spiritual maturity and discernment. His dependence on the Spirit intensified during his student days, which convicted him of sin and the dangers of relying upon others but eventually provided the courage for him to live boldly for Jesus Christ. His awakening came in the spring of 1735, amid an intense seven weeks of sickness in which he reported, "The blessed Spirit was all this time purifying my soul."[51]

These four streams coalesced to bring Whitefield to his liberating discovery, thus making him the first member of the Oxford Methodists to experience an evangelical conversion, which he recorded in his journal:

> God was pleased to set me free in the following manner. One day, perceiving an uncommon drought, and a disagreeable clamminess in my mouth, and using things to allay my thirst, but in vain, it was suggested to me, that when Jesus Christ cried out, "I thirst," his sufferings were near at an end. Upon which, I cast myself down on the bed, crying out, I thirst! I thirst! Soon after this, I found and felt in myself that I was delivered from the burden that had so heavily oppressed me! The Spirit of mourning was taken from me, and I knew what it was truly to rejoice in God my Saviour, and, for some time, could not avoid singing Psalms wherever I was;

[50] Whitefield to Rev. Mr. S—, June 24, 1748, in *Works*, 2:144. Whitefield's revision is published in his *Works*, 4:375–437. Isabel Rivers provides a helpful summary of the evangelical ambivalence to Law. See Isabell Rivers, "William Law and Religious Revival: A Reception of *A Serious Call*," *Huntington Library Quarterly* 71, no. 4 (2008): esp. 636–44.
[51] *Journals*, 35, 38, 41, 54, 57. The final phrase was deleted in the 1756 *Journals*.

but my joy gradually became more settled, and, blessed be God, has abode and increased on my soul (saving a few casual intermissions) ever since! Thus were the days of my mourning ended. After a long night of desertion and temptation, the star, which I had seen at a distance before, began to appear again, and the day-star arose in my heart. Now did the Spirit of God take possession of my soul, and, as I humbly hope, seal me unto the Day of Redemption.[52]

Several key insights emerge from Whitefield's language, which echoes Christian in John Bunyan's *The Pilgrim's Progress* (1678) when his overwhelming burden of sin rolls off his back as he gazes at the cross. This exemplifies Whitefield's common practice of borrowing from Jesus or other biblical persons to describe his experience. The centrality of Jesus's crucifixion was also center stage when he cried out, "I thirst" (John 19:28), as was the star that led the magi to the baby Jesus (Matt. 2:2, 10) when "the day-star arose" in Whitefield's heart. Once again, the Holy Spirit was active in leading and confirming his experience of the new birth. An insightful comparison can be made between Whitefield's initial account of his conversion recorded in 1740 and his revised, 1756 account. The later entries removed the graphic language that identified him with Jesus Christ on the cross; and his faith, absent in the 1740 account, became prominent in 1756.[53]

After his conversion at Oxford, Whitefield returned to Gloucester and spent nine months recuperating from the effects of his excessive spiritual introspection.[54] While at home, he chronicled his new freedom in the Spirit when he wrote, "I felt that Christ dwelt in me, and I in him, and how did I daily walk in the comforts of the Holy Ghost, and was edified and refreshed in the multitude of peace," and the Holy Spirit "led me into the knowledge of divine things."[55] Guidance and impressions from the third person of the Trinity continued to grow in importance as Whitefield began his ministry.

The day after his ordination, he struggled to write a sermon until he perceived the Spirit's guidance. In his journal, he recounted the way the words "speak out, Paul" flooded his soul with great power, and "immediately," he wrote, "my heart was enlarged. God spoke to me by his Spirit, and I was no longer dumb." His newfound awareness of a "direct and immediate experience of God" and the "felt presence of the Holy Spirit" has been

---

52 *Journals*, 58. This entire section was deleted in the 1756 *Journals*.
53 McGever, *Born Again*, 130–33.
54 *Journals*, 48, 52, 54–60.
55 *Journals*, 61–62. This was also deleted in 1756.

attributed to Scougal's influence from *The Life of God in the Soul of Man*.[56] This was not an isolated occasion for Whitefield, as he recorded numerous entries in his unpublished diary, declaring that he was "full of the Holy Ghost" and that he experienced "joy in the Holy Ghost."[57] His first journal concluded by reminding his readers that by thirsting after Jesus Christ they would receive the "indwelling of his blessed Spirit in [their] heart[s]."[58]

A later sermon proclaimed that the indwelling of the Holy Spirit was the privilege of every believer in Christ.[59] Despite his 1756 deletion of many journal entries that mentioned his immediate experience of the Spirit, "this emphasis on the Holy Spirit would be a consistent theme in Whitefield's career, although he would in time back away from claims for his immediate guidance."[60]

Thus, of the four formative streams of influence on Whitefield, Oxford Methodism would gradually diminish in importance; following his conversion, Pietism, Puritanism, and the empowerment of the Holy Spirit would continue to expand.

Ordination and Early Ministry

Just as Whitefield struggled to find peace with God, he agonized over whether he should become a minister. In 1736, he wrote to John Wesley—then still in Georgia—of his dilemma, reporting that while his friends had urged him to seek holy orders, he believed it was unnecessary to be ordained to serve God. This, combined with his serious self-examination, convinced him that he was unqualified because he was a great sinner and came from a humble background.[61] In his discernment, and remembering Moses's resistance when God called him to lead the people of Israel out of Egypt, Whitefield felt he should not run ahead of God's possible call. He prayed fervently that God would prevent him from accepting this challenge unless he was conscious of divine confirmation. Eventually he concluded, "If God did not grant my request in keeping me out of it [the ordained ministry] I knew his grace would be sufficient to support and strengthen me whenever he sent me into the ministry."[62]

---

56 Hindmarsh, *The Spirit of Early Evangelicalism*, 33; cf. 34–36.
57 Kidd, *George Whitefield*, 35.
58 *Journals*, 71. This section was deleted in 1756.
59 Whitefield, "The Indwelling of the Spirit, the Common Privilege of all Believers," in *Works*, 6:89–102.
60 Kidd, *George Whitefield*, 36; for a helpful treatment of Whitefield's reliance on the Spirit, see pp. 35–37.
61 Tyerman, *George Whitefield*, 1:39.
62 *Journals*, 65. This was deleted in 1756.

Ordination for Whitefield required a conversation with Bishop Benson of Gloucester. Despite the bishop's policy not to ordain a man unless he was at least twenty-three, Whitefield received his approval at only twenty-one. Presumably, this exception was due to the strong impression his "character" and "behaviour at church" made on the bishop. Additionally, he gave Whitefield a gift of money to purchase a book, which confirmed his earlier dream in which he met the bishop and received a gold coin.[63] Like his dependency upon the immediate impressions of the Holy Spirit, his receiving guidance through dreams drew frequent criticism of Whitefield and was deleted from his 1756 revision of his *Journals*.[64]

The same intensity that characterized Whitefield's conversion marked his preparation for ordination. He carefully studied the Thirty-Nine Articles—the primary theological teaching of the Church of England—proving each point by Scripture, as well as the biblical qualifications of a minister. Prayerfully he pondered two questions the bishop would ask: "Do you trust that you are inwardly moved by the Holy Ghost to take upon you this office and administration?" and "Are you called according to the will of our Lord Jesus Christ?" Bishop Benson certified Whitefield's responses and agreed to ordain him on Trinity Sunday, June 20, 1736.[65] After his ordination, Whitefield confessed that the "good of souls" would be his primary motivation. He further proclaimed his unwavering commitment to Jesus Christ by writing, "I gave myself up to be a martyr for him, who hung upon the cross for me."[66] Gratitude was a primary impulse for Whitefield throughout his ministry as he would often take inventory of Christ's numerous provisions for him and how he could respond more faithfully.

In the week leading up to his first sermon, which he delivered at his home church in Gloucester, Whitefield felt considerable trepidation. He wrote to a woman and expressed his fears that people might not appreciate his message. But, he declared, "I must tell them the truth, or otherwise I shall not be a faithful minister of Christ."[67] The commitment to always proclaim the truth, regardless of the consequences, created frequent trouble for him. This initial sermon—"The Necessity and Benefit of Religious Society"—explored how small groups could assist believers in growing into deeper maturity in Christ.[68] Reports reached the bishop that Whitefield

---

[63] *Journals*, 66–67. Much of this was deleted in 1756.
[64] *Journals*, 66.
[65] *Journals*, 68–69.
[66] Whitefield to Mr. S—, June 20, 1736, in *Letters*, 15–16.
[67] Whitefield to Mrs. H—, June 28, 1736, in *Letters*, 17.
[68] Whitefield, "The Necessity and Benefit of Religious Society," in *Works*, 5:107–22.

drove fifteen listeners mad during his sermon, to which the bishop "wished that the madness might not be forgotten before next Sunday."[69] In due course, not all reactions from the Anglican hierarchy would be nearly as appreciative of Whitefield's passionate and confrontational homiletical style.

Nonetheless, British ministers were warned of spiritual anorexia, owing to their anemic preaching, which produced "a starvation of the souls for Jesus Christ."[70] Whitefield quickly comprehended the same danger and addressed this tepid spiritual condition in his second sermon, preached on the new birth. This message would become his signature sermon. While it stressed the necessity of being born again, the sermon lacked awareness of justification by faith or grace.[71] Despite this absence, he proclaimed the redeeming power of Jesus's life, death, and resurrection. The popularity of this radically new message was confirmed by a third edition, published in October 1737.[72] Regardless of the topics, many of his sermons stressed the necessity of the new life in Christ. It was also frequently woven into his correspondence; for example, "Indeed we may flatter ourselves, that we may go to heaven without undergoing the pangs of the new birth; but we shall certainly find ourselves desperately mistaken in the end."[73]

Whitefield soon became convinced that he should join the Wesleys in Georgia as a missionary to this newly established British colony. While waiting to cross the Atlantic, he engaged in various short-term ministries in and around London, which provided frequent opportunities for preaching in diverse settings. In the final months of 1737 before his departure, he preached an average of nine times a week, becoming a preaching sensation and achieving celebrity status. He acknowledged that his meteoric rise from a lowly servitor at Oxford to an admired Anglican preacher created the temptation to pride. This popularity soon restricted his movement through the streets of London and forced him to travel by coach.[74] While mass crowds thronged to hear him wherever he spoke, Anglican clergymen became increasingly incensed by his message of the new birth.

Celebrating the New Birth

But the new birth continued to empower Whitefield's preaching and life, and he would never grow weary of proclaiming this message. He examined

---

69 *Memoirs*, 10.
70 Watts, *Humble Attempt*, 47.
71 Whitefield, "On Regeneration," in *Works*, 6:257–72.
72 Whitefield to Mr. H—, October 25, 1937, in *Letters*, 30.
73 Whitefield to Mrs. H—, June 28, 1736, in *Letters*, 18.
74 *Journals*, 70, 89.

this in his sermon on new life in Christ, titled simply "On Regeneration," which reveals how Scougal shaped both his theology and spirituality. Exegeting 2 Corinthians 5:17, "If any man be in Christ, he is a new creature," Whitefield declared, "To be in him not only by outward profession, but by an inward change and purity of heart" leads to "the cohabitation of his Holy Spirit." Further, to be in Christ is "to be mystically united to him by a true and lively faith" that introduces a person to all of the benefits of being joined with Jesus, just as the branches receive all of the nourishment of the vine.[75] The themes of union with Christ, the indwelling of the Holy Spirit, and the emphasis on inward transformation would continue to resonate throughout his entire ministry.

The burning desire of Whitefield's life was to become a new creation, shedding the past and being born into the newness of life in Christ Jesus. He reiterated the centrality of the Spirit's work in applying Christ's redemption, "that we should have a grant of God's Holy Spirit to change our natures, and so prepare us for the enjoyment of that happiness our Saviour has purchased by his precious blood."[76] This was Whitefield's experience; the new birth, after all, had brought him into a new relationship of enjoying the triune God. There was little wonder that whenever he visited Oxford he could not resist, in his own words, "running to that place where Jesus Christ first revealed himself to me, and gave the new birth."[77]

---

[75] Whitefield, "On Regeneration," 259.
[76] Whitefield, "On Regeneration," 265.
[77] Whitefield, "All Mens Place," 360.

CHAPTER 2

THEOLOGIAN OF THE HEAD AND HEART

By his own admission, George Whitefield was not a theologian—at least, not of the conventional sort. Indeed, he never aspired to be one. In much the same way that his Methodist field-preaching compatriot John Wesley has been famously dubbed a "folk-theologian"[1]—a practical theologian as opposed to a systematic theologian—Whitefield might aptly be described as an *occasional* theologian. In other words, he tended to avoid abstract theological discourse in favor of expressing his theology through the medium of letters, treatises, and, above all else, sermons.

Whitefield was convinced that theology belongs in the pulpit. He preferred to communicate theology through sermons he delivered to live gatherings in specific locations and times rather than through attempting to produce timeless systematic theological treatises. His sermons were geared toward the spiritual transformation of his listeners (and readers), not the mere transfer of theologically oriented information, even theologically orthodox information. For example, after spending the bulk of his landmark sermon entitled "The Lord Our Righteousness" carefully defining and defending the doctrines of justification by faith and its corollary, imputation, Whitefield pivoted toward application, thereby illustrating his conviction that an unapplied theology is not merely impoverished but dangerous to the soul: "I have been too long upon the

---

[1] Albert C. Outler, "John Wesley: Folk Theologian," *Theology Today* 34, no. 2 (1977): 150–60.

doctrinal part. To preach to your head without preaching to your heart is doing you no good."[2]

Taken in isolation, quotes like this could easily be construed as evidence of the way Whitefield prioritized matters of the heart over and against the head. Well-worn pejorative tropes abound regarding his lack of theological acumen (at best) and cavalier disinterest in theology (at worst). Then there is the "old jibe": "that Whitefield must have been eloquent indeed to make such utterances as his seem eloquent."[3]

Some have contended that "almost any single sermon states the whole of [Whitefield's] formal theology. His ideas are few; they are bluntly put and endlessly repeated."[4] Indeed, there is more than a grain of truth to this assessment. But what is no doubt intended here as a critique would almost certainly have been taken by Whitefield as a compliment—an accurate appraisal of his single-minded pursuit of a preaching ministry heavily focused on evangelism. In other words, if it is true that Whitefield's sermon corpus does not span the whole counsel of God in the manner of a preacher in a settled pastorate with a long tenure, then that was by his itinerant evangelistic design: planting, not watering, the seed of God's word was his chosen ministry course. He also intentionally utilized "plain language" in a bid to be understood by as many as possible, even if that meant running the risk of being labeled unsophisticated and anti-intellectual. Forewarning his audience, he wrote: "If any here do expect fine preaching from me this day, they will, in all probability, go away disappointed. For I came not here to shoot over people's heads; but, if the Lord shall be pleased to bless me, to reach their hearts." He was up-front and unashamed about his tone: "If the poor and the unlearned can comprehend, the learned and rich must."[5]

Of course, Whitefield did not always help his cause in being taken seriously as a theologian—practical, occasional, or otherwise. At points, he expressed his commitment to *sola Scriptura* with a simplicity that verged on the simplistic (and arguably even reductionistic), as though the Bible were his solitary (as opposed to his normative) source of theological authority. For example, he wrote in 1742, "I embrace the calvinistical scheme, not because of Calvin, but Jesus Christ, I think, has taught it to me."[6] A few years

---

[2] George Whitefield, *The Lord Our Righteousness* (Glasgow, 1741), 16.

[3] David Crump, "The Preaching of George Whitefield and His Use of Matthew Henry's *Commentary*," *Crux* 25, no. 3 (1989): 19.

[4] Stuart Henry, *George Whitefield: Wayfaring Witness* (Nashville: Abingdon, 1957), 97.

[5] Whitefield, "Christ the Believer's Husband," in *Works*, 5:174.

[6] Whitefield to the Reverend Dr. C—, September 24, 1742, in *Letters*, 442.

earlier, he declared to John Wesley, "Alas, I never read any thing that Calvin wrote; my doctrines I had from Christ and his apostles."[7]

But even if Whitefield never directly engaged with Calvin's literary legacy, he was certainly familiar with many of his theological descendants. For instance, in 1735 Whitefield purchased a copy of Matthew Henry's *Commentary* (1706), and it is hard to overstate the influence the seventeenth-century nonconformist's exegesis—and Calvinistic theology—exerted upon Whitefield's developing intuitions. Some have gone so far as to suggest that "Puritan theology, passed on as it was through the writings of Matthew Henry, may well have enjoyed the period of its greatest influence during the ministry of George Whitefield."[8]

Whitefield's Calvinism was nurtured during his time in New England in the fall of 1740, though he had already been exposed to this tradition before his second transatlantic voyage. His reading diet during the year leading up to his departure for America seems to have had an especially Calvinistic flavor. He read the sermons of the Scottish seceder Ralph Erskine, and they left a positive theological impression. So too did the sermons of the Cambridge divine John Edwards. On September 29, 1739, Whitefield wrote:

> This afternoon, I was greatly strengthened by perusing some paragraphs out of a book called *The Preacher*, written by Dr. Edwards, of Cambridge. . . . There are such noble testimonies given . . . of justification by faith only, the imputed righteousness of Christ, our having no free-will, &c., that they deserve to be written in letters of gold.[9]

Whitefield might have had a lifelong allergic reaction to unapplied and abstract theology, decrying "letter-learned" professing Christians who wrote about the new birth but had experienced "no more of it than a blind man does of colours"; and yet, beneath this polemical rhetoric lurked a preacher who, when he arrived at Calvinistic convictions, was willing to expend significant time and energy proclaiming and defending them in the public arena.[10] While strenuously avoiding jargon, Whitefield's sermons nonetheless assume a high degree of theological literacy. He regularly cited and censured Arian, Socinian, Arminian, papist, and antinomian

---

[7] Whitefield to the Reverend Mr. J— W—, August 25, 1740, in *Letters*, 205.
[8] Crump, "Preaching of George Whitefield," 24.
[9] *Journals*, 335.
[10] Whitefield, "The Folly and Danger of Being Not Righteous Enough," in *Works*, 5:135.

heterodoxy; he appealed to pastor-theologians ranging from Augustine to Solomon Stoddard as purveyors of orthodoxy. Indeed, as Thomas Kidd observes, "For those who only know Whitefield as a powerfully emotional preacher, the intellectual heft of his sermons may come as a surprise."[11]

If "the revival theology the moderate evangelicals preached was basically Reformed theology (Calvinism) cast in a pietist accent," then it would be hard to find a more public and vocal exemplar of these convictions during the eighteenth century than Whitefield.[12] This theological trajectory typically emphasized a series of themes: conviction of sin, conversion (including justification and regeneration), and the pursuit of sanctification (or, as it has sometimes been styled, "consolation").[13] These doctrines all appear repeatedly and prominently in Whitefield's writings, and we shall explore how each of them was expressed in his public ministry.

Conviction of Sin

Theological anthropology and soteriology were tightly interwoven in Whitefield's proclamation of the gospel. Echoing Wesley's pithy encapsulation of this theological relationship ("Know your disease! Know your cure!"[14]), Whitefield was adamant that the doctrine of original sin was "the very foundation of the Christian religion."[15] Motivating stark assertions like this was a belief that the "glad tidings of the gospel" are good news only to those who have first embraced the bad news of their utterly desperate plight and dire need of God's gracious salvific intervention. In one sermon, he offered his audience a peek behind the curtain of his theological priorities, contending that responsible preaching of the gospel entails avoiding the offer of "healing before we see sinners wounded." He continued, "Secure sinners must hear the thunderings of Mount Sinai, before we bring them to mount Zion."[16] Elsewhere, in his sermon "The Gospel, a Dying Saint's Triumph," Whitefield declared, "You cannot preach the gospel without preaching the law; for you shall find by and by, we are to preach something that the people must be saved by: it

---

11 Thomas S. Kidd, *George Whitefield: America's Spiritual Founding Father* (New Haven, CT: Yale University Press, 2014), 156.
12 Robert Caldwell, *Theologies of the American Revivalists* (Downers Grove, IL: IVP Academic, 2017), 19–20.
13 The eighteenth-century Massachusetts pastor Peter Thatcher summarized these doctrines succinctly as conviction, conversion, and consolation. See Caldwell, *Theologies*, 20.
14 John Wesley, "Original Sin," in *The Works of John Wesley: Bicentennial Edition*, vols. 1–4, *Sermons*, ed. Albert C. Outler (Nashville: Abingdon, 1984–1987), 2:185.
15 Whitefield, "Of Justification by Christ," in *Works*, 6:218.
16 Whitefield, "The Seed of the Woman, and the Seed of the Serpent," in *Works*, 5:13.

is impossible to tell them how they are to be saved, unless we tell them what they are to be saved from."[17]

Whitefield held that no aspect of human nature remains unpolluted by the effects of the fallen nature every individual inherits from our first parents. That is, while Whitefield's theology of original sin emphasized the imputation of the second Adam's righteousness by faith as the antidote to the imputation of the first Adam's sin to his posterity, it also stressed that Adam's fall resulted in the depravity of his sinful nature being imparted to the entire human race. For instance, he declared, "We all stand in need of being justified, on account of the sin of our natures: for we are all charge-able with original sin, or the first sin of our parents." Responding to the accusation that his theology renders God unjust, as well as the active cause of sin, he appealed to Paul's argument in Romans 5, "where we are told that 'in Adam all died'; that is, Adam's sin was imputed to all . . . [and] this point seems to be excellently summed up in the article of our church, where she declares, 'Original sin . . . is the fault and corruption of every man.'"[18]

On another occasion, Whitefield referred to the account of the fall in Genesis 3 as the origin of universal and inherent human depravity: "Our first parents contracted it [a prevailing enmity against God] when they fell from God by eating the forbidden fruit, and the bitter and malignant con-tagion of it hath descended to, and quite overspread, their whole posterity."[19] In addition to Scripture and tradition, Whitefield also appealed to empirical experience in support of the doctrine of original sin. For instance, he con-tended: "If we look inwardly, we will see enough of lusts, and man's temper contrary to the temper of God. There is pride, malice, and revenge, in all our hearts; and this temper cannot come from God; it comes from our first parent, Adam, who, after he fell from God, fell out of God into the devil."[20]

So important was a right understanding—and experiential convic-tion—of sin to Whitefield that he was prepared to assert, "If you have never felt the weight of original sin, do not call yourselves Christians."[21] For in-stance, in his sermon "The Lord Our Righteousness," he was not content simply to rehearse the "mournful account" of Adam and Eve's covenant-breaking transgression, one that rendered them—and by implication, their

---

[17] Whitefield, "The Gospel a Dying Saint's Triumph," in *Eighteen Sermons*, 86.
[18] Whitefield, "Of Justification by Christ," 217–18, quoting art. 9 of the Thirty-Nine Articles.
[19] Whitefield, "Walking with God," in *Works*, 5:23.
[20] George Whitefield, "The Method of Grace," in *Select Sermons of George Whitefield, with an Account of His Life by J. C. Ryle* (Edinburgh: Banner of Truth, 1997), 80.
[21] Whitefield, "The Method of Grace," 81.

descendants—"in need of a better righteousness than their own." Nor was it sufficient merely to assert the theological mechanics of imputation and Jesus's active and passive obedience, whereby "Christ not only died, but lived; not only suffered, but obeyed for; or instead of, poor sinners." Indeed, he warned, "Entertaining this doctrine in your heads, without receiving the Lord Jesus Christ savingly by a lively faith into your hearts, will but increase your damnation."[22]

Instead, as he drew his sermon toward its rhetorical climax, Whitefield felt compelled to impress upon his listeners that unless they availed themselves of what he had earlier described as "divine philanthropy," the existential reality of a looming eternity experiencing the horrors of a just divine judgment awaited them. Signaling his homiletical turn toward eliciting a personal conviction of sin among his listeners, he announced, "But it is time for me to come a little closer to your consciences." In what would become a familiar feature of Whitefield's sermons, he exhorted: "O Christless sinners, I am distressed for you . . . for whither would you flee, if death should find you naked? . . . O think of death! O think of judgment! Yet a little while, and time shall be no more; and then what will become of you, if the Lord be not your righteousness?" Vividly imagining the day of judgment when "Christ himself shall pronounce the irrevocable [damnatory] sentence" on those yet to experience the new birth, Whitefield empathized with his audience, imploring them to "close with Christ": "You need not fear the greatness or number of your sins. For are you sinners? So am I. . . . And yet the Lord (for ever adored be his rich, free and sovereign grace) the Lord is my righteousness."[23]

If Whitefield considered a right understanding of the doctrine of sin to be integral to a right proclamation of the gospel, then he also considered the doctrine of unconditional election to be an inextricable corollary of his solidifying Calvinist doctrine of salvation. In a letter to the Arminian John Wesley written in February 1741 he declared, "But I must preach the gospel of Christ, and that I cannot *now* do, without speaking of Election."[24] Given humanity's fallen state and inherent lack of capacity or desire to initiate salvation, by 1739 Whitefield had become convinced of the doctrinal necessity of unconditional election as an expression not of divine arbitrariness

22 Whitefield, "The Lord Our Righteousness," in *Works*, 5:219–20, 229.
23 Whitefield, "The Lord Our Righteousness," 219, 228, 231–32.
24 John Wesley, *The Works of John Wesley: Bicentennial Edition*, vols. 25–26, *Letters I–II*, ed. Frank Baker (Nashville: Abingdon, 1980–1982), 26:48–49 (italics in the original).

but of God's everlasting love. Emphasizing God's free grace in election—by which he meant *God's* freedom to dispense or withhold grace—he wrote to a fellow believer: "Oh how doth the free, the distinguishing grace of God excite the love of those, who are made partakers of it! What was there in you and me . . . that should move God to chuse us before others? Was there any fitness foreseen in us, except a fitness for damnation? I believe not." Reflecting a thoroughly Calvinistic interpretation of the so-called chain of salvation in Romans 8:29–30, Whitefield continued: "No, God chose us from eternity, he called us in time, and I am persuaded will keep us from falling finally, till time shall be no more. Consider the Gospel in this view, and it appears a consistent scheme."[25]

Nowhere does Whitefield's commitment to a Calvinistic conception of predestination come into sharper relief than in his very public doctrinal dispute with John Wesley between 1739 and 1742, one that eventually re sulted in the fracturing of the Methodist movement along Arminian and Calvinist theological fault lines. In Whitefield's estimation, to deny unconditional election (as was Wesley's settled theological stance) was to deny the doctrine of original sin. This in turn, he argued, threatened the cherished Reformation principle of *sola gratia*: salvation by grace alone. In his published response to Wesley's "Free Grace" sermon, Whitefield leveled a stunning charge against his one-time mentor: "You plainly make salvation depend not on God's *free-grace*, but on man's *free-will*."[26] Wesley recorded in his journal, "[Whitefield] told me he and I preached two different gospels, and therefore he not only would not join with me, or give me the right hand of fellowship, but was resolved publicly to preach against me and my brother wheresoever he preached at all."[27]

Responding to Wesley's characterization of Calvinist theology—that "by virtue of an eternal, unchangeable, irresistible decree of God, one part of mankind are infallibly saved, and the rest infallibly damned; it being impossible that any of the former should be damned, or that any of the latter should be saved"—Whitefield cast unconditional election as a necessary doctrinal implication of holding to an orthodox conception of original sin. He wrote, "But who ever asserted, that thousands and millions of men, without any preceding offence or fault of theirs, were unchangeably

---

[25] Whitefield to Mr. O—, November 10, 1739, in *Letters*, 90.

[26] *Journals*, 587 (italics in the original).

[27] John Wesley, *The Works of John Wesley: Bicentennial Edition*, vols. 18–24, *Journals and Diaries I–VII*, ed. W. Reginald Ward and Richard P. Heitzenrater (Nashville: Abingdon, 1988–1997), 19:188–89.

doomed to everlasting burnings?" Whitefield's ensuing argument reflects his familiarity with Reformed confessional statements like the Westminster Confession of Faith and the Canons of Dort. Both of these statements describe God's decision to actively elect some to salvation and pass by the reprobate using asymmetrical language, whereby the nonelect are ultimately judged for their sin rather than their nonelection. In this way, God is exonerated from the charge of being the author of unbelief. Whitefield continued, "Surely Mr. Wesley will own God's justice, in imputing Adam's sin to his posterity; and also, that after Adam fell, and his posterity in him, God might justly have passed them all by, without sending his own Son to be a saviour for any one." In sum, he perceived any denial of unconditional election as evidence of unwarranted optimism in one's theological anthropology: "Unless you heartily agree to both these points, you do not believe original sin aright."[28]

Whitefield the theologian might have been a zealous defender of unconditional election, but it is questionable how well he understood the nuances of Wesley's anthropology. Indeed, if Wesley's critique of Calvinism would appear to be more appropriately leveled toward hyper-Calvinism's diminishment of genuine human responsibility, then Whitefield's critique of Arminianism would seem to be more appropriately leveled against semi-Pelagianism, a stance from which Wesley explicitly distanced himself. After all, in one sense, he believed in original sin much as Whitefield did. For instance, in his 1759 sermon "Original Sin," Wesley contended:

> Is man by nature filled with all manner of evil? Is he void of all good? Is he wholly fallen? Is his soul totally corrupted? Or, to come back to the text [Gen. 6:5], is "every imagination of the thoughts of his heart evil continually"? Allow this, and you are so far a Christian. Deny it, and you are but a heathen still.[29]

That being said, Wesley always qualified his doctrine of sin with a theology of divinely and universally bestowed prevenient grace—a grace that would enable every person to respond positively, though nonmeritoriously, to the free offer of the gospel. For example, in his 1752 treatise

---

[28] *Works*, 4:67. The Westminster Confession of Faith 3.7 states, regarding reprobation, "The rest of mankind, God was pleased, according to the unsearchable counsel of His own will, whereby He extendeth or withholdeth mercy as He pleaseth, for the glory of His sovereign power over His creatures, to pass by, and to ordain them to dishonor and wrath for their sin, to the praise of His glorious justice."
[29] Wesley, "Original Sin," 183–84.

"Predestination Calmly Considered," Wesley clarified, "*Natural free will*, in the present state of mankind, I do not understand: I only assert, that there is a measure of free will *supernaturally* restored to every man, together with that *supernatural* light, which 'enlightens every man that cometh into the world.' "[30] If Whitefield was aware of this nuance in Wesley's theology—one that affirmed a graciously *freed* will rather than a will partially free from the effects of the fall, he failed to acknowledge it. In other words, whatever genuine theological disagreements existed between Wesley and Whitefield when it came to the doctrine of election, these doctrinal differences were compounded and exacerbated by terminological misunderstandings—willful or otherwise.

Contrary to Wesley's fears that Calvinist theology inevitably disincentivizes evangelism and "tends to destroy the comfort of religion, the happiness of Christianity," the doctrine of unconditional election was a consistent source of encouragement for Whitefield, both in his preaching ministry and in his experience of divine assurance of salvation. For example, in response to Wesley's charge that Calvinism renders "all preaching vain" (it being "needless to them that are elected," since "they, whether with preaching or without, will infallibly be saved," and "useless to them that are not elected," since "they cannot possibly be saved"), Whitefield distinguished between primary and secondary causes in the actualization of God's foreordained purposes. In this instance, God uses preaching as a proximate cause to accomplish the ultimate end of drawing his elect to himself. Whitefield wrote, "Hath not God, who hath appointed salvation for a certain number, appointed also the preaching of the word, as a means to bring them to it?" In this way, he was liberated to "preach promiscuously to all," confident that God's word will not fail to accomplish the purpose for which he has sent it forth.[31]

And far from undermining his sense of assurance, the doctrine of unconditional election brought Whitefield tremendous spiritual consolation. In his experience, the two doctrines were inextricably linked. He wrote to one correspondent, "Oh the excellency of the doctrine of election, and of the final perseverance of the saints, to those who are sealed by the Spirit of promise."[32] Acutely aware of the frailty and fickleness of his faith,

---

[30] John Wesley, *The Works of John Wesley: Bicentennial Edition*, vol. 13, *Doctrinal and Controversial Treatises II*, ed. Paul W. Chilcote and Kenneth J. Collins (Nashville: Abingdon, 2013), 287 (italics in the original).
[31] *Journals*, 575.
[32] Whitefield to Rev. Mr. H—, November 10, 1739, in *Letters*, 101.

Whitefield discovered immeasurable solace in God's commitment to finish the good work he has begun in his elect. He wrote to Wesley,

> As for my own part, this doctrine is my daily support: I should utterly sink under a dread of my impending trials, was I not firmly persuaded that God has chosen me in Christ from before the foundation of the world, and that now being effectually called, he will suffer none to pluck me out of his almighty hand.[33]

Justification and the New Birth

The doctrine of original sin was thus an ever-present feature of Whitefield's theology. Bemoaning ministers "who never preach up the law" as lacking the necessary theological foundation for then delivering "the glad tidings of the gospel," he made it his first priority to "shew people they are condemned." But assuming this initial posture of a "Boanerges, a son of thunder," was never an end in itself. Instead, it was a precursor to his ultimate desire of being a "Barnabas, a son of consolation," to those who saw their need for a Savior. Indeed, Whitefield had an irrepressible and contagious joy in showing convinced sinners "how they must be saved."[34]

His soteriology can be summarized as an appreciative eighteenth-century rendition of the Reformation and Puritan-era commitment to salvation by grace alone through faith alone. He believed and taught that while fallen humanity possesses genuine responsibility for their actions, every person without exception is both unwilling and incapable of contributing anything meritorious toward his or her salvation. In Whitefield's theology, humanity must be saved. It is God, and God alone, who takes the initiative in conceiving of this rescue in eternity past, who achieves it historically through the atoning death and resurrection of Jesus, and who promises to preserve and glorify his elect and thus fulfill the good work he has begun in them.

Two doctrines appear especially prominently in Whitefield's theology of salvation. First, the objective, external work of God in justifying guilty sinners; and second, the internal, subjective work of God in bringing about the experience of the new birth, or regeneration, in the lives of fallen people otherwise spiritually dead in their transgressions. We shall explore each of these in turn.

---

[33] *Journals*, 578.
[34] Whitefield, "The Seed of the Woman," 13.

Justification

Whitefield's mature theology of justification was heavily influenced by the apostle Paul's juridical language found especially in his epistle to the Romans. In his sermon "Of Justification by Christ," Whitefield painted a picture of justification that focuses on divine forgiveness and acquittal. Justification means "you have your sins forgiven, and are looked upon by God as though you never had offended him at all. . . . This word justified, implies a blotting out of all our transgressions." Encouraging his audience to envisage a courtroom scene in which God as Judge longs to declare sinners not guilty on account of Jesus's merits, Whitefield continued: "It is a law term, and alludes to a judge acquitting an accused criminal of the thing laid to his charge. . . . By being justified, we are to understand, being so acquitted in the sight of God, as to be looked upon as though we had never offended him at all."[35]

His conception of justification evolved to eventually incorporate a characteristically Reformed emphasis on imputation. Before his exposure to robust Calvinist influences, Whitefield gave the impression that he understood the doctrine simply in terms of a mere forgiveness of sins. Indeed, this was the essence and extent of John Wesley's lifelong conception of justification, which limited the extent of God's forgiveness to sins committed in the past. But come the late 1730s, this "low sense" in which Whitefield initially understood justification was augmented by a conviction that God also gifts those he has justified with "a federal right to all good things to come."[36]

From this point onward, he championed the double-faceted nature of imputation—the great exchange—whereby the transgressions of the justified are imputed to Jesus while Jesus's righteousness is imputed to undeserving sinners. Responding to the question implied in the language of "how the Lord is man's righteousness," he stated, "In one word, by imputation." He continued: "Christ not only died, he lived; not only suffered, but obeyed for, or instead of, poor sinners. And both these jointly make up that complete righteousness which is to be imputed to us, as the disobedience of our first parents was made ours by imputation."[37]

Just as the apostle Paul countered the accusation that the doctrine of justification theologically legitimizes licentiousness, Whitefield too

---

[35] Whitefield, "Of Justification by Christ," 216.
[36] Whitefield, "Christ, the Believer's Wisdom, Righteousness, Sanctification, and Redemption," in *Works*, 6:196.
[37] Whitefield, "Of Justification by Christ," 219–20.

responded to what he styled this "stale, antiquated objection." For instance, in his sermon "What Think Ye of Christ," after rehearsing the nature of justification by grace alone through faith alone, he wrote: "But I am afraid, numbers are ready to go away contradicting and blaspheming. Tell me, are there not many of you saying within yourselves, 'This is a licentious doctrine; this preacher is opening a door for encouragement in sin.'" With Paul's reasoning in Romans 6 serving as an inspired precedent, Whitefield attempted to cut this objection off at the pass, concluding that far from encouraging unholy living, the doctrine of justification "is not destroying, but teaching you how to do good works, from a proper principle."[38]

Elsewhere he argued that antinomian misappropriations of justification not only obscure the true intent of the doctrine but also perversely give "enemies of the Lord . . . cause to blaspheme." Whitefield stated: "The only question should be, whether or not this doctrine of an imputed righteousness does in itself cut off the occasion for good works, or lead to licentiousness? To this we may boldly answer, In no wise." He continued, "It excludes works, indeed, from being any cause of our justification in the sight of God; but it requires good works as a proof of our having this righteousness imputed to us, and as a declarative evidence of our justification in the sight of men."[39]

Grotesque parodies of Whitefield's doctrine of justification and supposed antinomian sympathies appeared from some unlikely sources during his lifetime. No doubt resentful of his frequent excoriation of the ills of the secular theater—not to mention feeling intimidated by the threat he posed to their market share of potential audiences—playwrights like Samuel Foote lambasted Whitefield's character, typically casting him as a charlatan preacher named Dr. Squintum (an allusion to his vision disorder, which affected the appearance of his eyes). Foote also took aim at his theology. For instance, in his highly successful 1760 play *The Minor*, Foote deployed the character of Mrs. Cole, the proprietor of a house of prostitution and one of Squintum's most prominent "converts," as a not-so-subtle vehicle for slandering Whitefield's doctrines as providing a cover for immorality. When asked how she could possibly reconcile her "vocation" with her evangelical "conversion," in a scurrilous distortion of Whitefield's theology, Foote's Mrs. Cole confidently replied, "Why, the Doctor knows that

38 Whitefield, "What Think Ye of Christ," in *Works*, 5:363.
39 Whitefield, "The Lord Our Righteousness," 221.

Works are of no Consequence toward a Future State, and that Faith is all."[40] Not even John Wesley, who was often hasty in drawing what he perceived to be a short and straight theological line between Calvinism and antinomianism, could quite bring himself to tar Whitefield, whose conspicuous godliness he knew firsthand, with this licentious brush.

Regeneration

If Whitefield understood justification to signify a believer's new legal standing before God—that, by grace through faith, God declares sinners no longer guilty in his sight and clothes them with an alien righteousness—then regeneration signified to him the new inward spiritual life God simultaneously imparts to believers. He understood these two doctrines to be conceptually discrete but nonetheless inextricably linked facets of salvation. God never justifies individuals without also sanctifying them, and that process of sanctification begins with the new birth. Whitefield wrote: "Is Christ your sanctification, as well as your outward righteousness? . . . These two, God has joined together. He never did, he never does, he never will, put them asunder. If you are justified by the blood, you are also sanctified by the Spirit, of our Lord."[41]

Whitefield's conversion became a template for the experience of the new birth he exhorted his audiences to undergo. A crucial turning point for him—both doctrinally and experientially—came in 1735 when, at Charles Wesley's recommendation, Whitefield read Henry Scougal's *The Life of God in the Soul of Man*. The Scotch Puritan's emphasis on a changed heart as the nonnegotiable marker of authentic Christian life left a dramatic impression on Whitefield and convinced him of his own need to undergo a radical inward transformation. Thereafter, he acknowledged that "true religion" does not consist in fulfilling religious duties. Instead, it consists of the "union of the soul with God, and Christ formed within." He wrote, "From that moment, but not till then, did I know that I must be a new creature."[42]

From 1737 onward, the theme of spiritual regeneration became a signature feature of Whitefield's proclamation of the gospel. For instance, in his sermon "On Regeneration," he went so far as to describe the "doctrine of our regeneration" as "the very hinge on which the salvation of each of

---

[40] Quoted in Albert M. Lyles, *Methodism Mocked: The Satiric Reaction to Methodism in the Eighteenth Century* (London: Epworth, 1960), 53.
[41] Whitefield, "The Lord Our Righteousness," 229.
[42] *Journals*, 46–47.

us turns." Such is the dire nature of humanity's spiritual plight that any attempt at self-wrought moral reformation is destined to fail. Given our predicament, Whitefield preached that nothing short of a "total renovation of [one's] depraved nature" is required, echoing Scougal in contending that a "bare outward profession of being called after His name" is insufficient. Rather, "he is a true Christian, who is one inwardly, whose baptism is that of the heart, in the Spirit." Appealing to a plethora of passages teaching the necessity of regeneration, Whitefield posed the rhetorical question, "Now what can be understood by all these different terms of being *born again* [cf. John 3:3–8], of *putting off the Old Man* and *putting on the New* [Eph. 4:22–24], of being *renewed in the spirit of our minds* [Rom. 12:2] and becoming *new creatures* [2 Cor. 5:17], but that Christianity requires a thorough, real, inward change of heart?"[43]

The new birth was by no means an abstract, theoretical truth for Whitefield, and he attested to its reality from personal experience. Not long before his death, he recounted the way he had known the effects of regeneration "for about thirty-five years as clear as the sun is in the meridian."[44] Just as Wesley told of how his "heart strangely warmed"[45] at Aldersgate Street on May 24, 1738, Whitefield detailed the spiritually visceral nature of his new birth. He described the way those who had undergone regeneration should be able to attest to a "spiritual, as well as a corporeal feeling; . . . it is as real as any sensible or visual sensation, and may truly be felt and discerned by the soul, as any impression from without can be felt by the body."[46]

But as certain as he was of the reality of regeneration, befitting Jesus's teaching on the subject to a perplexed Nicodemus in John 3, Whitefield's preaching on the new birth left room for mystery surrounding its precise spiritual mechanics. He conceded, "The truth of the matter is this: the doctrine of our regeneration, or new birth in Christ Jesus, is hard to be understood by the natural man." Indeed, "how this glorious change is wrought in the soul cannot easily be explained. For no one knows the ways of the

43 Whitefield, "On Regeneration," in *Works*, 6:257, 259–60, 262 (italics in the original).
44 Whitefield, "God a Believer's Glory," in *Eighteen Sermons*, 380.
45 Wesley, *Works of John Wesley*, 18:250.
46 Whitefield, "What Think Ye of Christ?," 369. Stout contends that for all eighteenth-century evangelical revivalists, regardless of their precise theological orientation, "individual experience became the ultimate arbiter of authentic religious faith. . . . As sensation represented the only avenue for natural knowledge in Lockean epistemology, so the supernatural experience of the New Birth became the sole authentic means to spiritual knowledge in the evangelical revivals." Harry S. Stout, *The Divine Dramatist: George Whitefield and the Rise of Modern Evangelicalism* (Grand Rapids, MI: Eerdmans, 1991), 205.

Spirit, save the Spirit of God Himself. Not that this ought to be any argument against this doctrine."[47]

Sanctification and Perfection

Thus far we have seen the way Whitefield's moderate Calvinism expressed itself in doctrinally predictable ways, including a commitment to unconditional election, an orthodox doctrine of original sin, justification by grace alone through faith alone, double imputation, and the necessity of spiritual rebirth as the threshold of a life of progressive sanctification. He also contended for God's preservation of his elect and, as we shall now observe, against the possibility of attaining what Arminian revivalists like John Wesley styled "Christian perfection." And yet, Wesley's distinctive stance on the extent to which a believer can be fully sanctified in this life was not the only position on the nature of the postregenerate Christian life that Whitefield challenged in the public sphere. He also emphatically rebutted what he styled the "sin-soothing" doctrines espoused by one of his most strident critics of the day, the prominent Church of England clergyman and professor of poetry Dr. Joseph Trapp (1679–1747). In other words, Whitefield's theological utterances on the subject of perfection were far from monochrome. Instead, they were characterized by a pronounced multivocality that revealed him to be a far more sophisticated and agile theologian than is often recognized.

Whitefield was unsurprisingly forthright in preaching against the perfectionism championed by John Wesley. At the same time that he was striving to reclaim the evocative language of "free grace" from Wesley and reapply it in terms compatible with his Calvinistic convictions (emphasizing God's sovereign freedom to give and withhold grace), he was also challenging Wesley's monopolization of the language of perfection. For instance, in a letter to Wesley penned in 1740, Whitefield lamented: "I am sorry to hear . . . that you seem to own a sinless perfection in this life attainable."[48] "Sinless perfection" was the typical term he used to describe Wesley's theology of sanctification, which Whitefield interpreted as Wesley's claim that a believer can attain an unimpeachable and irrevocable legal standing before God.

---

[47] Whitefield, "On Regeneration," 260–61.
[48] Whitefield to Rev. Mr. J—W—, September 25, 1740, in *Letters*, 211. Throughout 1740, Whitefield consistently described Wesley's position using the terminology of "sinless perfection." See *Journals*, 459; *Letters*, 208.

For his part, though, Wesley strenuously sought to distance himself from this doctrinal characterization. Contrary to Whitefield's assessment, Wesley consistently defined "Christian"—not "sinless"—perfection, as a dynamic reality, where "neither perfection nor imperfection is a fixed state."[49] He declared that there is no such thing as "absolute perfection on earth . . . none which does not admit of a continual increase."[50] As for the language of "sinless perfection," Wesley clarified: "[It] is a phrase I never use. . . . I believe a person filled with the love of God is still liable to . . . involuntary transgressions. . . . Such transgressions you may call 'sins' if you please. I do not."[51]

But if Whitefield failed to grasp the admittedly subtle nuances embedded within Wesley's perfectionism, then Whitefield's Calvinist theology—augmented by his experience of the Christian life—attested to what Wesley was unable to fathom: how Whitefield's doctrine of indwelling sin in the life of a believer could coexist with a zealous pursuit of holiness. Perhaps Whitefield was insinuating that an Arminian doctrine of perfection afforded scope for spiritual pride when he appealed to the spiritually invigorating effects of his awareness of a need for further sanctification: "I do not expect to say indwelling sin is finished and destroyed in me, till I bow down my head and give up the ghost. There must be some Amalekites left in the Israelite's land, to keep his soul in action, to keep him humble, and to drive him continually to Jesus for pardon and forgiveness."[52]

And yet, while Whitefield was a vocal critic of Wesley's perfectionism, he was just as emphatic in his opposition toward what he perceived to be the "im-perfectionism" sanctioned by Anglican contemporaries like Joseph Trapp, whom he cast as a dangerous libertine.[53] As Whitefield went about London during the middle of 1739 preaching and rapidly growing in popularity, Trapp was just as busy, going about the city on his own anti-Whitefield publicity tour. In a series of sermons, based on Ecclesiastes 7:16 and subsequently printed under the collective title *The Nature, Folly, Sin, and Danger of Being Righteous Over-much*, Trapp scolded Whitefield for setting the bar of holiness excessively high: "But why must we allow ourselves no Pleasure in worldly Things? Is there no such Thing as innocent Diversion?"[54]

---

49 Theodore Runyon, *The New Creation: John Wesley's Theology Today* (Nashville: Abingdon, 1998), 88.

50 Wesley, "Christian Perfection," in *Works of John Wesley*, 2:104.

51 Wesley, *Works of John Wesley*, 13:170.

52 Whitefield to Rev. Mr. J—W—, September 25, 1740, in *Letters*, 211.

53 See also Ian J. Maddock, "George Whitefield: Christian Perfectionist?," *Reformed Theological Review* 74, no. 3 (2015): 147–61.

54 Joseph Trapp, *The Nature, Folly, Sin, and Danger of Being Righteous Over-much* (London: S. Austen, 1739), 24.

Whitefield's response was both swift and theologically pugnacious, immediately preaching and then printing two sermons respectively entitled "The Folly and Danger of Being Not Righteous Enough"[55] and "A Preservative against Unsettled Notions and Want of Principles, in Regard to Righteousness and Christian Perfection." Both sermons involved vigorous defenses of holy living, as Whitefield attempted to chart a middle course between the Scylla of what he styled Trapp's "irreligion" and the Charybdis of enthusiasm. "True piety," Whitefield contended, "like the centre of an infinite line, is at an equal infinite distance from the one and the other and therefore can never admit of a coalition with either. The one erring by defect, the other by excess."[56]

In the second of these sermons, Whitefield openly embraced and adopted the language of perfection—noteworthy and not incidental, given his concurrent repudiation of Wesley's perfectionism during the years 1739 and 1740. Throughout "A Preservative against Unsettled Notions," Whitefield addressed his exhortations to his "beloved lovers of Christian perfection" and urged his readers "to never give over pursuing and thirsting after the perfect righteousness of Christ, until we rest in him." He prayed to God, "Lead us on perpetually towards that perfection to which thou hast taught us to aspire" and "which thou hast promised to all such as shall endeavour to be perfect, even as the Father who is in heaven is perfect." He even went so far as to cast himself—no doubt, for those with ears to hear, in an implicit critique of Wesley—as a singularly orthodox defender of Christian perfection. He justified the polemical nature of his sermon on the grounds that Trapp's "sin-soothing" doctrines "have given so great a shock to the sound religion of Christian perfection, that unless I had opposed him, I verily believe the whole flock who listened to his doctrine would have been scattered abroad like sheep having no shepherd."[57]

That is, if Whitefield was opposed to Wesley's insistence that all traces of indwelling sin might successfully be eradicated during a Christian's lifetime, he nonetheless exhorted believers to pursue perfection and avoid the moral complacency he understood Trapp to be advocating. Contrary to Wesley's fears that Calvinist soteriology inevitably encouraged antinomianism and discouraged the pursuit of holiness, Whitefield embraced

---

[55] In 1715, Trapp had published a treatise under the title *A Preservative against Unsettled Notions and Want of Principles in Religion*, no doubt prompting Whitefield's choice of title.

[56] Whitefield, "A Preservative against Unsettled Notions, and Want of Principles, in Regard to Righteousness and Christian Perfection," in *Works*, 5:141.

[57] Whitefield, "A Preservative against Unsettled Notions," 142–43, 155, 157.

the language of perfection, so long as it was appropriately configured in a manner palatable to his Calvinistic theological tastes. In this way, for all of the partial shortcomings in his understanding of Wesley's theology, Whitefield's spoken and printed sermons on the doctrine of sanctification nonetheless reveal him to be a dexterous theologian, adept at responding to what he instinctively perceived to be threats to sound doctrine and practice.

Whitefield's Experiential Calvinism

Whitefield's theology was a prime example of the "moderate Calvinism" prevalent during the eighteenth-century evangelical revivals.[58] Eventually coming to cherish the Calvinist theology he discovered in the years following his conversion and in the lead-up to his first preaching tour of the American colonies, he expressed his doctrine "with a strong emphasis on piety, devotion, and religious experience." He embodied a Calvinism that must "be experienced, felt, and known in the heart."[59]

Abstract theological reflection and doctrinal innovation were anathema to Whitefield. He used his God-given creativity to imaginatively present what he considered to be the doctrinal essence of the Bible's metanarrative—namely, "our fall in Adam, and the necessity of our new birth in Christ Jesus."[60] Read through a Reformed lens, he habitually identified the doctrines of original sin, justification by faith, and the new birth as constituting the settled core of his evangelistic, conversion-oriented sermons.

Indeed, less than a year before his death at the relatively young age of fifty-five—and in a moment of candid theological self-reflection—he recollected, "The second sermon I ever preached, was on these words, *He that is in Christ is a new creature*: I was then about twenty years and a half old. The next sermon I preached upon, *Ye are justified*; the next sermon, *Ye are glorified*." Contemplating these unchanging doctrinal convictions with much satisfaction, he reflected,

> Though I am fifty-five years old, yet, thank God, I am so far from changing my principles . . . that if I was to die this moment, I hope I should have the strength and courage given me to say, I am more convinced of the efficacy

[58] Mark K. Olson, "Whitefield's Conversion and Early Theological Formation," in *George Whitefield: Life, Context and Legacy*, ed. Geordan Hammond and David Ceri Jones (Oxford: Oxford University Press, 2016), 45.
[59] Caldwell, *Theologies*, 20.
[60] Whitefield, "The Duty of Searching the Scriptures," in *Works*, 6:80.

and the power of those truths which I preached when I was twenty years old, than when I first preached them.[61]

Soon afterward, in a memorial sermon delivered in London on November 18, 1770, none other than John Wesley concurred: "The new birth" and "justification by faith" were "the fundamental doctrines which he everywhere insisted on."[62]

---

[61] Whitefield, "Neglect of Christ the Killing Sin," in *Eighteen Sermons*, 269 (italics in the original).
[62] Wesley, "On the Death of George Whitefield," in *Works of John Wesley*, 2:343.

CHAPTER 3

TRUE RELIGION

If George Whitefield were living today and picked up any volume in this Crossway series, "Theologians on the Christian Life," he would be delighted to read the "Series Preface." He would certainly proclaim a hearty *amen* to the goal of "learning about and practicing discipleship" and distilling "wisdom for living the Christian life." Inspired throughout his life by this conviction—which was reinforced through his deep commitment to Scripture—he challenged anyone with whom he had contact to examine his or her life and to know the distinction between being an "almost Christian" and an "altogether Christian."

Early in his ministry, he discerned that the nature of a true Christian consists of four different marks of a faithful disciple. First, a believer is someone who understands and cultivates true religion. Second, Jesus's disciples must be filled with the Holy Spirit; and, third, they must seek to consistently deny themselves, take up their cross, and be Christ's followers. The fourth and most difficult indicator is persecution for the cause of Christ, or at least willingness to suffer for him if needed.

Nature of True Religion

Once Whitefield experienced the new birth, he recognized that many people who claim to be Christians lack the essential biblical vitality of the new life in Christ. To speak of true religion implies that false religion also exists. Not surprisingly, this judgmental attitude against the authenticity of others' faith generated opposition from those whom Whitefield called "almost Christians." He addressed the nature of true religion through a broad linguistic spectrum including *vital religion,*[1] *heart religion,*[2] *inward religion,*[3] and the *divine life.*[4] He proclaimed that a person is a "true Christian" only if he or she is inwardly born of God, is raised to new life by the Holy Spirit, and experiences a "thorough newness both of heart and life."[5]

Preaching on Romans 14:17 ("For the kingdom of God is not meat and drink; but righteousness, and peace, and joy in the Holy Ghost"), Whitefield expounded the nature of the kingdom of God.[6] He warned against the persistent problem of divisions within the body of Christ and the human tendency to dispute with others holding different positions. Whitefield articulated the need for a catholic spirit that embraced others who were born again, regardless of their denomination, because unity rather than division exists in heaven. He defined the kingdom of God as "true and undefiled religion, heart and soul-religion." In other words, true religion identifies those belonging to God's reign. As the sermon unfolded, he first examined what God's kingdom is not. Many of his listeners were shocked when he repudiated the common assumption that simply belonging to a specific church or worshiping God by observing certain external religious practices made a true believer. According to Whitefield, this was not the means to enter heaven.[7]

He also claimed that baptism alone is insufficient to make a Christian. The Anglican teaching of baptismal regeneration had convinced many that they were true believers, even though they had been baptized only in water and not of the Holy Spirit (Matt. 3:11; Acts 1:5). Whitefield dismantled the common assumptions of what constitutes a true believer, including having your name recorded in the church membership book. This means nothing unless it is also entered into the book of life. Nor does speaking intelligently about the truths of the gospel validate believers unless they have

---

[1] Whitefield to Rev. Mr. M—, November 10, 1748, in *Works,* 2:200; Whitefield, "Recommendatory Preface to the Works of Mr. John Bunyan," in *Works,* 4:306.

[2] Whitefield, "Law Gospelized," in *Works,* 4:391; Whitefield, "Christ the Only Rest for the Weary and Heavy Laden," in *Works,* 5:310. For a helpful treatment of Whitefield's heart religion, see David Ceri Jones, "George Whitefield and Heart Religion," in *Heart Religion: Evangelical Piety in England and Ireland, 1690–1850,* ed. John Coffey (Oxford: Oxford University Press, 2016), 93–112.

[3] Whitefield, "Benefits of Early Piety," in *Works,* 5:161; Whitefield, "Christ the Believer's Husband," in *Works,* 5:174.

[4] Sean McGever observes that Whitefield used this term over fifty times in his corpus as synonymous with the new birth. McGever, *Born Again: The Evangelical Theology of Conversion in John Wesley and George Whitefield* (Bellingham, WA: Lexham, 2020), 127n129.

[5] Whitefield, "The Power of Christ's Resurrection," in *Works,* 6:323.

[6] George Whitefield, *The Kingdom of God* (Glasgow: Robert Smith, 1741).

[7] Whitefield, *The Kingdom of God,* 8–9, 11–12.

experienced the truth deeply in their hearts. A person might even know the church's catechism and hold orthodox beliefs yet have "the devil in [his or her] heart."[8]

After reviewing these unreliable signs of true religion, Whitefield confessed his earlier ignorance: "I know how much I was deceived with a form of godliness." Much like the apostle Paul, who reported his conversion three times (Acts 9:1–19; 22:3–16; 26:4–18), Whitefield rehearsed his conversion more than once. On each occasion, he stressed that he had fasted twice a week, often prayed nine times a day, and received the Lord's Supper weekly, yet was still ignorant in grasping the truth that "inward religion" required his transformed heart. His early confusion created empathy for his listeners as he passionately proclaimed the good news whenever and wherever he preached. The transatlantic evangelist never tired of affirming Scougal's *The Life of God in the Soul of Man*, which had introduced him to the nature of true religion. He no longer believed that religion is simply a matter of performing spiritual activities but became fully convinced of the necessity of the new birth. To dramatize his conviction, he reminded his auditors that Paul had followed a similar consuming external religiosity before his conversion (Phil. 3:2–16).[9]

Further, Whitefield announced that receiving the Spirit is not to impress people with amazing signs and wonders but to sanctify the soul.[10] To correct their distorted impressions of what it meant to be a true Christian, he appealed to the various needs of his listeners. Some were already true Christians and desired to renew their faith. Others attended church, thinking they were true believers, and quickly discovered they did not fit the biblical paradigm of Whitefield's message. Still others were antagonistic to the gospel and came only to heckle him. Regardless of the crowd's motivation, God could change their resistant hearts. From start to finish, Whitefield declared that only a converted person could experience the reality and benefits of true religion.

His sermon "The Almost Christian" further clarified the distinctive nature of true religion and explored several questions, including the nature, attraction, and dangers of being an "almost Christian."[11] First, Whitefield parsed the nature of this partial believer. Such a person possesses an

---

8 Whitefield, *The Kingdom of God*, 31.
9 Whitefield, *The Kingdom of God*, 13–14, 19–22.
10 Whitefield, *The Kingdom of God*, 21, 23, 27.
11 Whitefield, "The Almost Christian," in *Works*, 6:174–86. John Wesley preached on the same text using the same title on July 25, 1741, three years after Whitefield did.

unstable nature that can oscillate between Jesus Christ and the world. This individual is superficially attracted to a biblical understanding of salvation but finds wealth and the works of darkness more alluring than God's transforming light. Further, Whitefield decried individuals "fond of the form" of godliness who have nonetheless never experienced the power of the new birth in their hearts. Counterfeit Christians are also preoccupied with making an impression on others, especially those who are wealthy or in powerful places of leadership. They seek to be noticed through public displays of charity, as long as little is required of them, and they avoid the difficult acts of visiting those who are sick or in prison. Weaving these themes together, Whitefield critiqued the "almost Christian" as being "guided more by the world, than by the word of God." He hoped that some of his listeners would identify with at least one of his descriptions of this distorted image of a true believer and prayed that it would convict them to seek to be an "altogether Christian."[12]

Whitefield proclaimed that there are five reasons why people might be "almost Christians." Variations of these erroneous beliefs appear throughout his corpus. The first parallels his "Kingdom of God" sermon and warns of the danger of relying on morality, belonging to a specific church, or performing religious duties to satisfy oneself and impress God. He clarified that only a "thorough inward change of nature, a divine life, a vital participation of Jesus Christ, an union of the soul with God" can produce an "altogether Christian," that is, a true, complete Christian. Next, those who are timid fear what others might think of them if they believe in Jesus, and they desire the praise of people more than the affirmation of God. Third, some are consumed by a love for money, like the rich young man from Scripture (Mark 10:17–27); despite following all of the commandments, he needed to "renounce the self-enjoyment of riches" and follow Jesus. Still others do not embrace Christ because of their "love of pleasure." Whitefield acknowledged that some people give their money to those in need but lack the deeper surrender of idols and refuse to take up their cross and follow Jesus. Whitefield would later examine the importance of the cross for "altogether Christians" in his teaching on discipleship. Fifth, some are "almost Christians" because they lack a consistent lifestyle—they have begun the journey out of novelty but have soon discovered the road was too narrow or too long—and lose interest in following Jesus.[13]

---

12 Whitefield, "The Almost Christian," 176–79.
13 Whitefield, "The Almost Christian," 179–82.

This sermon concluded with a reminder of the futility of being an "almost Christian." There can be no salvation for anyone who rejects Christ's message, since God accepts no rivals: a divided heart will remain continually empty. Further, this path reveals a rejection of and ingratitude toward Jesus. When one considers what it cost Christ to purchase the souls of humanity by shedding his precious blood, the required human response becomes clear. Whitefield reasoned that surrendering a mere portion of one's heart to Christ displays the height of ungratefulness. Therefore, if God's presence provides fullness of joy, why would anyone chance missing it by clinging to the superficial substitutes of living an "almost Christian" life?[14]

Seven years later, Whitefield wrote to a wealthy man and stressed the urgency of total dedication to Jesus as he encouraged him to be a "good soldier of Jesus Christ." While the circumstance of the person was unknown, he was facing difficult challenges in being consistent in his faith, and Whitefield sought to bolster his confidence. Whitefield admonished his friend that it is a "blessed thing to be engaged in fighting his [Jesus's] battles; and not only to be almost, but altogether a Christian." Ignoring this admonition to total commitment would produce a "half-way religion" and contradict the profession of committed Christians.[15]

The Indwelling Presence of the Holy Spirit

In a sermon preached to a London religious society, Whitefield expanded his instruction on the nature of true religion to include "a thorough, real, inward change of nature, wrought in us by the powerful operations of the Holy Ghost, conveyed to and nourished in our hearts, by a constant use of all the means of grace, evidenced by a good life, and bringing forth the fruits of the spirit." He proclaimed that this is "real, inward religion" and is dependent on God's Trinitarian salvific intervention. Although the individual experiences the new birth in Jesus Christ, the unfolding renovation is dependent on the Holy Spirit, who refashions the inner life to produce an outward expression of holy living. God also actively inspires the use of spiritual disciplines to deepen this process of maturity.[16]

Further, Whitefield emphasized that the radical transformation of the new birth is possible only as the Holy Spirit is "felt" in a person's soul.[17]

---

[14] Whitefield, "The Almost Christian," 183.
[15] Whitefield to Lord R—, November 10, 1748, in *Works*, 2:198.
[16] Whitefield, "The Benefits of Early Piety," 161.
[17] Whitefield, "The Folly and Danger of Being Not Righteous Enough," in *Works*, 5:126.

Scripture affirms this gift of the indwelling presence of the Spirit in a born-again person's heart (Rom. 8:9, 11; 1 Cor. 3:16; Gal. 4:6; 2 Tim. 1:14). The transatlantic evangelist taught this essential truth in his 1739 Pentecost Sunday sermon, "The Indwelling of the Spirit, the Common Privilege of All Believers," based on John 7:37–39.[18] Some of his critics challenged him that the Holy Spirit was given only to Jesus's initial followers. He countered by reminding his fellow Anglican critics that they had confessed this truth at their ordination.

He also explained that this vital experience of the Holy Spirit is not reserved for ministers alone but is for every person who believes in Jesus Christ—no one can experience the new life in Christ without being born of the Spirit (John 3:8). Foundational to Whitefield's understanding was the doctrine of union with Christ. The Spirit is the person responsible for bringing believers into union with Christ, who further joins them with God. Furthermore, "the Holy Spirit is the common privilege and portion of all believers in all ages; and . . . we also as well as the first Christians, must receive the Holy Ghost before we can be truly called the children of God." For Whitefield, "child of God" was synonymous with "altogether Christian." Therefore, the proof of being a genuine believer is the indwelling presence of God's Spirit.

That raised the practical question of how we can recognize "the operation of God's Spirit upon the hearts of believers." Whitefield responded by asserting that individuals should be able to "feel" the Holy Spirit. This sent shock waves of trepidation into his opponents, who warned of the potential danger of subjectivity and countered that a person can have the Holy Spirit but not feel him. Whitefield considered this nonsense, because to have the Spirit and not be able to feel him denies the living presence of the Spirit in a person's life.[19]

Similarly, Whitefield was frequently reviled for not being a faithful Anglican minister. To refute those charges, he quoted the liturgy of the Church of England, reminding his opponents that the collect for Christmas Day stressed God's daily renewal through the Spirit. Also, the prayer for the Sunday before Pentecost requested that the comforts of the Holy Spirit might bring joy to all believers. Since the ordination orders for deacon and priest underscored the prerequisite of the third person of the Trinity for

---

18 Whitefield, "The Indwelling of the Spirit, the Common Privilege of All Believers," in *Works*, 6:89–102.
19 Whitefield, "The Indwelling of the Spirit," 89–93.

conducting one's ministry, Whitefield reminded his fellow clergymen once again what they had professed in their vows. Deacons were required to acknowledge that they were "inwardly moved by the Holy Ghost." And the bishop pronounced these words over priests: "Receive thou the Holy Ghost, now committed unto thee, by the imposition of our hands." Therefore, according to Whitefield, the need to experience the felt presence of the Holy Spirit was not aberrant theology but something true of every ordained member of the Church of England.[20]

Whitefield enumerated other benefits every believer should expect from the Spirit's indwelling. Jesus's high priestly prayer included the Holy Spirit's desire to unite "all true followers" of Jesus together (John 17:11, 21, 23). Once more Whitefield highlighted the importance of union with Christ, a theme he absorbed from his reading of the Puritans. As he expanded this truth, he asserted that God's Spirit joins Christians in a "real, vital, and mystical" union. Christian unity is dependent on a catholic spirit, a truth that created Whitefield's lifelong desire for increased cooperation among believers. While there can be many manifestations of unity, he particularly prayed for a shared passion for proclaiming the new life in Christ. Scripture is dependent on the Spirit's inspiration, and without this revelation, there will be no comprehension of God or the awareness of freedom from sin. The dynamic power of the Holy Spirit guides believers in sanctification by urging the process of dying to sin and rising afresh in Christ. Whitefield also reasoned that anyone who does not receive the Spirit cannot "dwell with and enjoy God." This translates into a deepening communion with God that begins on earth and will reach fulfillment in heaven. Another principle of this sermon was Whitefield's practice of referring to Christians as Jesus's followers, which leads to the third mark of a true Christian.[21]

Walking with Jesus in Discipleship

While the language of discipleship was not common in Whitefield's time, the principles of discipleship were nevertheless significant for him. He once referred to himself as a "disciple" when he reached his destination after a long day of traveling and preaching. Because of his itinerant ministry, he was dependent on newly made friends who provided accommodations. When he retired late that evening, he compared himself to Jesus, who

20 Whitefield, "The Indwelling of the Spirit," 94–95.
21 Whitefield, "The Indwelling of the Spirit," 93, 97, 99.

had no place to "lay his head" (Matt. 8:20).[22] Just as he made a distinction between true religion and the many counterfeit expressions of it, he also qualified that not all who follow Jesus outwardly are his "true disciples."[23] One key determination of a genuine disciple is whether the person faithfully follows Jesus's commands and fulfills them out of love rather than mere duty.[24]

Some of Whitefield's listeners lacked clarity on the proper nature of discipleship, believing that it implied a higher level of Christianity, but for him the terms *disciple* and *Christian* were synonymous.[25] Occasionally he employed the term *disciples* to refer to fellow ministers, but more often it was a designation of laypeople.[26] During a visit outside of Philadelphia, he examined the different denominations and churches represented in the area. "About four in the afternoon, we went with many dear disciples of the Lord" to visit an elderly person.[27] In his preaching he distinguished between the nature and the action of Christ's followers. The nature relates to the character or being of a disciple and provides instruction regarding a person's identity in Christ. The action concerns what Jesus Christ expects his followers to do, and how to live out their lives in the world through imitation of him.

The Nature of a Disciple

The "Grand Itinerant," as Whitefield's contemporaries dubbed him, talked frequently about developing Jesus's attitude of humility and illustrated this through Mary, declaring, "She seated herself at the feet of Jesus, in the posture of a humble disciple." Many writers throughout history have elevated Mary above Martha. While Jesus rebuked Martha for her distracted inattentiveness, it was clear that she loved Jesus as much as Mary and that serving Christ was just as important as times of quiet attentiveness spent with him. Whitefield believed that Martha would have gladly joined her sister at Jesus's feet but that someone needed to prepare the dinner. Nonetheless, he praised Mary's wiser choice and affirmed, "I rather recommend [Mary] to your imitation, and caution you, and all my other friends, to be much on

---

22 *Journals*, 474.
23 Whitefield, "Blind Bartimaeus," in *Works*, 5:406; Whitefield, "The Great Duty of Charity Recommended," in *Works*, 6:238.
24 Whitefield, "The Lord Our Righteousness," in *Works*, 5:225.
25 Michael J. Wilkins, *In His Image: Reflecting Christ in Everyday Life* (Colorado Springs: NavPress, 1997), 35–38.
26 *Journals*, 344.
27 *Journals*, 358; see also 212, 310, 313, 468 for further usage of Whitefield's discipleship language.

your guard" so that "in the midst of your worldly cares, you do not lose sight of what much better deserves your attention." Whitefield was cognizant that regardless of life's responsibilities, all Christians must be aware of the temptation to miss Jesus amid the busyness of their lives.[28]

Whitefield found in Mary's humble posture a powerful image of a disciple. Her sensitivity created a greater receptivity than Martha's to hearing Christ's words. This prompted Whitefield's assessment that a disciple must be prepared to receive both "the law and the gospel from [Jesus's] mouth." This critical balance reflects the teaching of Scripture that if either component is ignored, it creates an unhealthy Christ follower. Excessive reliance on the law without the gospel frequently creates a bitter, highly judgmental, or even melancholy person. Likewise, a narrow emphasis on the gospel, to the exclusion of the law, can leave a person without the proper perspective of sin or the reality of his or her own divided heart; it can lead to a presumptuousness about Christ's mercy that takes forgiveness for granted. The proper balance of law and gospel confronts a person with the necessity for regeneration, or new birth, and according to Whitefield, the new birth is the one thing that is needful.[29]

Whitefield was often a polarizing figure, creating opposition wherever he went. This was frequently due to his perception that many Anglican ministers were unconverted and ignorant, at least in the practical sense, of the Holy Spirit's enabling power and guidance. In 1739, Edmund Gibson, bishop of London, wrote a pastoral letter to the Church of England clergymen, though his intended audience was Whitefield and John Wesley. Whitefield responded by thanking the bishop for his care of the souls under his supervision and for recognizing the serious temptations of both lukewarmness and enthusiasm. Enthusiasm sought the direct guidance of the Holy Spirit and often included a highly charged emotionalism and volatile behavior. It carried excessive baggage from the seventeenth century and was usually associated with religious and political fringe groups that stirred fears of political instability. Whitefield declared that his response to the bishop was inspired by "love and meekness" that was reflective of "a disciple of Jesus Christ." Both of these terms imply a humble receptivity to listen to a person who has greater spiritual authority. Conscious of being only twenty-four years old, Whitefield saw the wisdom of replying with "humility and reverence" to

---

[28] Whitefield, "The Care of the Soul Urged as the One Thing Needful," in *Works*, 5:456–57.
[29] Whitefield, "The Care of the Soul Urged," 458.

the bishop. These four qualities of a disciple—love, meekness, humility, and reverence—reinforce the general principle of eager receptivity. Any disciple who embodies them will exhibit greater awareness of Jesus and be more fully transformed by the power of the Holy Spirit.[30]

The Doing of Discipleship

When Jesus inaugurated his earthly ministry, he read the words from Isaiah 61:1–2, which are recorded in Luke 4:18–19. Isaiah provided him with an expansive spectrum for his ministry, including proclaiming the good news to the poor, binding up the brokenhearted, announcing freedom for the captives, releasing the prisoners bound by darkness, and declaring the year of the Lord's favor. The Gospels reveal the compassion and deep empathy of Jesus throughout his public life (Matt. 9:36; 14:14; 20:34), and he drew near to people because they were like sheep without a shepherd (Mark 6:34). Whitefield reinforced the Christian's responsibility to care for the poor, as taught in the parable of the sheep and the goats (Matt. 25:31–46). Caring for one's neighbor was central to Jesus's teaching, though, according to Whitefield, it was so commonly ignored during his day that one might think Scripture were silent on this topic.[31]

Whitefield described his practice from his earliest Oxford days when he sought, "in imitation of my Lord's disciples," to follow Christ's example of compassion. This included visiting one or two sick people daily. While his financial resources were limited as a servitor, he sought donations from the wealthy to assist those who were poor.[32] In 1737, before his first voyage to Georgia, he began the practice of taking collections for prisoners and regularly expounded Scripture to them. He also frequently preached charity sermons to gather donations for less fortunate children.[33]

In 1739, Whitefield demonstrated the necessary social responsibility of a Christ follower by his regular visits to the sordid Newgate Prison in Bristol, England.[34] He continued this pattern in America, preaching in the prisons and taking collections for his underprivileged children at Bethesda, his Georgian orphanage.[35] During his final decade of life, he

---

[30] Whitefield, "Answer to the Bishop of London's Last Pastoral Letter," in *Works*, 4:5.
[31] Whitefield, "The Almost Christian," 177–78.
[32] *Journals*, 61–62. This was deleted from the 1756 *Journals*.
[33] *Journals*, 75, 77, 82, 87, 184.
[34] *Journals*, 214–15, 220. For the conditions at Newgate, see Thomas S. Kidd, *George Whitefield: America's Spiritual Founding Father* (New Haven, CT: Yale University Press, 2014), 67.
[35] *Journals*, 345, 402.

spoke from Matthew 25 in a New York City prison. A newspaper article reported afterward that he had donated his money to help debtors purchasing firewood for the winter and had paid the fines to release those jailed for smaller debts.[36] He again demonstrated his compassion for a London prisoner in 1768, and prayed and administered the Lord's Supper to him before he went to the gallows.[37] Even more compelling was what he called God's "peculiar providence" two months before his own death, when he encountered a horse stealer and received permission to speak to him before his execution. Whitefield even walked the final half-mile journey with him, stood "upon" his coffin, prayed, and gave a blessing.[38] His persistent empathy was also on display when he designed his Tottenham Court Road Chapel in London and constructed twelve small houses surrounding the church for the exclusive use of widows.[39]

The most focused treatment of Whitefield's teaching on discipleship appeared in "The Nature and Necessity of Self-Denial," first preached on October 9, 1737, based on Luke 9:23, "And he said to them all, if any man will come after me, let him deny himself." Its central message was the eternal nature of God's kingdom, built on the "doctrine of the cross," which, he said, required a "constant state of voluntary or self-suffering and self-denial."[40] Elsewhere, he claimed that Christianity had always been a "doctrine of the cross."[41] To indicate the seriousness of this commitment, he clarified that all who desire to share in Christ's honor first need to participate in his sufferings through self-denial. For Whitefield, denying oneself meant renouncing one's total life for the cause of Christ. This was not optional but rather "the grand secret of our holy religion." Self-denial is one of the most accurate diagnostic tools for distinguishing a moralistic and formal approach from that of a faithful follower of Jesus. "Holy religion," another synonym for true religion, confirms that a person is an "altogether Christian." Regardless of worldly enticements, Whitefield charged his listeners with the necessity of self-surrender, which should be done cheerfully. He was grieved by the addiction to "self-indulgence," the "reigning love of riches," and the abundant "greediness of sensual

---

[36] Kidd, *George Whitefield*, 235.

[37] Luke Tyerman, *The Life of the Rev. George Whitefield*, 2 vols. (London: Hodder and Stoughton, 1876–1877), 2:550–51.

[38] Whitefield to Mr. R— K—, July 29, 1770, in *Works*, 3:425.

[39] *Memoirs*, 226–27.

[40] George Whitefield, *The Nature and Necessity of Self-Denial* (London: James Hutton, 1738), 1.

[41] Whitefield, "The Almost Christian," 174.

pleasure" that saturated Britain. Any attempt to follow Jesus that revolves around the satisfaction of earthly desires is doomed to failure and will destroy self-denial.[42]

Some who heard Whitefield averred that self-renunciation was only intended for Jesus's first disciples. Leaving no room for doubt, he clarified that this was Christ's expectation for anyone who would follow him, regardless of time and place. He reaffirmed the necessity of self-denial when he proclaimed that the very essence of religion is a "recovery from our fallen estate in Adam, by a new birth in Christ Jesus." To refuse to surrender oneself confirms that a person is blinded by sin that has contaminated his or her whole life. Acting as a spiritual physician, Whitefield argued that the only remedy for a person bound by sin and imprisoned by the temptations of the world, the flesh, and the devil is Jesus Christ. Therefore, he prescribed "self-denial, mortification, and renunciation" of the self to experience the freedom that only God can provide.[43]

The sermon concluded with guidance and motivation for his hearers to apply the Scripture to their lives. First, he encouraged frequent meditation on the life of Jesus, who displayed the perfect model of self-surrender to God, which was evident throughout his life. Peter claimed Jesus "also suffered for you, leaving you an example, so that you might follow in his steps" (1 Pet. 2:21 ESV). Next, Whitefield called for a recovery of the lifestyle of early Christians, in particular, the "noble army of martyrs," who demonstrated how everyday disciples, both ministers and laypeople, followed Jesus, regardless of the cost.[44] Whitefield was likely already aware of John Foxe's *Book of Martyrs*—which provided a historical review of martyrs from the early church until Foxe's time in the sixteenth century—though Whitefield did not indicate reading it until his second voyage to America, in 1739, one year later.[45]

Whitefield's third motivation reflected on the "pains of hell," which revealed parallels to Ignatius of Loyola's use of spiritual imagination.[46] Just as Whitefield sought to challenge his listeners to be Christ's disciples,

---

[42] Whitefield, *The Nature and Necessity of Self-Denial*, 2, 5–6, 11. One detects echoes of Martin Luther's theology of the cross in this paragraph and in Whitefield's treatment of persecution. While he quoted Luther frequently, there is no explicit indication that he knew this foundational principle of the Reformer's theology. For a helpful summary of Luther's theology of the cross, see Stephen J. Nichols, *Bonhoeffer on the Christian Life: From the Cross, for the World* (Wheaton, IL: Crossway, 2013), 38.

[43] Whitefield, *The Nature and Necessity of Self-Denial*, 12–13, 15, 19.

[44] Whitefield, *The Nature and Necessity of Self-Denial*, 21–22.

[45] Whitefield to Mr. —, August 16, 1739, in *Letters*, 64.

[46] Whitefield, *The Nature and Necessity of Self-Denial*, 23–24.

Ignatius's *Spiritual Exercises* were developed to guide his fellow Jesuits in making a good decision to follow Jesus. Both utilized vivid retelling of Scripture passages to confront readers with desired actions to take. While there is no evidence of Whitefield having direct knowledge of Ignatius, his use of spiritual imagination followed a similar pattern.[47] However, it is more likely that Whitefield was influenced by his frequent reading of the Puritans from the previous century, who also created detailed meditations that employed sanctified or spiritual imagination for both reading and preaching Scripture.[48]

Whitefield's fourth motive was the converse of the third and invited his listeners to "meditate on the joys of heaven."[49] Once more he employed a vivid use of the imagination to create an attractive picture of heaven to influence his hearers. This demonstrated his awareness of the Puritan use of composition of place to help frame the biblical context so that listeners might better enter into and apply the Scripture to their lives.[50]

Whitefield's emphasis on self-surrender was based on Christ's crucifixion and focused on Jesus as the Lamb of God who freely shed his blood on the cross to save sinners. One of Whitefield's most successful publishing ventures was his *Hymns for Social Worship*. While he did not compose texts like his gifted poetic friend Charles Wesley, he compiled the hymns of others for use in his London Tabernacle. His selection of these hymns confirms that they resonated with his theology. One selection was Isaac Watts's "When I Survey the Wondrous Cross," which captured the significance of the cross and was entitled "Glorying in the Cross":

> When Saints survey the wondr'ous Cross,
> On which the Prince of Glory dy'd,
> Their richest gain they count but loss,
> And pour contempt on all their pride.

The first stanza, while not mentioning Christ's blood, clearly recognizes Jesus's death through the brutal means of execution typically reserved for the most dangerous criminals. A common human fallacy is to proudly take

---

47 D. Bruce Hindmarsh, *The Spirit of Early Evangelicalism: True Religion in a Modern World* (New York: Oxford University Press, 2018), 283n37; see also 19–20.
48 Tom Schwanda, *Soul Recreation: The Contemplative-Mystical Piety of Puritanism* (Eugene, OR: Pickwick, 2012), 138–42.
49 Whitefield, *The Nature and Necessity of Self-Denial*, 24.
50 Charles E. Hambrick-Stowe, *The Practice of Piety: Puritan Devotional Disciplines in Seventeenth-Century New England* (Chapel Hill: University of North Carolina Press, 1982), 31–32, 38–39.

more credit than is due for one's accomplishments. Watts, who was shaped by a Puritan theology, understood the divided heart, which he exposed in his second stanza:

> Forbid it then that we should boast,
> Save in the Death of Christ, O God;
> All the vain Things that charm us most,
> We'd sacrifice them to his blood.

Whitefield reminded his listeners that financial wealth was temporary and vain and could distract their hearts from Jesus.[51] The fourth stanza completes the cycle of self-denial and asks how to respond to Jesus's sacrificial death:

> Were the whole realm of nature mine,
> That were a present far too small:
> Love so amazing, so divine,
> Demands my soul, my life, my all.[52]

Those who have cultivated self-denial have surrendered not only the allure of the world's goods but their soul, their life, and all to Jesus. Whitefield ably demonstrated the nature of self-renunciation through the many deprivations he experienced during his itinerant travels. Even when he was afforded the more luxurious accommodations of the Countess of Huntingdon, his primary patron, and other nobility, these were minor exceptions to his dedicated lifestyle of self-surrender.

Persecution as a Mark of Discipleship

Whitefield was a realist and recognized, despite the attractive nature of the Christian life, that it is far from easy; many obstacles—in particular, persecution—confront those who seek to follow Jesus. His most sustained treatment of this appeared in his "Persecution Every Christian's Lot," published in 1742 and based on 2 Timothy 3:12, "Yea, and all that will live godly in Christ Jesus shall suffer persecution."[53] The initial sentence

---

[51] See especially Whitefield, "Worldly Business No Plea for the Neglect of Religion," in *Works*, 5:299–307.
[52] Isaac Watts, "Glorying in the Cross," in *A Collection of Hymns for Social Worship*, comp. George Whitefield (London: Henry Cock, 1770), no. 62, sts. 1, 2, 4 (p. 174). For a helpful study of Whitefield's hymnbook, see Mark A. Noll, "Whitefield, Hymnody, and Evangelical Spirituality," in *George Whitefield: Life, Context and Legacy*, ed. Geordan Hammond and David Ceri Jones (Oxford: Oxford University Press, 2016), 241–60.
[53] Whitefield, "Persecution Every Christian's Lot," in *Works*, 6:345–60.

proclaimed that Jesus warned his disciples to expect "many distresses, afflictions, and persecutions . . . for his name's sake." Whitefield articulated that non-Christians have no fear of suffering for their beliefs, since they do not have any personal relationship with Jesus. But the person born again, who confesses to be "in Christ" and "led by his Spirit," must expect to suffer.

Whitefield recognized that few people suffer persecution "because so few live godly in Christ Jesus." Unlike modern-day residents of oppressive countries that punish Christians for practicing their faith, very few who lived in eighteenth-century Britain and the American colonies had such a fear. But for Whitefield, persecution provided a helpful means of monitoring whether a person was an "altogether Christian" and maturing in faith. In other words, hardship is experienced only by those who are intentional about being Jesus's followers. This again prompted Whitefield's reminder of the true nature of a Christian. Many can call themselves disciples—they can practice outward spiritual activities and even live moral lives—yet not experience persecution, because they have not been born again in Christ.[54]

Whitefield expanded the application of persecution to prepare his listeners for the variety of ways they might experience it. Sometimes a person will be assaulted through evil speech. Whenever a Christian's life is out of step with the typical behavior of the world, he or she should expect to be ridiculed. Whitefield cited Matthew 5:11, "Blessed are ye, when men shall revile you, and persecute you, and shall say all manner of evil against you falsely, for my sake," to reinforce this truth. The most serious expression involves physical attacks and bodily harm. Whitefield illustrated this in terms of a person fired from a job and the long history of Christian martyrs.[55] Though he named no specific person in this sermon, elsewhere he referenced both Stephen (Acts 7:54–60), the first Christian martyr, and Ignatius, the first-century bishop of Antioch. A well-known saying of Ignatius from his epistle to the Romans declared, "Now do I begin to be a disciple."[56] In a 1743 letter, Whitefield recounted the attacks he had experienced while preaching one day and confessed he had "very little natural courage" but was strengthened in

54 Whitefield, "Persecution Every Christian's Lot," 345, 347.
55 Whitefield, "Persecution Every Christian's Lot," 348–49, 352.
56 Whitefield, "Saul's Conversion," in *Works*, 6:158; Whitefield, "Christians, Temples of the Living God," in *Works*, 6:279. Philip Schaff, *A Select Library of Nicene and Post-Nicene Fathers*, series 2, vol. 1 (New York: Christian Literature Company, 1890), 168.

God through Ignatius's motto and declared, "I begin to be a disciple of Jesus Christ."[57] He later voiced this exact phrase when attacked by a vicious mob.[58]

In a 1739 letter, four years after his conversion, he wrote of his desire to grow in deeper intimacy with Jesus, yet confessed, "I am only beginning to begin to be a Christian."[59] He also alluded to the reality that suffering is part of the Christian school of formation; the more a person faces the world's animosity, the more that individual needs to depend on Christ for survival. Whitefield imagined some of his listeners would object to such pointed teaching on persecution, since they believed that the world had become more civilized since the days of the early church and that disciples no longer needed to fear attacks. But he clarified that until the human "heart is changed, the enmity against God (which is the root of all persecution) remains" and condemnation will continue.[60] Another hymn from Whitefield's hymnbook vividly portrays what the suffering Christians should expect as Christ's disciples:

> Jesus, the despis'd and mean,
> Our Master let us own;
> He the sacrifice for sin,
> The Saviour he alone:
> Let us take and bear his cross,
> Despis'd disciples let us be;
> Mock'd and slighted, as he was
> For you, my friends, and me.[61]

As Whitefield concluded his message "Persecution Every Christian's Lot," he reiterated that persecution for righteousness' sake produces the strongest evidence of a faithful Christ follower. The Grand Itinerant declared that Christians possess the ability not only to believe in Jesus but also to suffer for his sake. Again, Whitefield emphasized that suffering should not be avoided, because, he assured his listeners, it is "a mark of your discipleship, evidence that you do live godly in Christ Jesus." Instead,

---

57 Whitefield to Mr. B—, July 25, 1743, in Works, 2:36.
58 Whitefield to Mr. H—, July 23, 1739, in Letters, 54.
59 Whitefield to Rev. Mr. Mc L—, July 28, 1742, in Letters, 412–13; Whitefield to Governor B—, January 11, 1754, in Works, 3:59.
60 Whitefield, "Persecution Every Christian's Lot," 352.
61 "Calling to Follow Jesus" (aka "Come, My Father's Family"), in A Collection of Hymns for Social Worship, comp. George Whitefield (London: William Strahan, 1753), no. 3, st. 2 (p. 112).

he added that he had often experienced maltreatment from a variety of sources, including Satan, who desired to sift him as wheat (Luke 22:31). Because of the intensity of his frequent episodes of harassment, Whitefield requested the prayers of his listeners that he might always be faithful and never ashamed of Jesus and, above all, that "Christ may be glorified in" his life.[62]

Whitefield corresponded with a man engulfed in great turmoil and sought to encourage him in his struggles so that his oppressed friend could affirm, "Now I begin to be a disciple of Jesus Christ." Sometimes his letters utilized a hymn text to reinforce his counsel, and on this occasion this person needed to be reminded that both Jesus and his disciples faced suffering and that this man should not be surprised when he also experienced it.

> For this let men revile my name,
> I shun no cross, I fear no shame;
> All hail reproach, and welcome pain,
> Only thy terrors, Lord restrain.

One possible reason for this person's troubles was that anyone who faithfully serves Jesus will be attacked by Satan, but the corresponding good news is that God "will never leave nor forsake" any who follow him (Heb. 13:5).[63]

In 1744, Whitefield replied to the bishop's attack on the Methodists. In the eighteenth century, the term *Methodist* described anyone who was an evangelical. Those who supported Whitefield were called the Calvinist Methodists, and those who associated with the Wesleys were named the Wesleyan Methodists. When Whitefield addressed his fellow Methodists, he reminded them that affliction, while unpleasant, always produces growth in both the number of Christians and the in-depth faith of individual believers. Despite any persecution, God abundantly supplies all of their needs, a truth that prompted the affirmation "Persecution is your privilege: it is a badge of your discipleship: it is every Christian's lot in some degree or other."[64] These were not the words of an alarmist: Whitefield and his close associates had already experienced

---

[62] Whitefield, "Persecution Every Christian's Lot," 354, 356–59.

[63] Whitefield to Mr. S—, March 11, 1749, in *Works*, 2:245.

[64] Whitefield, "Letter to Reverend Clergy of Lichfield and Coventry," September 20, 1744, in *Works*, 4:196. For more on the conditions that prompted this exchange of letters, see Tyerman, *George Whitefield*, 1:99–100. Whitefield declared the same principle in another sermon, proclaiming it was not a "disgrace to be spoken evil of by them" (the enemies of Christ) and that persecution was "the privilege of their discipleship." Whitefield, "Walking with God," in *Works*, 5:33–34.

numerous violent mobs. The most tragic case involved William Seward, Whitefield's publicist, who also assisted him in fundraising. When Seward and Howell Harris (1714–1773), a Welsh evangelist who became one of Whitefield's top associates and friends, were preaching in Wales, Seward was injured by a rock that nearly blinded him. A short time later, in October 1740, he and Harris were again attacked by a vicious mob. This time a stone was better aimed and hit Seward's head so forcefully that he collapsed and died a few days later.[65] Through this tragic act, Seward became the first Methodist martyr of the evangelical revival. Unfortunately, it was not an isolated occurrence, and Harris and John Cennick, another close friend of Whitefield, also found themselves caught in the bitter crossfire of an angry mob.[66]

The Necessity of True Religion

Weaving these principles of persecution together reinforces Jesus's teaching on the nature and dynamics of discipleship (Luke 14:25–33). Whitefield synthesized this when he clarified all that is involved in following Christ:

> Seriously count the cost, and ask yourselves again and again, whether you count all things but dung and dross, and are willing to suffer the loss of all things, so that you may win Christ. . . . All that live godly in Christ Jesus, shall suffer persecution. . . . This is a mark of your discipleship, and evidence that you do live godly in Christ Jesus.[67]

While persecution is not the only mark of discipleship, it reinforces Whitefield's consistent contrast between a vital inward transformation that originates in the new birth and the outward display of mere talk yet intense efforts to impress others that one's hollow piety is genuine.

Whitefield clarified this more broadly when he warned of the folly of not being righteous enough. He cited Nicodemus as an example of one who knew much of the teachings of Scripture yet was devoid of the new life in Christ. During their clandestine encounter, Jesus sought to reeducate this learned teacher of the law in the basic principles of true religion. Jesus criticized the "letter-learned pharisees" of his day who were not born again.

---

[65] Arnold A. Dallimore, George Whitefield: The Life and Times of the Great Evangelist of the Eighteenth-Century Revival, 2 vols. (London: Banner of Truth, 1970, 1980), 1:583–84.
[66] Dallimore, George Whitefield, 2:161–63.
[67] Whitefield, "Persecution Every Christian's Lot," 356–57.

Whitefield drew a stark contrast to correct any confusion about what Jesus expected of his followers: "Now till the Spirit of God is felt on our souls as the wind on our bodies, indeed, my dear brethren, you have no interest in him: religion consists not in external performance, it must be in the heart, or else it is only a name, which cannot profit us."[68] For Whitefield, this was vital and true religion!

---

[68] Whitefield, "The Folly and Danger of Being Not Righteous Enough," 125–26.

CHAPTER 4

WHITEFIELD'S EXPERIENCE OF GOD

Throughout his life, Whitefield sought to know the breadth and length and height and depth of God's presence. Shortly after his conversion in 1735 at age twenty, he recorded these words in his journal:

> Oh, what sweet communion had I daily vouchsafed with God in prayer after my coming again to Gloucester! How often have I been carried out beyond myself when sweetly meditating in the fields! How assuredly have I felt that Christ dwelt in me, and I in Him! and how did I daily walk in the comforts of the Holy Ghost, and was edified and refreshed in the multitude of peace! Not that I was always upon the mount; sometimes a cloud would overshadow me; but the Sun of Righteousness quickly arose and dispelled it, and I knew it was Jesus Christ that revealed Himself to my soul.[1]

This Trinitarian passage focuses on each member of the Godhead and strongly reflects the Puritan piety that influenced Whitefield's life. The language of being "carried out beyond myself" is shorthand for the intense experience when a person is overwhelmed by the love of God. Meditating in the fields refers to Genesis 24:63, one of the popular Puritan texts for teaching meditation. The mutual indwelling that Whitefield experienced with Jesus is an allusion to Song of Solomon 2:16 and 6:3 and reflects the

---

[1] *Journals*, 61.

foundational principle of union with Christ, which he occasionally referred to as spiritual marriage.[2] He confessed that his delightful, sweet communion was not a habitual experience because he still knew the painful separation of living in the valleys of life. Perhaps most importantly, he was convinced beyond any doubt that Jesus Christ had initiated this experience and revealed himself to him. His delight in God produced peace and comfort over the range of these experiences. This time in Gloucester inspired Whitefield in his future preparation for ministry. He deleted this passage from his 1756 revision of his journal because of its intense spiritual ardor, which could be interpreted as enthusiasm and would have made him suspect to his fellow Anglican clergy.

Communion with God is possible only because of union with Christ, which Whitefield dramatically experienced during his conversion at Oxford. Union and communion have been a common theme in the history of Christian spirituality, encapsulating the new life of the believer born again in Christ. While Whitefield frequently described his experience of God in terms of communion, he often added the modifier "sweet" to magnify the depth of this relationship with God.

Though the experience in Gloucester was a personal one, he also tasted the same delight in fellowship with others who had also experienced the new birth. He wrote: "Early in the morning, at noonday, evening, and midnight, nay, all the day long, did the blessed Jesus visit and refresh my heart. Could the trees of a certain wood near Stonehouse speak, they would tell what sweet communion I and some others enjoyed with the ever blessed God there." Given the choice, he acknowledged that "communion with God's children is sweet; but communion with God himself is infinitely sweeter."[3] Further, while he typically reserved the language of sweet communion for his personal experiences with God, he used the variation of "sweet fellowship" to speak of his intimate spiritual encounters with other believers.

Whitefield felt this spiritual refreshment not only directly with God but also in reflecting on God through interacting with others. When he read August Hermann Francke's *Piety of Halle*, it led him to "sweet communion with God." Initially, he perceived God intellectually, but Francke's treat-

---

[2] See for example, Whitefield to Mr. C—, April 10, 1740, in *Letters*, 162; Whitefield, "Christ the Best Husband," in *Works*, 5:66; and Whitefield, "Christ the Believer's Husband," in *Works*, 5:176. The first sermon was based on Ps. 45, which the Puritans understood as a summary of the Song of Songs, and the second used Isa. 54:5.
[3] Whitefield to Mrs. A—, October 6, 1747, in *Works*, 2:132.

ment of Abraham's willingness to sacrifice Isaac to God also stimulated his longing for a renewed "fervour in Evening prayers."[4] This illustrates how a person can experience God through both love and knowledge; healthy relationships should contain both. Though knowing God includes intellectual and experiential dimensions, knowledge is often associated more with the cognitive and doctrinal, and love with the affective and devotional.[5] Reviewing Whitefield's Gloucester experience reveals that not only was he overcome by the love of Jesus, but this was inspired by his meditation on Scripture, which enlarged his knowledge of Jesus.

Another example that combines both love and knowledge took the form of an apparent out-of-body experience of God:

> Sometimes, as I was walking, my soul would make such sallies as though it would go out of the body. At other times, I would be so overpowered with a sense of God's Infinite Majesty, that I would be constrained to throw myself on the ground, and offer my soul as a blank in His hands, to write on it what He pleased.

On this occasion Whitefield tasted a cognitive awareness of "God's Infinite Majesty," but he also spoke of a fresh encounter with God's love. Once, he and a friend longed for Jesus's return and wondered when he would be "revealed from heaven in a flame of fire!" Whitefield exclaimed, "Oh that my soul may be in a like frame, when He shall actually come to call me!"[6] Beyond love and knowledge, a person can experience God broadly, depending upon the need of the hour, including joy and peace or conviction and correction.

Experiencing the Presence of the Holy Spirit

We have explored Whitefield's immediate or direct experience of the Holy Spirit after his conversion and his teaching on the indwelling of the Spirit. Here we turn to how he sensed the guidance of the third person of the Trinity. Whitefield would later proclaim that a primary means of grace is

---

[4] D. Bruce Hindmarsh, *The Spirit of Early Evangelicalism: True Religion in a Modern World* (New York: Oxford University Press, 2018), 25.

[5] For a helpful summary of this, see Tom Schwanda, "Knowing God with Head and Heart: The Dynamics of Christian Experience," C. S. Lewis Institute, September 5, 2019, https://www.cslewisinstitute.org/. The classic study of this for the Puritans and early evangelicals is Archibald Alexander, *Thoughts on Religious Experience* (Edinburgh: Banner of Truth, 1967).

[6] *Journals*, 83–84. For other examples of Whitefield's personal and group experiences of sweet communion, see *Journals*, 338, 354, 377.

watching for the motions or movements of the Holy Spirit.[7] To counter the fissiparous tendency, which fragmented early eighteenth-century evangelicalism, he advised a "close adherence to the motions of the Holy Spirit, and a constant watching over the corruptions of our own hearts, in order that we may walk before God as very little children." This demonstrates how responsiveness to the impressions of the Spirit for spreading the gospel creates an expanding outreach of the gospel. Consistent with his normal pattern, he cultivated a "close adherence to the motions of the Holy Spirit and a constant watching over the corruptions" of his heart. The desired result was to walk with God as a child of faith.[8] There were other ways in which Whitefield sensed the presence of the Spirit, including writing sermons.[9] After a full day of preaching to large crowds and counseling many others, he rejoiced that his "soul was full of ineffable comfort and joy in the Holy Ghost." As he reached his destination for the night, he recognized that one specific way the Holy Spirit was working in him was inspiring him to "intercede most earnestly" for his "dear friends."[10]

While crossing the Atlantic, Whitefield narrated that the Holy Spirit took advantage of his more relaxed schedule to convict him of "pride, sensuality, and blindness of [his] own heart," as well as instructing him how Satan had sought to tempt him. He also acknowledged his gratitude for being "enlightened to see into the mystery of godliness." Given the powerful insights he had discovered, he prayed that he might be attentive to "the still small voice of the Holy Spirit."[11] Shortly after his conversion at Oxford, he testified how instrumental the Spirit was in his growth of knowledge. His practice consisted of comparing the biblical commentaries of William Burkitt and Matthew Henry while reading Scripture. With delight he confessed that the Spirit of God had led him "into the knowledge of Divine things," and he had "been directed, by watching and reading the Scripture in this manner."

Unfortunately, he later forgot this critical element of discerning his experiences of the Holy Spirit through the written word of God.[12] On February 9, 1744, he wrote of the untimely death of his four-month-old son, John, on the previous day. This created confusion, since he had believed that

---

[7] Whitefield, "Walking with God," in Works, 5:30.
[8] Whitefield to Mr. Thomas N—, February 26, 1742, in Letters, 372.
[9] Journals, 508. See also Journals, 69.
[10] Journals, 210.
[11] Journals, 336.
[12] Journals, 62.

his child would "be a preacher of the everlasting gospel." In fact, Whitefield named him after John the Baptist, convinced that he would "be great in the sight of the Lord." He had baptized his son a week after his birth, in his London Tabernacle, and solemnly committed him to God's service. Initially, he took comfort that his early prophecies about his son appeared to be confirmed by several incidences, including the protection of his wife from a serious carriage accident. Reviewing his predictions, he lamented that "satan was permitted to give" him "some wrong impressions" about which he later recognized he had "misapplied several texts of scriptures." Whitefield grieved that his misunderstanding of God's gift of a son, so soon taken away from him and his wife, threw him into "very solemn and deep reflection." In the end, he trusted that this sorrowful loss of John gave him greater wisdom and discernment of "satan's devices" and would better prepare him for future ministry.[13]

Four years later, while crossing the Atlantic, Whitefield confessed to a minister: "In how many things have I judged and acted wrong.—I have been too rash and hasty in giving characters, both of places and persons. Being fond of scripture language, I have often used a style too apostolical, and at the same time I have been too bitter in my zeal." He used the term "wildfire" to describe how the spirit of his flesh had distorted his ability to speak according to the Holy Spirit's guidance and confessed, "I have likewise too much made inward impressions my rule of acting, and too soon and too explicitly published what had been better kept in longer, or told after my death." He acknowledged his hastiness had "stirred up needless opposition" that had tarnished his ministry.[14] This brutally honest confession expressed Whitefield's self-awareness of the destructive nature of zeal without knowledge, and this stark awareness confronted him with the complexity of discerning whether an inward impression was from the Holy Spirit or his spirit.

Whitefield typically recognized the importance of relying on the Holy Spirit for discernment, though he neglected this regarding his hasty prophecy of his son, John. John's heartbreaking death forced Whitefield to reevaluate how he perceived God's guidance and how to approach it in a more biblical and balanced manner going forward. In addition to receiving direction from the impulses of the Holy Spirit, Whitefield also had several

---

[13] Whitefield to Mr. D— T—, February 9, 1744, in *Works*, 2:50–52.
[14] Whitefield to Rev. Mr. S—, June 24, 1748, in *Works*, 2:144. Whitefield later inserted this letter in his *Remarks on a Pamphlet . . . Enthusiasm*, in *Works*, 4:243.

significant dreams at strategic points in his life. Chapter 1 recounted his early experiences of seeing God on Mount Sinai—which encouraged him before his conversion to continue to pursue God—and of Bishop Benson offering him a gold coin before his ordination, apparently confirming a dream.[15] Whitefield also dreamed, following his conversion, that he should continue the prison ministry he had developed during his student days at Oxford.[16] Later, when he revised his *Journals*, he would delete all but the first dream of seeing God on Mount Sinai. He described one more dream he had at age thirty after being condemned by the faculty of Harvard for sharply judging them. Whitefield took comfort from Joseph's example of being mistreated by his brothers.[17] Unlike Whitefield's dependence on the reading of the motions of the Holy Spirit, he reassured the faculty that his dreams did not control him but rather connected him with God's providence in his life.[18]

Watching and Waiting for God's Presence

In the next chapter, we will examine Whitefield's teaching on how to cultivate the spiritual life through the means of grace, but it is instructive to first notice that he experienced what he taught. Isaac Ambrose (1604–1664), a British Puritan minister read by Whitefield, taught that "watchfulness is the first and principal help to all exercises of religion . . . and therefore we set it in the front of all duties." Ambrose taught that this alertness includes being watchful in prayer and attentive in all aspects of life.[19] Since God is omnipresent (Ps. 139:7–12), one can experience God through noticing his presence at any time or any place. Whitefield fully embraced this and proclaimed that "believers keep up their walk with God, by watching and noting his providential dealings with them."[20]

In his own life he appealed to Moses's example of guiding the people of Israel to the promised land through the cloud during the day and pillar of fire at night (Ex. 13:21–22). Whitefield frequently applied biblical metaphors to himself as he sought to emulate the lives of those in Scripture. Early in his ministry, he confessed to a friend that he needed patience for the "Lord's leisure, and to wait for the moving of the cloud of

---

15 *Journals*, 41–44, 66–67.
16 *Journals*, 63.
17 *Journals*, 545.
18 Whitefield to Harvard College, January 23, 1745, in *Works*, 4:204.
19 Isaac Ambrose, *Media: The Middle Things in Reference to the First and Last Things . . .* , 3rd ed. (London: Nathanael Webb, 1657), 43.
20 Whitefield, "Walking with God," 29.

his providence."[21] He could become restless when "the cloud" stopped, as it created uncertainty in predicting his arrival at his next preaching venue to prepare his listeners. However, he quickly realized that when "the cloud" paused, God stopped him for a reason, and he resumed his travels, like Moses and the Israelites, only when it moved again.[22] On another occasion, he felt the freedom to continue traveling, saying, "The cloud seems to be moving" and he expected to see his correspondent in the spring.[23]

Four years before his death, Whitefield still used the same language. The context implies that he was again waiting for "the cloud" to move but took advantage of this opportunity to preach, though he hoped to travel to a more strategic region once it resumed moving.[24] He understood the importance of humbly watching and waiting earlier in his ministry, when he wrote: "When I find the cloud of divine providence moving your way, I trust the language of my heart will be, Lord, I come to do or suffer thy will! In the meanwhile, I watch unto prayer."[25] The reference to suffering indicates that obeying the movement of "the cloud" required courage. Once, Whitefield recognized opposition awaited him in Ireland, but in obedience to God he pledged his desire to move forward only when "the cloud" moved, and so he waited patiently in a posture of watchfulness.[26]

As Whitefield cultivated his attentiveness to "the cloud's" movement, it enabled him to experience God's presence and peace and created a deep sense of trust in God's faithful provisions. He observed the Lord's guidance and grace as he watched and waited for God to lead him. It also instructed him on the importance of recognizing God's proper timing, not his own.[27] More specifically he declared that by following "the cloud," he "enjoyed much of the divine presence" as he returned to England.[28] It can be frustrating for us that he did not indicate more clearly how he discerned the movement of "the cloud," but this practice is one more example of him embodying biblical stories, this time Paul's experience of being blocked by the Holy Spirit from entering the regions of Asia and Bithynia (Acts 16:6–10).

---

[21] Whitefield to Mr. E—, May 22, 1740, in *Letters*, 177.
[22] Whitefield to Rev. Mr. J— K—, March 6, 1742, in *Letters*, 377–78.
[23] Whitefield to Mr. I—, September 26, 1740, in *Letters*, 214.
[24] Whitefield to Rev. Mr. K—, June 19, 1766, in *Works*, 3:338–39.
[25] Whitefield to Rev. Mr. A—, July 12, 1742, in *Letters*, 407.
[26] Whitefield to Rev. Mr. A—, July 12, 1742, in *Letters*, 407.
[27] Whitefield to Mrs. C—, October 25, 1757, in *Works*, 3:215.
[28] Whitefield to Rev. Mr. C—, January 1, 1741, in *Letters*, 229–30. For additional examples of how Whitefield depended upon the movement of the cloud for God's guidance, see Whitefield to Mr. S— M—, May 26, 1742, in *Letters*, 391; Whitefield to Mr. J— H—, November 12, 1742, in *Letters*, 451; Whitefield to Mr. I—, December 21, 1742, in *Letters*, 477.

Retiring to Be with God

Early in life, Whitefield recognized the importance of spending time alone with God. In one letter he declared, "Proper retirement and solitude" are not obstacles "but rather great helps to a religious life. We find, our Saviour was led into a wilderness, before he entered on his public ministry, and so must we too, if we ever intend to tread in his steps."[29] Even before his conversion, Whitefield was intentional about retiring from his studies and responsibilities of waiting on the wealthy Oxford students as a servitor. Initially, he found it difficult to establish "regular retirements" in the morning and evening, but soon he formed the habit to know and love God more fully.[30] He spoke more specifically of his evening practice to retire for two hours to pray over his Greek New Testament and "Bishop Hall's most excellent *Contemplations*."[31] He also followed Jesus's frequent example of withdrawing before significant events to create a more focused time of prayer. On the night before his ordination, Whitefield retired to a hill "and prayed fervently for about two hours, on behalf of [him]self and those who were to be ordained with [him]."[32] On another occasion, he withdrew to a garden while in Georgia for solitude to sense God's presence and also found retirement in a person's home while traveling through England, which allowed him to experience "great measures of [God's] Divine Presence."[33]

John Wesley had invited Whitefield to join him and his brother Charles as a missionary in Georgia. Whitefield realized one attraction would be the lengthy voyage, which could take up to three months. (It has been estimated that Whitefield spent a total of three years of his fifty-five-year life aboard ships.)[34] These periods of withdrawal typically consisted of reading and praying over Scripture while on his knees, refreshing his soul with great sweetness.[35]

Soon realizing that his vessel had become his parish, he quickly went about reading public prayers, expounding Scripture, catechizing those who were interested, and offering spiritual direction to those who wrestled with

---

[29] Whitefield to Mr. H—, June 12, 1735, in *Letters*, 10.
[30] *Journals*, 47.
[31] *Journals*, 57.
[32] *Journals*, 69.
[33] Whitefield to Mr. W— D—, June 28, 1740, in *Letters*, 195; *Journals*, 286.
[34] The exact duration of his third voyage to the American colonies was eleven weeks. *Journals*, 28. Stephen R. Berry, "Whitefield and the Atlantic," in *George Whitefield: Life, Context and Legacy*, ed. Geordan Hammond and David Ceri Jones (Oxford: Oxford University Press, 2016), 207.
[35] *Journals*, 87.

issues of the Christian faith. Amid these activities, Whitefield sought time alone to focus on his spiritual life.[36] He declared on this first voyage that before God called him to a specific ministry, God always sent him "into some retirement." Filled with great expectation, he imagined what God might do and concluded his journal entry by praying, "Lord, fit and prepare me for it."[37]

Whitefield's journal provides several illuminating accounts of how his seafaring retirement profited his soul. It taught him the importance of surrendering his desires and plans for ministry to God as he prayed, "Break my will, purify my heart, and fit me for the great work that lies before me."[38] He also learned that severe storms that lengthened his journeys brought insights that he needed to learn. For example, the Holy Spirit convicted him of "pride, sensuality, and blindness of [his] own heart." The more relaxed pace of life which sharply contrasted with his normal frenetic pattern of preaching permitted him to notice the danger of the "hurry of business" that awaited him on shore. This inspired his prayer that his compulsive nature would not drown out the "still small voice of Thy Holy Spirit." Additionally, his solitude permitted him to better recognize the "mystery of godliness" and convinced him to emulate Enoch as he desired to walk more closely with God.[39]

As a result, one scholar has called Whitefield's nautical withdrawal his "cloister," which stimulated the contemplative side of his piety.[40] But there were other benefits to his "blessed retirements," including preparing for the conflicts that awaited him. He recounted numerous biblical stories of how God equipped his servants for difficult challenges, and on one occasion Whitefield was reminded of the great promise, "Fear thou not; for I am with thee: be not dismayed; for I am thy God: I will strengthen thee; yea, I will help thee; yea, I will uphold thee with the right hand of my righteousness" (Isa. 41:10).[41]

This, like many other dimensions of Whitefield's spirituality, indicates his balanced posture of devotion. On the one hand, retirement created "a sweet means to keep and quicken the Divine Life," and therefore he prayed, "Lord, grant I may never be afraid to converse with Thee and myself."[42] On the other hand, he understood that solitude came with a

---

[36] *Journals*, 102–3.
[37] *Journals*, 166.
[38] *Journals*, 166.
[39] *Journals*, 336.
[40] Berry, "Whitefield and the Atlantic," 217–18.
[41] *Journals*, 506.
[42] *Journals*, 399.

cost as he acknowledged that the devil never attacked more than when a person was confined to a ship with more time alone and in greater isolation from others.[43]

Celebration of the Lord's Supper

Whitefield typically referred to the Lord's Supper as the "holy sacrament" or "blessed sacrament." He also called it "holy communion" and "breaking of the bread," and once he joyfully announced, "We have been favored with delightful Passover feasts."[44] During the eighteenth century, the Church of England mandated that the sacrament be celebrated three times a year, though its observance had increased in some regions, depending on local bishops and clergy. Evangelicals like Whitefield regularly sought more frequent, even weekly, observance, when possible.

Before his conversion, he had already been strongly inspired through his reception of the Lord's Supper. While visiting his brother in Bristol, he reported that God had blessed him with "great foretastes of his love" through the Lord's Supper. When he revised his *Journals* in 1756, he altered this, using the words "great sensible devotion." However, he described this overwhelming experience as being filled with "unspeakable raptures" in which he "was carried out beyond [him]self." Having been inspired by the living presence of Jesus through holy Communion, he declared his "great hungerings and thirstings after the blessed sacrament." Indeed, this early experience would continue to shape his desire to receive the Lord's Supper.[45] Visiting Gibraltar in 1738 while traveling to Georgia, he reported, "[I] received (what my soul longed after) the Sacrament of Christ's Most Blessed Body and Blood." That was an unusual reference for Whitefield to make regarding Communion, no doubt inspired by his attendance that day at a Roman Catholic mass, in which he commented on its "pageantry, superstition, and idolatry of their worship."[46]

In his earlier, unpublished, diary, he reported: "Surely grace is given at the sacrament."[47] This reality was later reaffirmed in his published *Journals* when he confessed that he had received grace at the Lord's Table.[48] More specifically, Whitefield proclaimed that he experienced "grace in a very

---

43 *Journals*, 334–35.
44 Whitefield to Rev. Mr. S—, April 1, 1769, in *Works*, 3:384.
45 *Journals*, 41.
46 *Journals*, 136.
47 Hindmarsh, *The Spirit of Early Evangelicalism*, 34; cf. 17.
48 *Journals*, 199.

affecting manner . . . in abundant measure" in his soul that assisted him to face his frequent trials.[49] Contemporary readers from a more memorialist tradition might be surprised by the deep spiritual experience about which he gushed with delight, describing the "sweet communion" he had tasted through the celebration of the Lord's Supper.[50]

One of Whitefield's more dramatic experiences of the Lord's Table occurred at Cambuslang.[51] This small town on the outskirts of Glasgow, Scotland, was the location of a 1742 revival during a celebration of the Lord's Supper. People traveled for miles to festivals there, known as sacramental occasions. These gatherings often lasted four days, beginning on Friday with a combination of sermons, singing, self-examination, and prayers in preparation, and reaching their zenith on Sunday. Those who confessed or renewed their faith in Jesus gathered around long tables and received the bread and wine of Communion. The gatherings concluded on Monday with additional sermons on gratitude and encouragement to live as faithful disciples of Jesus. Whitefield's Calvinist theology, equally shared by his Scottish Presbyterian friends, recognized the important combination of preaching and observance of the Lord's Supper. He struggled to describe the overwhelming sense of God's ineffable presence at Cambuslang and simply sought to capture his experience, writing, "The power of God came down and was greatly felt." An estimated twenty thousand people had gathered for this festival. Many were "bathed in tears," while others were "almost swooning" in mourning over their sins, but also in gratitude for Jesus's sacrificial death. Whitefield concluded, "I must not attempt to describe" this experience and added that it was "like the Passover in Josiah's time" when he eradicated Israel's idolatry and turned their hearts back to true worship of God (2 Chron. 35:1–19). Another account from an observer reported the effect this had on Whitefield: "While he was serving some of the tables, he appeared to be so filled with the love of God, as to be in a kind of ecstasy, and he communicated with much of that blessed frame."[52] Reminiscent of the transformative power of the Lord's Supper on his life, Whitefield later jubilantly rejoiced that God's divine presence was so evident and difficult to bear that he could actually "see and feel" God's "inexpressible" presence.[53]

---

[49] *Journals*, 56.
[50] Hindmarsh, *The Spirit of Early Evangelicalism*, 34.
[51] Thomas S. Kidd, *George Whitefield: America's Spiritual Founding Father* (New Haven, CT: Yale University Press, 2014), 161–69.
[52] Luke Tyerman, *The Life of the Rev. George Whitefield*, 2 vols. (London: Hodder and Stoughton, 1876–1877), 2:30.
[53] Whitefield to Lady H—, September 11, 1753, in *Works*, 3:29.

Yet Whitefield's overpowering experience of the Lord's Supper was common among many early British evangelicals.

Trials and Temptations

Just as Scripture honestly reveals the struggles of biblical characters, warts and all, Whitefield acknowledged the afflictions he experienced along his pilgrimage of faith. Sin has always been understood as the primary barrier to spiritual maturity with God, but unlike John Wesley, Whitefield believed that Romans 7 describes the postconversion believer's struggle to overcome indwelling sin. He consistently confessed he was the chief of sinners, following the apostle Paul's original claim (1 Tim. 1:15).[54] This self-awareness led to his perennial claim that he was "less than the least of these," which he considered his motto. Near the end of his life—including his final letter just seven days before his death—he used this for his closing signature.[55]

Whitefield frequently struggled with the effects of his indwelling sin. In a revealing letter, he recounted his recent success in preaching, which humbled him, yet he was concerned about grieving the Holy Spirit owing to his unfruitfulness and pride. He confessed he had gone to sleep angry with himself primarily because he felt he had accomplished so little for Christ, given all of the abilities he had received. As he awoke, a new attitude emerged, and he exuberantly declared: "My soul is swallowed up in God. His presence is filling my soul, and renewing my bodily strength." Imagining that his friend was with him, he said, "I think I could now warm your heart with a lecture upon the unparalleled love of Jesus." Although many of his afflictions began with such discouragement, they were eventually transformed into fresh experiences of God's presence and sustaining strength.[56]

On another occasion, he found himself in "inexpressible agonies of the soul for two or three days" as he recognized the depth of his indwelling sin. Even though he was confident of God's forgiveness, he struggled to forgive himself. He confessed he could identify with David after David's conviction of adultery, and with Peter after his threefold denial of Jesus; and

---

[54] References to this are abundant in Whitefield's corpus; see, for example, *Journals*, 207, 462, 515.

[55] Whitefield to Mr. C—, June 7, 1755, in *Works*, 3:122; Whitefield to Mr. R— K—, September 23, 1770, in *Works*, 3:427.

[56] Whitefield to Mr. S— C—, September 2, 1742, in *Letters*, 430–31. "Swallowed up" meant to be filled with the fullness of God. See Whitefield to Lady H—, May 27, 1755, in *Works*, 3:120.

Whitefield imagined Christ's loving gaze on him, which, he said, "broke my rocky heart" as he wept bitterly. This brought comfort and assurance of a renewed relationship with God, and joy to continue preaching.[57]

Pride was a major internal trial for Whitefield his entire life. Being touted as a preaching sensation by the age of twenty-two did not help, nor did the continued applause from many of his listeners. Early in his ministry, God warned him of this danger, and he quickly realized his vulnerability to spiritual pride and prayed against this temptation.[58] Soon he recognized he was unable to resist pride solely by himself and was grateful for a friend who kept watch over his soul.[59] A few months later he wrote more specifically of his struggle with vanity and affirmed that he was often blind to the "self-pride and self-love" that flooded his life. Wisely, rather than ignore this, he earnestly sought out friends who would lovingly rebuke him. He even scolded one correspondent who did not reprove him sooner: "When I am unwilling to be told of my faults, dear Sir, correspond with me no more."[60]

Whitefield was no stranger to spiritual combat; his first episode was in May 1738, and his last recorded encounter came in November 1769, less than a year before his death.[61] One early account is particularly illuminating regarding the nature and effects of his struggle: "I had many violent conflicts with the powers of darkness, who did all they could to disturb and distract me; but Jesus Christ prayed for me." At various times, it seemed as if God had later forgotten him and Satan were in control, until God "rebuked the tempter, and from that moment," Whitefield sensed victory over his enemy. He interpreted the intensity of his temptation as validation that God would perform a mighty work through him, since he felt the most "extraordinary conflicts and comforts" in his life. This enabled him to taste the delights of heaven, and he thought of nothing earthly. Instead, he "earnestly desired to be dissolved and go to Christ." Eventually he came to realize that his time had not yet come, and God graciously renewed his strength to continue his earthly ministry.[62] He often applied to himself

---

[57] *Journals*, 334–35.

[58] *Journals*, 70. See also *Journals*, 332.

[59] Whitefield to Mr. —, August 7, 1739, in *Letters*, 60.

[60] Whitefield to Rev. and Dear Sir —, November 10, 1739, in *Letters*, 82. For a similar letter inviting the same loving reproof regarding his struggle with pride, see Whitefield to Mr. H— H—, June 6, 1741, in *Letters*, 268–69.

[61] Whitefield to Mr. —, May 6, 1738, in *Letters*, 43; Whitefield to Mr. R— K—, November 30, 1769, in *Works*, 3:408.

[62] Whitefield to Mr. —, May 6, 1738, in *Letters*, 43.

Jesus's words to Peter that the devil would sift him as wheat, but that Jesus would deliver and restore him (Luke 22:31).[63] Despite Satan's best efforts to disrupt Whitefield's preaching, these inward trials renewed his confidence in God. To one friend he confessed that Satan sought to disturb him, but Jesus refreshed him and overcame the powers of darkness.[64]

Significantly, Whitefield perceived afflictions not as God's punishments but, instead, as gifts to further his spiritual maturity. Traveling to Georgia, he described how seasickness from the raging storms prevented him from his daily practice of reading prayers to those on the ship. Always optimistic, he asserted, "Suffering times are a Christian's best improving times; for they break the will, wean us from the creature, [and] prove the heart."[65] On another voyage, which had extended to over nine weeks and he described as "long and perilous," he concluded that it had been profitable to his soul and had reminded him of the necessity of ministers learning to endure hardships for the cause of Christ. "Many inward trials" had been sent by God, which, he declared, had produced great sanctification in his soul. Further, he recognized that he would face trials until he reached heaven and that they were particularly beneficial to "heal the pride" of his heart.[66]

The Grand Itinerant argued that when his troubles increased, so did his consolations. He received great encouragement from 1 Samuel 30:6: "David strengthened himself in the LORD his God."[67] Whitefield later returned to this text when he wrote to a minister, "It [the message of 1 Samuel 30:6] came with sweet power to my soul," and he observed, "The nearer I come to Christ, the closer my trials are."[68] There was a connection between Whitefield's experience of temptation and his earlier practice of cultivating an awareness of God's providence. Both required a spiritual sensitivity not to dismiss or ignore what provided either an invitation to follow God more closely or a warning that the temptation was close at hand and could lead him astray.

Longing for Heaven

For Whitefield, these spiritual battles created an intense longing for heaven, which he often expressed throughout his correspondence as a desire to

---

63 Whitefield to Rev. and Dear Sir —, November 10, 1739, in Letters, 76; Whitefield to Rev. Mr. D—, August 15, 1740, in Letters, 202; Whitefield to Mr. Peter S—, January 7, 1742, in Letters, 306.
64 Whitefield to Mr. J— S—, July 26, 1744, in Works, 2:63–64.
65 Journals, 139.
66 Journals, 179; see also Whitefield to Mr. N—, August 15, 1740, in Letters, 202.
67 Journals, 448.
68 Whitefield to Mr. N—, August 15, 1740, in Letters, 202.

die. Frequently, when he learned of someone's death, he wished it could have been him instead. (He first recorded this sentiment when he was only twenty-three.)[69] Before dismissing this morbid tendency, we need to realize his close identification with the apostle Paul, who captured the same longing when he wrote, "For I am in a strait betwixt two, having a desire to depart, and to be with Christ; which is far better" (Phil. 1:23).

In a revealing letter to Anne Dutton, Whitefield disclosed his motivation for wanting to die:

> My dear Sister, pray that I may patiently wait till my change shall come. I want to leap my seventy years. I long to be dissolved to be with Christ. Sometimes it arises from a fear of falling, knowing what a body of sin I carry about me. Sometimes, from a prospect of future labours and sufferings, I am out of humour, and wish for death as Elijah did: At others, I am tempted, and then I long to be freed from temptations. But it is not thus always: There are times when my soul hath such foretastes of God, that I long more eagerly to be with him; and the frequent prospect of the happiness which the spirits of just men made perfect now enjoy, often carries me as it were into another world.[70]

While his desire to enjoy Jesus more fully was only one of several reasons for longing for death, elsewhere Whitefield gave it greater prominence. His primary yearning to die was not to be freed from his many "crosses," but, he said, "that I may be with Christ, [because] he draws me more and more to him every day."[71] Employing the devotional language of the Song of Solomon, he again affirmed his eagerness to be united with Christ, because his view of heaven was so clear that he sought to be dissolved and be with Christ: "My soul was sick of love."[72] Whitefield also sought heaven because of health problems, including uncontrolled vomiting after preaching, which began when he was twenty-four. And he sought to exchange the strife and divisions that had marked his life for unity among fellow Christians.[73]

Regardless of his desires, he understood, like Paul, that his ministry was not yet finished, for it was better for him to continue preaching "in

---

[69] Whitefield to Mr. —, May 6, 1738, in *Letters*, 43.
[70] Whitefield to Mrs. Ann D—, November 10, 1739, in *Letters*, 91.
[71] Whitefield to Mr. N—, August 15, 1740, in *Letters*, 202. See also Whitefield to Honoured Sir —, July 24, 1739, in *Letters*, 54; Whitefield to Mr. William D—, November 10, 1739, in *Letters*, 109.
[72] *Journals*, 517.
[73] Whitefield to Mr. William D—, November 10, 1739, in *Letters*, 109; *Journals*, 211; Whitefield to Mr. J— H—, November 24, 1740, in *Letters*, 224.

the hopes of bringing more souls to Jesus Christ."[74] Over time he showed a growing awareness that God's timetable, not his, would determine when his nascent joy would be fulfilled. Confessing the challenge of waiting for God's timing and surrendering his own will, he wrote, "Nevertheless, through grace, the prevailing language of my heart is, 'Not my will, but thine be done.'"[75]

Whitefield took additional comfort in waiting because he had already tasted the joys of heaven while still on earth. Writing to Howell Harris, he declared that he had been "in the suburbs of heaven. Blessed be God!" he wrote, "I live in heaven daily."[76] This became clearer during his successful preaching tour in Savannah, Georgia, when he described the "manifestation of God's glory" as abundantly evident. He gushed as he proclaimed: "Every day he fills me with himself, and sometimes brings me even upon the confines of eternity. Methinks I often stand upon Mount Pisgah, and take a view of the heavenly Canaan, and long to be gathered to my people." But again, he accepted that there was still much preaching to be done before he would "enter into glory." The allusion to Mount Pisgah is reminiscent of God permitting Moses to climb the mountain and gaze over the promised land he would not enter (Deut. 34:1), but Whitefield had in view the heaven that awaited him.[77]

Even as a young man, he possessed a deep desire for heaven. He once requested prayers from a friend that he might be more aware of what God had done for him so he could be more grateful. Cognizant of the value of engaging in "heart-transforming divine exercises," he sought to "be gradually trained up for eternal uninterrupted communion with that heavenly choir, who cease not chanting forth day and night hallelujahs to Him that sitteth upon the throne and to the Lamb for ever."[78] This sense of thankfulness equipped him for deep communion with God. When asked what heaven would be like, he confessed, "I am lost in contemplation of it."[79] He documented this while crossing the Atlantic; as previously mentioned, periods of retirement often created more heightened awareness and enjoyment of God.

---

[74] Whitefield to Rev. Mr. A—, July 12, 1742, in *Letters*, 408.
[75] Whitefield to Mr. T— A—, October 18, 1747, in *Works*, 2:140; Whitefield to Mr. J— S—, October 6, 1747, in *Works*, 2:131; *Journals*, 415.
[76] Whitefield to Mr. Howell Harris, September 3, 1742, in *Letters*, 516.
[77] Whitefield to Rev. Mr. J— B—, June 13, 1740, in *Letters*, 188.
[78] Whitefield to Dear Sir —, January 25, 1738, in *Letters*, 36.
[79] Whitefield to Mr. G—, September 15, 1769, in *Works*, 3:399.

In preaching on the radical transformation of shedding the old nature and being reborn in newness in Christ, Whitefield spoke autobiographically: "O what an unspeakable blessing is this! I almost stand amazed at the contemplation thereof." The object of his gratitude was God, who, through his Son and with the Holy Spirit, makes sanctification a reality for believers. He continued by asking his hearers to ponder this mystery and reflect upon the love of God that had filled their souls. Inviting them to realize what God was doing in their lives, Whitefield rhetorically asked: "Is not the joy you feel unspeakable? Is it not full of glory? I am persuaded it is; and in secret communion, when the Lord's love flows in upon your souls, you are as it were swallowed up in, or, to use the apostle's phrase, 'filled with all the fulness of God.'"[80] In the process, he captured the nature of contemplation: gazing at God with attentive gratitude, which is always a gift of God's grace that saturates the believer with God's love. This experience is not reserved for a select few; Whitefield taught that "heavenly-mindedness is the very life of a Christian."[81]

He understood that people can prepare themselves for heaven through spiritual disciplines. Therefore, he counseled a friend aware of his many sins that God had "already vouchsafed some assurances of love" and that the friend should "continually keep faith in exercise, till it be entirely swallowed up in the boundless ocean of the beatific vision." Consequently, meditation on Jesus and his redeeming love led Whitefield to gaze eternally on the Savior's face in heaven.[82] Seeing Jesus face-to-face, or the beatific vision, has been a consistent theme throughout the history of the church for those desiring sweet communion with God.[83] In a further eschatological reflection shared with a fellow minister, Whitefield waxed eloquent about his experience of God. Though only twenty-six, he declared that it would not be long before he would see Jesus. If his sight of Christ by faith had already enthralled him, then how much more, he reflected, "shall I be ravished when I see him face to face!"[84] This language, common to both the medieval devotional writers and Puritans, draws upon Song of Solomon

---

[80] Whitefield, "Christ the Believer's Wisdom," in *Works*, 6:193.

[81] Whitefield to the Right Honourable the Lord R—, August 11, 1741, in *Letters*, 311. Others have noticed the contemplative and even mystical shape of Whitefield's spirituality. See Hindmarsh, *The Spirit of Early Evangelicalism*, 38–40; Samuel C. Smith, *A Cautious Enthusiasm: Mystical Piety and Evangelicalism in Colonial South Carolina* (Columbia: University of South Carolina Press, 2013), 53, 57–58.

[82] Whitefield to Mr. H—, November 10, 1739, in *Letters*, 118. Whitefield also spoke expectantly of the beatific vision in Whitefield to Mr. —, December 5, 1752, in *Works*, 2:457.

[83] For a helpful treatment of this, see Hans Boersma, *Seeing God: The Beatific Vision in Christian Tradition* (Grand Rapids, MI: Eerdmans, 2018).

[84] Whitefield to Rev. Mr. C—, October 13, 1741, in *Letters*, 333.

4:9: "Thou hast ravished my heart, my sister, my spouse; thou hast ravished my heart with one of thine eyes, with one chain of thy neck." One scholar has recently observed that Whitefield's "heart-ravishing joys of knowing God in Christ" were a result of God's grace.[85] Elsewhere Whitefield spoke of being "carried out beyond [him]self," which contains the same depth of being transported with ecstatic joy by the love of God and vividly excavates the depths of Whitefield's experience of God.[86]

He also alluded to Matthew 5:8 and prayed, "Lord, purify me, even as thou art pure; for only the pure in heart see thee!"[87] Aware of this future delight, he grasped for words to express what was on his heart and asked when he might "be swallowed up in the vision and full fruition of the glorious Godhead." He added: "The bunch of grapes make me long to eat of the full clusters in the heavenly Canaan. The first-fruits make me pant after the full harvest." He continued, using the language of the Song of Solomon: "My soul is sick of love" [Song 5:8]. Nothing can satisfy it, but the full sight and enjoyment of Christ."[88]

Sweet Communion

This chapter has opened the window into Whitefield's soul and revealed the depth of his desire for and enjoyment of God. It began with his union with Christ, fueled by his desire for deeper intimacy that ushered him into a transforming communion with God, which he often called "sweet communion." His various spiritual disciplines, cultivated not so much to gain something from God as to taste and experience God, flooded his soul with a heavenly-mindedness that brought him into "the suburbs of heaven" and generated a consuming love to surrender all his life to Christ, who had already offered his life totally to him.

Therefore, because of his spiritual pilgrimage, Whitefield longed for its fulfillment, "panting daily," he said, "after the full enjoyment of my God."[89] Before his *Communion Morning's Companion* (1755) had been published, he realized that the means of grace were still necessary. Still, he mused to a friend that someday books would no longer be needed to sense God's pres-

---

[85] Michael A. G. Haykin, *The Revived Puritan: The Spirituality of George Whitefield* (Dundee, ON: Joshua, 2000), 75.
[86] *Journals*, 61. This is from the opening quotation of this chapter.
[87] Whitefield to Rev. Mr. C—, October 13, 1741, in *Letters*, 332–33. See also Whitefield to the Right Honourable Lady Mary H—, December 24, 1741, in *Letters*, 350–51.
[88] Whitefield to Mr. J— B—, February 17, 1741, in *Letters*, 244–45.
[89] Whitefield to Lady H—, July 11, 1755, in *Works*, 3:128.

ence and that he would "be admitted into an uninterrupted communion and fellowship with the blessed Trinity for evermore."[90] This motivated his life personally but also overflowed in his ministry to others. He summarized his advice to a friend based on his daily experience of life, "Let us keep close to our loving Lord, and not suffer the noise and hurry of business [*sic*], to rob us of one moment's communion and fellowship with the ever-blessed God."[91]

---

[90] Whitefield to Mr. C—, June 7, 1755, in *Works*, 3:123.
[91] Whitefield to Mr. R— K—, April 18, 1753, in *Works*, 3:11.

CHAPTER 5

THE MEANS OF GRACE

The goal of the Christian life is fullness of joy and complete union and communion with Jesus Christ in heaven. In a letter to a person of nobility, Whitefield detailed the depth of that delight and the challenges of maturing through life to attain this blessed hope. He confessed, "My heart's desire and continual prayer" is "that your Ladyship, having put your hand to the plough, may be kept from looking back!" One must be warned of the devil's efforts to "divert [believers] from the cross" and to tempt Christians into believing that they can simultaneously love two masters: God and the world. Whitefield was confident that his friend understood these real temptations and would be able to "fight the good fight of faith, and run with patience the glorious race" set before her. This happiness could be further strengthened by cultivating a life devoted to Jesus and "spent in communion and fellowship with the ever-blessed God." Such intentional living creates a foretaste of heaven on earth that inspires one's desire to enjoy God's presence even more fully. Whitefield emphasized that while the Christian life should be looking upward to heaven, it is never automatic or simple, but the required efforts are always worth the investment. Recognizing the competing allure of the world and fallen humanity's proclivity to seek the path of least resistance, Whitefield continually preached and taught how to use the means of grace to experience union and communion with Christ.[1]

---

[1] Whitefield to Lady F— S—, May 12, 1749, in *Works*, 2:254–55.

The Nature of Walking with God

Whitefield proclaimed the nature and dynamics of the means of grace most clearly in "Walking with God," a sermon based on the example of Enoch (Gen. 5:24). Walking with God meant that the "prevailing power of enmity" that separated Enoch from God needed to be removed. Second, a person experiences reconciliation to live in peace with God. Third, and most significant for the remainder of his sermon, walking with God implies "a settled, abiding communion and fellowship with God." This echoes the necessity of abiding in Christ (John 15:4–10). Whitefield summarized that Enoch "kept up and maintained a holy, settled, habitual, though undoubtedly not altogether uninterrupted communion and fellowship with God, in and through Christ Jesus." Finally, building on the previous principles, to be in communion with God requires that a person "advance in the divine life." Walking requires movement and challenges the believer to display a "progressive motion" to grow in grace.[2] This instruction was dependent upon an inner experience of grace that stressed the new birth, in contrast to the common New England colonial emphasis on "godly walking" that was more externally focused.[3]

Whitefield used a phrase similar to "a settled, abiding communion and fellowship with God" in another sermon, "Christ the Best Husband," originally preached to the women's society at Fetter Lane in London. Throughout this and other sermons, he used the metaphor of spiritual marriage to illustrate union with Christ. Simply stated, a person cannot walk with God unless he or she is married to him. Both the Old and New Testaments communicate this intimate union between Christ and the individual believer, or the church (e.g., Isa. 54:5; 62:5; Hos. 2:19–20; Matt. 9:15; 22:1–14; 25:1–13; 1 Cor. 6:17; 2 Cor. 11:2; Rev. 21:2.). This language was used to declare Christ's desire and longing for union and communion with fallen humanity. Whitefield sought to woo his listeners with the message that without new life in Christ "sin is [their] husband," but when they are "married to Christ, when [they] are born again" they are "espoused unto the Lord Jesus Christ." This espousal creates a mutual desire for affection and longing so that the believer, or bride of Christ, will "endeavour to keep up a daily communion with him." Consistent with Luther's, Calvin's, and the Puritans' teaching on spiritual marriage, this union, which begins on

---

[2] Whitefield, "Walking with God," in *Works*, 5:23–26.
[3] Douglas L. Winiarski, *Darkness Falls on the Land of Light* (Chapel Hill: University of North Carolina Press, 2017), esp. 18, 116–21, 135, 147, 149.

earth, is never fully realized until heaven; or in Whitefield's language, "The nuptials between you shall be solemnized" when you reach the "mansions of everlasting joys" in heaven.[4]

While some might think this bridal imagery is more appropriate to women, Whitefield utilized the same metaphor for men in his sermon "Christ the Believer's Husband." Before we can claim "our Maker is our husband," we must be "legally freed from all pre-engagements whatsoever," and especially "be divorced from our old husband the law." Further, before anyone is "married or united to him [Christ] by faith" in "spiritual marriage," there must be mutual consent, which creates the "betrothing, or espousal." This reflects the Pauline usage of "the marriage state" to conceptualize "the real, vital union, between Jesus Christ and regenerate souls." In human marriage, one can experience great delight and intimacy, but spiritual marriage transcends those joys as one can exult "in a rapture of holy surprise, and ecstasy of divine love," saying, "My beloved is mine, and I am his" (Song 2:16). Consequently, faithful walking with God provides the strongest possibility for the enjoyment of God.[5]

Whitefield turned to this same metaphor to motivate a man to mature in grace and "grow in the knowledge of Christ Jesus [his] Lord." He reminded the man that he was "truly married to the dear Lord Jesus" only when he believed in Christ through faith and could call him Lord. This belief is more than head knowledge; it requires confirmation in a person's heart. Only then can people be called "true children of the bridegroom, and real partakers of the supper of the Lamb."[6] Almost a year later, Whitefield corresponded with a minister and inquired, "How is it with your heart?" He warned him of the potential distractions of life: "Let nothing intercept, or interrupt your communion with the bridegroom of the church." Whitefield also comforted him with the assurance that he was praying for the minister's soul, that he would have the strength to overcome anything that would compete with his love for Christ.[7]

The Central Means of Grace

Whitefield examined seven practices to encourage this spiritual progress: reading Scripture, secret prayer, frequent meditation on Scripture,

---

[4] Whitefield, "Christ the Best Husband," in *Works*, 5:65–78, quotations at pp. 70, 77.
[5] Whitefield, "Christ the Believer's Husband," in *Works*, 5:171–96, quotations at pp. 174–75, 177, 181. The bridal and spiritual-marriage imagery appeared in other sermons as well: Whitefield, "The Marriage of Cana," in *Works*, 5:64–78; Whitefield, "The Wise and Foolish Virgins," in *Works*, 5:373–91.
[6] Whitefield to Mr. C—, April 10, 1740, in *Letters*, 162.
[7] Whitefield to the Rev. Mr. T—, February 17, 1741, in *Letters*, 242.

observing God's providential dealings, watching the motions of the Holy Spirit, making full use of God's ordinances, and keeping company with other Christians who were walking with God. This was not intended to be an exhaustive list. The first five were more personal, though they could be performed in public settings, while the last two were communal. Whitefield's teaching of these spiritual practices were expanded through his other sermons and letters on each topic. Additionally, he argued that spiritual disciplines "are means; but then they are only means; they are part, but not the whole of religion." He stressed that if the means were automatic, then the Pharisees would have been the most religious of all people.[8] Nevertheless, when the "powerful operations of the Holy Spirit" enliven the means of grace, the results are the "fruits of the spirit."[9]

Reading Scripture

Whitefield reinforced his first discipline, reading Scripture, through several biblical passages that stressed both the nature of God's word and the necessity and benefit of regular interaction with it. If someone neglects Scripture and allows anything else to supplant it as the supreme guide in life, such a person is deluded and in danger of making a "shipwreck of [his or her] faith." Whitefield affirmed the inspired nature of Scripture, calling it "the lively oracles of God" not only because it prepares one to experience new life in Christ but also because it assists a person to deepen life and "increase it in the soul." Drawing upon the example of Mary's attentiveness to Jesus in Luke 10:39, Whitefield proclaimed, "We must make his testimonies our counsellors, and daily, with *Mary*, sit at Jesus feet, by faith hearing his word." To cultivate this habit prepares believers to daily grow in awareness until they meet Jesus face-to-face. Those who saturate their souls with the living word of God will experience the delight of being renewed in their lives.[10] In "The Great Duty of Family Religion," the Grand Itinerant stressed the critical importance of reading Scripture as the first responsibility of a father. Whitefield understood that without the words of Scripture deeply planted within people's hearts, they are ill-equipped to speak to their children or others in life.[11]

Whitefield's most detailed treatment of reading the Bible for spiritual maturity was "The Duty of Searching the Scriptures." Since ignorance of God's

---

8 Whitefield, "On Regeneration," in *Works*, 6:266.
9 Whitefield, "Benefits of an Early Piety," in *Works*, 5:161.
10 Whitefield, "Walking with God," 27–28 (italics in the original).
11 Whitefield, "The Great Duty of Family-Religion," in *Works*, 5:56.

word is the cause of all error, he taught seven principles of how to study Scripture. The first principle, foundational to the others, was the recognition that the Bible was written to reveal the way of salvation in Jesus Christ. Whitefield affirmed a typological reading, maintaining that Christ can be found in the Old Testament, and therefore he instructed his listeners to always search for Christ to guide them in understanding difficult passages. Second, he taught readers to approach the word with a "humble child-like disposition," because God hides his truth from the proud. Mary again provides an example of receptivity to God's revelation, as does young Samuel when he learned to hear God's voice by surrendering himself with the invitation, "Speak; for thy servant heareth" (1 Sam. 3:10).[12]

Whitefield's next two principles are related to the internalization of Scripture. Third, one must be intentional to grasp the mysteries of the kingdom of God, for those who ignore this counsel will never understand God's message. The reader's motivation is crucial, for if a person reads the Bible only for entertainment or to criticize it, then it will fall on deaf ears. Fourth, Whitefield taught that to "make an application of every thing you read to your own hearts" will increase your effectiveness in studying Scripture. While the Bible is an ancient book, what was written in the past is just as relevant for contemporary readers as for those who first heard it. To guide the application to our hearts, we must "diligently seek the assistance of the Holy Spirit." This naturally overflows into the fifth principle, of depending upon the Holy Spirit. Whitefield illustrated this through Nicodemus: though he was a "teacher of Israel" who should have understood "the doctrine of regeneration," he was ignorant, since he lacked the illumination of the Spirit. The natural man cannot grasp the "hidden sense and meaning" of the Bible, for his eyes cannot read it as it was intended. Therefore, according to Whitefield, "if we are strangers to the Spirit we will be strangers to [God's] word."[13]

This fifth principle could have been first, as Whitefield stressed the aid of the Holy Spirit to encourage the reader to pray before engaging Scripture so that Christ would remember his promise to send the Spirit "to guide you into all truth" (John 16:13). Sixth, Whitefield counseled his readers to pray frequently throughout the reading—pausing to "pray over every word and verse, if possible"; and after reading, "earnestly beseech God," so that what

12 Whitefield, "The Duty of Searching the Scriptures," in *Works*, 6:82–83.
13 Whitefield, "The Duty of Searching the Scriptures," 83–86.

has been read "may be inwardly engrafted in your hearts, and bring forth in you the fruits of a good life." Whitefield often claimed that he was a faithful Anglican and quoted the familiar collect from the Book of Common Prayer that the Holy Spirit would guide so that "you will then not only read, but mark, learn, and inwardly digest" the words of the passage. His seventh and final principle was that one must read Scripture continually with an intensity that resembles someone searching for buried treasure. He concluded that one can never discover the richness of Scripture "by a careless, superficial, cursory way of reading them, but by an industrious, close, and humble application" of them.[14] Whitefield's approach was consistent with the emergence of eighteenth-century evangelicalism, which prioritized the foundational nature of the Bible.[15]

Secret Prayer

Whitefield combined his second discipline, secret prayer, with what he called "ejaculatory prayer," often called "arrow prayers" today, and he compared prayers of this kind to sending "short letters . . . to heaven upon the wings of faith." Given the spontaneous nature of such prayer, it was intended to guide believers as they went about their daily business. It reflected God's omnipresence with those who sought him and fulfilled the Pauline admonition to "pray without ceasing" (1 Thess. 5:17). Personal prayer is instrumental in drawing near to God because it is the "fan of the divine life, whereby the spark of holy fire kindled in the soul by God, is not only kept in, but raised into flame." Among other benefits, this ad hoc prayer serves as a protection against temptation, and those who neglect it are more likely to experience spiritual diseases. Regardless of the form of prayer, it creates a way for uniting the believer with God. Whitefield maintained that it raises a person to God and brings God down to those who pray, and he personally claimed that he had experienced "sweet communion" with God through prayer.[16]

Whitefield counseled a man about the benefits of this practice: "If you could be brought once to love secret prayer, and to converse feelingly with God in his word, your heaven will begin on earth; you will enjoy more

---

[14] Whitefield, "The Duty of Searching the Scriptures," 83–87.
[15] Tom Schwanda, *The Emergence of Evangelical Spirituality: The Age of Edwards, Newton, and Whitefield* (Mahwah, NJ: Paulist, 2016), 2–3, 112–52.
[16] Whitefield, *"Walking with God,"* 28–29. This imagery of fire was also significant in Whitefield's spirituality. D. Bruce Hindmarsh, *The Spirit of Early Evangelicalism: True Religion in a Modern World* (New York: Oxford University Press, 2018), 10.

pleasure than in all manner of riches."[17] This demonstrates both the benefit
of prayer in increasing one's intimacy with God and how one spiritual discipline—in this case, prayer along with reading Scripture—overflows with
other practices. Whitefield described how secret prayer works together
with "self-examination, and receiving the blessed sacrament."[18] He also
championed the importance of family prayer.[19] While he preached extem-
poraneously and often stressed the same freedom in prayer, he appreciated
the set forms of the Book of Common Prayer of his Anglican tradition. "For
Christianity does not require us to cast off all outward forms; we may use
forms, and yet not be formal: for instance, it is possible to worship God in
a set form of prayer, and yet worship him in spirit and truth."[20] This principle, coupled with his strong dependence upon the Holy Spirit, created a
lively personal relationship with God.

Faithful to these beliefs, Whitefield penned twenty-one prayers cover-
ing a variety of daily concerns, which exhibited rich biblical imagery. These
included prayers for a person entrusted with the education of children, for
a servant, for one undergoing spiritual desertion, for a person experiencing
persecution for his or her faith, for someone who desired the new birth,
and for one newly awakened to the Christian life. There were also prayers
for those who were poor or wealthy, a poor Negro, a man searching for a
wife, a woman's discernment whether to accept a marriage proposal, and a
pious soul longing for heaven. In a prayer of lament reminiscent of the Puritan teaching on desertion, he cried out, "Thou hast taken off my chariot-
wheels, and I drive heavily; thou hast permitted a cloud to overshadow
me and a horrible darkness, fearfulness and dread to overwhelm me." Yet
consistent with the biblical model of psalms of lament that concluded in
confident hope and trust in God, he continued, I "believe thou wouldst yet
turn again, and visit me."[21]

Meditation on Scripture

Whitefield separated holy and frequent meditation, his third spiritual
discipline, from reading Scripture. He compared meditation to the body's
digestion of food, employing the biblical examples of David and Isaac

[17] Whitefield to the Right Honourable the Lord L—, October 26, 1741, in *Letters*, 335.
[18] Whitefield to the inhabitants of Savannah, October 2, 1738, in *Letters*, 490.
[19] Whitefield, "The Great Duty of Family-Religion," 57–58.
[20] Whitefield, "The Wise and Foolish Virgins," 376.
[21] Whitefield, "Prayers," in *Works*, 4:457–90, quotation at p. 461.

(Gen. 24:63) to illustrate gathering and internalizing spiritual nutrients from Scripture to nourish the soul. More eloquently, he contended that meditation "is a kind of silent prayer, whereby the soul is frequently, as it were, carried out of itself to God, and in a degree made like unto those blessed spirits, who by a kind of immediate intuition always behold the face of our heavenly Father." In light of this benefit of divine communion and beatific vision, Whitefield urged his listeners to frequently engage in meditation, since it can both kindle "the fire of divine love" and "maintain a close and uniform walk with the most-high God." While meditation can be used in several ways, he stressed that the focus should be "on the works and word of God."[22] This was evident in his *Law Gospelized*, which was his revision of William Law's *Serious Call to a Devout and Holy Life* to make it more biblical and therefore suitable for evangelical readers. Here meditation had a heavenly focus on Jesus Christ and the angels. Later his guidance was enlarged "to meditate upon the perfection of the divine attributes, to contemplate the love of God in Christ, [and] the glories of heaven," which can create "souls advanced in piety."[23] In a sermon on self-denial, to encourage submission to God he admonished his hearers to meditate frequently "on the life of our blessed Lord and Master Jesus Christ" from the cradle to the cross, being attentive to Christ's consistent pattern of total submission to God the Father. Whitefield's final motivation challenged his listeners to "often meditate on the joys of heaven." Stephen followed this principle (Acts 7:55–56), realizing that the joys of heaven far surpass any rewards one can gain by submitting to the allure of the world.[24]

Being Attentive to God's Providence

Whitefield's fourth spiritual discipline, attentiveness to God's providence, extended to God's numbering the hairs of a person's head and God's awareness of even the sparrow that falls to the ground (Matt. 10:29–31).[25] Providence teaches that God is ever present and governs all of creation—nothing is by chance, given God's daily awareness and involvement. In a letter written from Dublin in 1751, Whitefield attested to his own experience of being guided by it: "I find that providence has wonderfully prepared my way, and over-ruled every thing for my greater acceptance. O that I could be more

---

22 Whitefield, "Walking with God," 29.
23 Whitefield, "Law Gospelized," in *Works*, 4:411, 431.
24 Whitefield, "The Extent and Reasonableness of Self-Denial," in *Works*, 5:437–38.
25 Whitefield, "Walking with God," 29.

humble and thankful!"[26] Driven to accomplish God's calling, he recognized that he needed to notice and discern how daily life might afford new opportunities for him to preach. This lesson was translated into guidance for his listeners: "Hear what the Lord has to say concerning [your life] in the voice of his providence." While it is one thing to receive the benefits of God, it is another thing to accept that "every cross has a call in it, and every particular dispensation of divine providence, has some particular end to answer in those to whom it is sent."[27]

In 1736, Whitefield reminded his correspondent that all the "dispensations of providence" are expressions of God's love and that afflictions are "not so much to punish, as to purify your soul."[28] Therefore, he taught his listeners to carefully observe the movements of providence in order to walk more closely with God. If this sounds subjective to our contemporary ears, Whitefield helpfully offered two examples of how it could be cultivated. First, he turned to Scripture and employed Abraham's commission to his servant to find a wife for Isaac (Gen. 24:10–22). The only qualification was that the woman could not be a Canaanite. The wise servant prayed, as he reached the destination, that the Lord would provide a woman who would fulfill the expectations of his prayer and draw water from the well for him. Rebekah was the answer to this prayer.

Second, Whitefield taught the necessity for sailors to be responsive to God's providential care: "Grant me a lively persuasion, that thy providence ruleth all things; that thou intendest every thing for my good, and enable me therefore patiently to tarry thy leisure, and to give thee thanks for all things that befall me, since it is thy will in Christ Jesus concerning me."[29] Reaching one's destination across often turbulent waters depended upon careful gazing on God's providence to chart one's course toward the harbor safely. Sailors' attentiveness could adjust to changing weather from moment to moment. Ignoring such conditions could lead to their peril. Despite the subjective nature of this practice, Whitefield taught more fully that surrendering to God's purposes is dependent upon being "guided by the word, providence, and the Spirit of the Lord."[30]

---

[26] Whitefield to Lady H—, May 30, 1751, in *Works*, 2:409. See also Whitefield to Mr. S—, August 18, 1749, in *Works*, 2:273.
[27] Whitefield, "Walking with God," 29–30.
[28] Whitefield to Mr. H—, October 14, 1736, in *Letters*, 21.
[29] Whitefield, "A Prayer for a Sailor," in *Works*, 4:484.
[30] Whitefield "Marks of a True Conversion," in *Works*, 5:344.

Sensing the Motions of the Holy Spirit

While observing God's providence is an external operation, Whitefield also taught the importance of recognizing the Spirit's guidance within a person's heart. This fifth spiritual discipline had been foundational to him since the beginning of his ministry. Just as a child is led by a parent, Jesus's disciples needed to be guided by the Holy Spirit. As previously noted, Whitefield's utter dependence on the Spirit's guidance frequently brought charges of enthusiasm. Conscious of his critics, he declared, "Though it is the quintessence of enthusiasm, to pretend to be guided by the Spirit without the written word; yet it is every Christian's bounden duty to be guided by the Spirit in conjunction with the written word of God." This interactive, twofold reliance on the word and Spirit was a central principle to Luther, Calvin, and other Protestant Reformers. Whitefield urged his listeners to intensely seek the Holy Spirit's guidance, which would be confirmed by their experiencing "enlightening, quickening, and inflaming" power "by the word of God" felt in their souls.[31] This description calls to mind the experience of the two disciples on the road to Emmaus on Easter evening (Luke 24:32). Therefore, believers are directed to monitor the motions of the "blessed Spirit" by testing them according to "the unerring rule of God's most holy word." Such discernment guards a person from falling into "diabolical and delusive" traps. Additionally, it enables Christians to chart a middle course between the twin dangers of enthusiasm, on one side, and deism or infidelity, on the other.[32]

On several occasions, the Grand Itinerant encouraged others with how the Spirit, working in cooperation with God's word, could sustain them. Whitefield reminded a fellow clergyman, whose initial success in preaching had later been replaced by opposition, of the strong prospect of a bountiful harvest. The preacher did not need to fear, since the Spirit would provide the words of utterance and "apply the word to the hearers," so that he might speak boldly with confidence.[33] Two women needed to receive encouragement of another kind. To one who had experienced doubt, Whitefield wrote that he had heard that by the "word and Spirit," God had "spoken to [her] soul" and reinforced the truth that God had "loved" her "with an everlasting love."[34] Another woman was mired deep in despondency and doubted God's

31 Whitefield, "The Duty of Searching the Scriptures," 86.
32 Whitefield, "Walking with God," 30.
33 Whitefield to Rev. Mr. R—, November 10, 1739, in *Letters*, 93.
34 Whitefield to Mrs. T—, February 12, 1741, in *Letters*, 236.

goodness. Whitefield was moved to remind her of God's "word applied by his Spirit" that God loved her "with an everlasting love."[35]

Writing to Anne Dutton, he acknowledged the difficulty of being attentive to the Spirit's motions, owing to the human tendency to quench those impressions.[36] He spoke about how he had experienced specific guidance amid the "various storms of opposition and reproach" in his life by "watching the motions of his blessed Spirit, word, providence." This triplex of spiritual resources combined to overshadow him with "safety and refuge."[37] He used similar language on other occasions when he counseled a person, "Commune with your own heart in your chamber, and be still, and you will then hear the secret whispers of the Holy Ghost."[38] Another person was instructed to avoid conflict, since it would hinder the "small still voice of the Holy Ghost."[39] While there is no specific reference to John 16:13 ("When he, the Spirit of truth, is come, he will guide you into all truth"), it is clear throughout all of these examples that Whitefield recognized that one of the central roles of the Spirit is to lead believers into God's truth. Taken together, noticing the movement of God's providence and the motions of the Holy Spirit assures Jesus's followers of God's presence and guidance in life. The greater that awareness, the closer one is able to walk with God and enjoy his fellowship.

Celebrating God's Ordinances

Whitefield's sixth discipline included various spiritual practices but typically focused on baptism and especially the Lord's Supper. He asserted that God's ordinances are "conduit-pipes, whereby the infinitely condescending Jehovah conveys his grace to [his people's] souls." This is the highest privilege extended by God and creates "delight to visit the place where God's honour dwelleth."[40] Such language articulates Whitefield's theology that the Lord's Supper communicates grace to its participants by reminding them of Christ's presence. This is clear in an early letter to a friend, in which he instructed him: "When you receive the sacrament, earnestly endeavour to be inwardly bettered by it the following week."[41] Later he asserted that

---

[35] Whitefield to Mrs. B—, February 17, 1741, in *Letters*, 243.
[36] Whitefield to Mrs. Ann D—, November 10, 1739, in *Letters*, 92.
[37] Whitefield to Mr. E—J—, October 6, 1742, in *Letters*, 446.
[38] Whitefield to the Right Honourable the Lord L—, October 26, 1741, in *Letters*, 335.
[39] Whitefield to Mr. F—, September 22, 1742, in *Letters*, 438.
[40] Whitefield, "Walking with God," 31.
[41] Whitefield to Mr. H—, April 2, 1736, in *Letters*, 14. See also Whitefield, "On Regeneration," 266.

he had administered the "Holy Sacrament to about two hundred and fifty communicants" and that "our Lord made himself known to many in the breaking of the bread."[42] Of the seven means of grace to cultivate walking with God, this was his shortest section and least developed, though his teaching was expanded through his sermons and detailed correspondence with others.

For Whitefield, the ordinances were an expression of God's tokens of love sent through his Holy Spirit; people could experience deep intimacy with Jesus through the Lord's Table because they were "espoused unto Christ." This bridal language, associated with union with Christ, attests to the covenantal joy of feasting with Jesus. In Communion, Christ's deepest love is dramatically displayed through the broken bread and poured out wine, and invites the recipients to surrender their love in response to Christ.[43] In a sermon preached from Isaiah 54:5, "For thy Maker is thine husband," Whitefield exhorted his listeners that the Church of England eucharistic liturgy required the minister to "acquaint all those who receive the sacrament worthily, that they are one with Christ, and Christ with them; that they dwell in Christ, and Christ in them." This indwelling of Christ was reinforced in the participation of the Lord's Supper, which was a profound mystery that he called an "ineffable union."[44]

Because of Christ's presence in the sacrament, it possesses the dynamic ability to transform people through the Spirit's power. Whitefield urged a friend to consistently make use of God's ordinances, for "by-and-by the loving Saviour may pass by and visit your soul." He inquired of this friend whether he had not earlier sensed God's "divine power in the use of the means." Whitefield sought to strengthen his friend's faith and anticipation by reasoning that if God met him in the past, should he not "expect more in the same way" now?[45] Consequently, one should not approach the Lord's Table casually but carefully prepare his or her heart for a proper reception of the holy sacrament. In his observations on John 11, structured around the style of a catechism, Whitefield urged that "Christians ought to study to prepare themselves by prayer and self-examination" to receive the Lord's Supper.[46]

---

[42] Whitefield to Mr. S—, October 25, 1743, in *Works*, 2:41.
[43] Whitefield, "Christ the Best Husband," 74.
[44] Whitefield, "Christ the Believer's Husband," 178. For a broader background of Whitefield's use of this sermon's bridal imagery, see Thomas S. Kidd, *George Whitefield: America's Spiritual Founding Father* (New Haven, CT: Yale University Press, 2014), 163–66.
[45] Whitefield to T— K—, February 20, 1741, in *Letters*, 251.
[46] Whitefield, "Observations on Select Passages of Scripture," in *Works*, 4:370.

In June 1755, Whitefield corresponded with a fellow clergyman and reported, "My little communion-book is not yet come out."[47] It was released later that year and was designed to prepare people for receiving the Lord's Supper. The popularity of *A Communion Morning's Companion* was evidenced by a fifth edition in 1767.[48] Whitefield confessed that very little in the book was original to him but that he drew upon the meditations of Bishop Ken on Christ's passion, which had powerfully stirred his soul earlier in life.[49] Additionally, the volume contained an order for celebrating the Lord's Supper, fifty-nine communion hymns, and seventeen doxologies. Looking ahead eschatologically, he mused that there would come a time "when we shall need books and ordinances no more, but shall be admitted into uninterrupted communion and fellowship with the blessed Trinity for evermore."[50]

Seeking Fellowship with Other Christians

The seventh and final means of grace that Whitefield emphasized was how "Christian societies, and fellowship meetings" have guided believers over the centuries in faithful discipleship. He discerned from church history that vibrant Christianity is dependent upon strong gatherings for mutual fellowship. Therefore, it was essential that believers "would walk with God, and keep up the life of religion, to meet together as they have opportunity, to provoke one another to love and good works."[51]

The importance of this was demonstrated by his earliest sermon, "The Nature and Necessity of Society in General, and Religious Society in Particular" (Eccl. 4:9–12), which argued that Adam needed a helper in the garden before the fall, since friendship was an essential dimension of life. Whitefield proclaimed three benefits of religious societies: when a person falls into temptation, there is someone to pick him or her up; another person can impart heat or enliven someone in need; and believers can preserve others from external enemies. He also set forth three duties for members: mutual reproof, mutual exhortation, and mutual protection from opposition.[52] In addition to this strong reliance on mutual support and responsibility, he declared that the purpose

47 Whitefield to Mr. C—, June 7, 1755, in *Works*, 3:122.
48 George Whitefield, *A Communion Morning's Companion* (London: Henry Cock, 1767), title page.
49 George Whitefield, *A Communion Morning's Companion* (London: W. Strahan, 1755), A2.
50 Whitefield to Mr. C—, June 7, 1755, in *Works*, 3:123.
51 Whitefield, "Walking with God," 31.
52 Whitefield, "Nature and Necessity of Society," in *Works*, 5:108, 111–19.

of the societies is to stir up love and holiness and "convince each other of the evil of sin."[53]

Like Wesley, who divided his societies into smaller groups of bands and classes, Whitefield experienced firsthand the benefits of small, intimate gatherings. He wrote of one occasion, "Spent the remainder of the evening with our bands, which are little combinations of six or more Christians meeting together to compare their experiences." Their purpose was to "confess your faults one to another, and pray for one another, that ye may be healed."[54]

Over time the societies became an increasing burden for Whitefield. He believed that his calling was "to go about and preach the gospel to all." And he added, "My being obliged to keep up a large correspondence in America, and the necessity I am under of going thither myself entirely prevents my taking care of any societies."[55] Arnold Dallimore was one of the first to conjecture that in addition to these reasons, Whitefield relinquished his leadership of these groups because of the bitter competition and tensions that they created in his relationship with Wesley.[56]

Other Means of Grace

Fasting

Whitefield's understanding of the means of grace was not restricted to the aforementioned seven disciplines. According to Jesus, fasting and giving to the needy were also standard spiritual practices (Matt. 6:2–4, 16–18). When one considers that fasting almost literally killed Whitefield during his Oxford student days of excessive asceticism, it is not surprising that he did not include it as a central means of grace. However, his marginalization of abstinence should not be understood as a rejection of this practice. A primary purpose for fasting, often combined with prayer, is to discern matters of life and faith.[57]

One of Whitefield's hesitations in championing fasting was that it could easily be abused and become a source of pride. Comparing the Pharisee and publican, he clarified that it could lead someone to assume he is superior to

---

[53] Whitefield, "Christ the Only Rest for the Weary and Heavy Laden," in *Works*, 5:314–15.
[54] *Journals*, 197–98.
[55] Whitefield to Mr. L—, November 22, 1749, in *Works*, 2:291.
[56] Arnold A. Dallimore, *George Whitefield: The Life and Times of the Great Evangelist of the Eighteenth-Century Revival*, 2 vols. (London: Banner of Truth, 1970, 1980), 2:249.
[57] *Journals*, 196.

his neighbor. Whitefield laid out a balanced position: the Pharisee was not condemned for fasting twice a week; in fact, Whitefield asserted, "I wish some Christians would imitate him more in this." Rather, the Pharisee's sin was depending on fasting for self-justification before God.[58] Elsewhere Whitefield warned of the danger of treating fasting in a superstitious manner and expecting God to reward valiant displays of abstinence.[59]

Acts of Charity

Whitefield devoted a full sermon to the spiritual discipline of almsgiving. He began by insisting, "Nothing is more valuable and commendable, and yet, not one duty is less practiced, than that of charity." He was conscious of the objection that being generous to others could bring a giver into poverty. Compassion does not require excessive sacrifice that would injure the benefactor; instead, each person is to contribute according to his or her ability. This is a universal practice, since Christians are created to help one another, being interdependent with each other, not independent. He challenged the rich, who wasted many precious resources the poor would gladly receive. Motivation is critical to the right practice of charity. Giving in order to impress others, especially wealthy friends, yields no benefit for a person's soul. Rather the proper impetus must be love to God. Christ displayed this through his love for souls, leaving heaven and dying upon the cross for lost humanity.[60]

Listening to Sermons

Whitefield taught that hearing sermons was another means of grace, and his teaching on how to listen to preaching was particularly appropriate for the listeners of his estimated eighteen thousand sermons. He understood preaching to be an ordinance of God, and therefore people should come with sincerity to hear God's word, not just a curiosity to be entertained. The power of preaching transcends external hearing and possesses the dynamic ability to work inwardly to enlighten and enflame a person's heart. Otherwise, these homiletical efforts are done in vain.

This means of grace was, for him, no different from any of the seven primary means in that it was participatory. Listeners should prepare themselves

---

[58] Whitefield, "The Pharisee and Publican," in *Works*, 6:41–42.
[59] Whitefield, "The Temptation of Christ," in *Works*, 5:263.
[60] Whitefield, "The Great Duty of Charity Recommended," in *Works*, 6:227, 229, 235–36.

by praying before, during, and after the message, and always remember to pray for the preacher. This preparation includes a diligent receptivity to what is proclaimed, since ministers are "sent of Jesus Christ" and the people should "hang upon them to hear" God's word. Whitefield warned against the common human tendency of allowing prejudice, either in favor of or against the preacher, to shape one's ability to hear the proclamation of Scripture. Central to the listeners' participation is applying the message to their hearts—the more this is faithfully done, the greater each hearer's benefit. The Holy Spirit is instrumental throughout this process, and Whitefield challenged the perceptions of his listeners so that they could recover the powerful results of preaching recorded in the Bible. He clarified that the "reason why we do not receive larger effusions of the blessed Spirit of God, is not because our all-powerful Redeemer's hand is shortened, but because we do not expect them, and confine them to the primitive times" of the early church.[61] No doubt this desired engagement and participation between Whitefield and his hearers accounted for his phenomenal success as a preacher.

Motives to Keep Walking with God

The final section of "Walking with God" contained a dual purpose—both the realistic reminder that those who seek to follow God will face persecution and affliction and that the final goal of enjoying God in heaven is worth more than the earthly challenges a person will experience. Whitefield imagined an objection from his listeners: if walking with God is so delightful, why were Jesus's disciples so "frequently afflicted, tempted, destitute, and tormented"? Whitefield turned to the Beatitudes and taught that "blessed" are those "who are persecuted, and have all manner of evil spoken against them falsely" (Matt. 5:11). These hardships are "the privilege of their discipleship," and "as afflictions abound, consolations do much more abound."[62]

Trials and Afflictions

Since he faced almost a continuous onslaught of afflictions and trials throughout his life, Whitefield wanted his listeners to be prepared when they faced distressing situations. His sermon "Glorifying God in the Fire" gives us a clearer perspective of his understanding. Against the background

---

[61] Whitefield, "Directions How to Hear Sermons," in *Works*, 5:418–27, quotations at pp. 422, 425.
[62] Whitefield, "Walking with God," 33–34.

of Israel's rebellion and resistance to God, this message dramatized, with the illuminating artistry of a painter's palette, the consequences of neglecting God's law and rejecting his covenant. Whitefield's two-pronged approach examined the purpose of the resulting afflictions and the desired response Christians should display when they are thrust into the furnace of afflictions. Biblically there is always a remedial function for suffering. Fire "separates one thing from another," and just as it purges metals to create greater purity, the furnace purges believers from their sin and rebellion. One can never "go to heaven upon a feather-bed" of ease. Instead, we all must face the intense challenges of the fires of affliction. These trials are not generic but are tailored to the uniqueness of each person's life. Whitefield contended, "God will not put you or me into the fire if there was not something to be purged away." Drawing upon the life of Abraham, he counseled that a person needs to pray for the strength of Abraham's faith but not for the intensity of his trials.[63]

Whitefield challenged his listeners to glorify God in response to fiery-hot afflictions not only when they were delivered from their troubles but also while they were deeply embedded in them. That included patiently waiting amid their turmoil, realizing that afflictions were a sign of God's love for a person's growth in sanctification, and not begging for them to be ended but entreating God to not "let the fire go out till it has purged away all [one's] dross." One should refuse to press God for reasons when suffering but seek instead to live by faith and not by sight. Additionally, a person glorifies God not by grumbling but by humbly submitting to trials. In summary, we glorify God when we have "patience, meekness, humility; learning to distrust ourselves, having a deeper knowledge of our weaknesses, and of God's omnipotence and grace." The resulting fruit of this faithful response according to Whitefield is a "heavenly-mindedness, deadness to the world, and liveliness to God.[64]

Enjoyment of God

Matthew Henry captured this principle of "liveliness to God" during his last earthly moments when he confessed, "A life spent in communion with

---

[63] Whitefield, "Glorifying God in the Fire; or, The Right Improvement of Affliction," in *Eighteen Sermons*, 134–54, quotations at pp. 143, 144, 145. Whitefield also addressed this topic in "The Furnace of Affliction," a funeral sermon for Rev. Middleton, in *Eighteen Sermons*, 179–201, and "The Burning Bush," in *Eighteen Sermons*, 250–71.
[64] Whitefield, "Glorifying God in the Fire," 149–50.

God, is the pleasantest life in the world." Later, Whitefield supplemented this with the delight of being heavenly-minded: "There is a heaven at the end of this walk" with God, and "the nearer you walk with God, the more you will enjoy of Him whose presence is life."[65] This delighting and enjoying of God was central in his prayer for a devout person thirsting for heaven. Those who hunger after God pray. "For these are the happy spirits, who offer a sacrifice of pure praise before the throne of God continually"— and, using language reminiscent of medieval Catholics and Puritans, he continued—"who are ever wrapt in the contemplations of his perfection; and see them, not like us" here on earth "through a glass darkly, but near at hand, and face to face." Those who continue to gaze at God will be ushered into the overwhelming "joy springing from the beatific vision" that will transform them into the very likeness of God.[66]

While ambition can typically be motivated by pride or envy, there is a spiritual form of ambition that reflects Paul's striving for the heavenly prize of Jesus's call (Phil. 3:12–14). Seeking to encourage a person of nobility, Whitefield confirmed that "the almighty God approves the ambition and the angels look down with pleasure to see" her effort to "obtain the prize" of her heavenly reward.[67] In his meditation on the wise and foolish virgins (Matt. 25:1–13), he equipped his listeners for what awaited them if properly prepared with their lamps trimmed and burning. The wise virgins who possessed the essential oil and "the wedding garment of an imputed righteousness" were admitted to the heavenly marriage banquet. He imagined what they tasted and saw and how it created ineffable "transports" as they were welcomed into the "presence and full enjoyment" of Jesus the divine bridegroom, "whom their souls hungered and thirsted after." What they had previously known only in part as they sat at the Lord's Table on earth expanded beyond their wildest expectations as they gathered "together to eat bread" in Christ's "heavenly kingdom."[68]

Whitefield's Invitation to Walk with God

The frenetic pace of Whitefield's itinerancy often precluded creative and original thinking. He frequently drew his inspiration from meditating on Scripture, biblical commentaries (especially by Matthew Henry), and other

[65] Whitefield, "Walking with God," 32–34, 36.
[66] Whitefield, "The Pious Soul Longing for Heaven," in *Works*, 4:488.
[67] Whitefield to Lady Fanny S—, June 16, 1758, in *Works*, 3:236.
[68] Whitefield, "The Wise and Foolish Virgins," 382.

popular works from both Puritan and early evangelical authors. Concerning this chapter's theme, Anne Dutton occupied center stage. Her *Walking with God* (1735) "had become a standard devotional text" to his friends at Bethesda, his Georgian orphanage, and Whitefield further rang out its praises for guiding "others in South Carolina." He added, "It hath also been serviceable to a dear friend now with me, as also to myself."[69] Dutton's treatise had left its indelible imprint on Whitefield as he in turn broadcasted the nature and dynamics of this possible fellowship with God. The overflow of this fueled the intensity of his relationship with God (revealed in the previous chapter) and was evident as he sought, through his preaching and correspondence, to invite others into what he tasted and experienced in his communion with God. This delight and enjoyment of God is not reserved for superior saints but is for everyone who takes seriously the biblical invitation to walk with God.

---

[69] Kidd, *George Whitefield*, 143; Whitefield to Mrs. A— D—, February 20, 1741, in *Letters*, 259.

CHAPTER 6

GUIDING SOULS TO JESUS

Whitefield was heralded as a great communicator of the gospel and frequently spoke to massive crowds numbering in the thousands, but he equally devoted great energy to guiding others toward greater maturity in Jesus Christ. This chapter examines his ministry through the lens of spiritual direction, thus viewing his role as what he would have called a physician of the soul or spiritual father. This theme has been a neglected area of study regarding the transatlantic evangelist. We catch a glimpse of it in a 1742 epistle in which he expressed his hope that his friend was growing in Christ and that the power of Scripture was transforming his soul. Whitefield stressed the stark distinction between knowing certain ideas about Christ cognitively and experiencing those truths in one's heart. He inquired: "Do you grow in grace? Is the world more under your feet than usual? Do you find a real, solid, abiding rest in Jesus Christ? Or is it only transitory and superficial?"[1]

These diagnostic questions invited self-examination of not just his friend's thoughts but how he lived with and for Christ. "Do you grow in grace?" Growing in grace meant that his correspondent was deepening his faith in Christ and maturing in sanctification. "Is the world more under your feet than usual?" challenged his earthly attachments, which could easily have restricted his ability to grow in grace. This question might also have reminded him that the world is one of the three main temptations, along with the flesh and devil, that seeks to derail the Christian life. Whitefield's

---

[1] Whitefield to Mr. R— S—, August 10, 1742, in *Letters*, 415.

third probe regarding abiding in Jesus would have sharpened his friend's focus on depending on Christ as demonstrated by John 15:1–17—that to bear much fruit, he must abide in Jesus, for apart from him this friend could accomplish nothing (John 15:5). Eighteenth-century Protestants would not have used the language of spiritual direction, though it was common among Roman Catholics. However, that does not mean evangelicals ignored the critical practice of soul care; they simply used different terms to convey the Spirit's guidance in shaping Christ's followers. To minimize repetition, the terms *physician of the soul, soul physician, spiritual director, spiritual guide,* and *spiritual father* will be used interchangeably in this chapter.

The Ministry of a Soul Physician

The term *physician of the soul* was commonly applied to identify seventeenth-century Puritan ministers and continued the longstanding practice of the care or cure of souls.[2] The "function" of the Puritan minister "was to probe the conscience of the downhearted sinner, to name and cure the malady of his soul, and then to send him out strengthened and emboldened for the continuance of his lifelong battle with the world and the devil."[3] For the Puritans, this included both the initial struggle of the new birth and the lifelong process of destroying sin and growing in holiness.[4]

Whitefield revealed a deep appreciation of Puritanism in many areas of his ministry, including his awareness of the role of the physician of the soul, grounded biblically on Jesus as the great physician (Matt. 9:12; Mark 2:17; Luke 5:31). Whitefield's sermon on Jeremiah 8:20–22, titled "The Balm of Gilead Displayed, or, Christ the Physician of Souls," claimed that such healing is possible and the only reason why people do not recover their health is their unbelief. Despite their hard hearts, Jesus is still willing to restore their lives. Speaking on behalf of Christ with deep compassion, he invited his listeners, "Come to Christ, he is a tender Physician, he will heal you of your diseases." Following his normal pattern, Whitefield directed his soul-searching invitation to the full range of listeners

[2] J. I. Packer, *A Quest for Godliness: The Puritan Vision of the Christian Life* (Wheaton, IL: Crossway, 1990), 43, 55; John T. McNeill, *A History of the Cure of Souls* (New York: Harper & Row, 1951).
[3] William Haller, *Rise of Puritanism* (New York: Harper & Row, 1957), 27.
[4] For a helpful survey of the Puritan understanding of soul physicians, see Haller, *Rise of Puritanism*, 26–48; McNeill, *A History of the Cure of Souls*, 192–269; Timothy J. Keller, "Puritan Resources for Biblical Counseling," *Journal of Pastoral Practice* 9, no. 3 (1988): 11–44; Peter Lewis, *The Genius of Puritanism* (Haywards Heath, UK: Carey, 1977), 63–135.

present: to those who came out of curiosity or desired to ridicule him, to those who were resistant and rebellious, to those who had begun to be awakened and wondered if Jesus might forgive them, and to believers for the renewal of their faith.[5] While Whitefield primarily dealt with sin as a prelude to conversion, many of his epistles examined the necessity of growing in sanctification.

In a 1749 letter, he vividly revealed the soul physician's concern for both saving grace and maturing grace when he wrote to a doctor in the hope that Christ had begun "a good work" in his soul. Whitefield reminded him that Jesus, "the great physician," would give him "many a bitter portion" to wean him from his excessive attachment to the world. While Whitefield did not explicitly state it, his correspondent understood that human doctors were often required to probe open wounds—causing great pain—before they were able to prescribe bitter-tasting medicine that could restore health. Similarly, Jesus engaged in the painful purging necessary for this man to be healed of his inappropriate self-worth. As a doctor of the soul, Whitefield concluded with this spiritual prescription: "Grow in grace, press forwards. . . . Be a consistent Christian, live above the world."[6]

A few years later, he wrote to a prominent woman in Scotland using this same imagery of a person maturing in Christ. He prayed for her, "May the great physician of souls vouchsafe to give you all thriving souls in healthy bodies." To encourage her, he reported the amazing power that God's gospel worked through his ministry on both sides of the Atlantic. This news of the advancement of God's kingdom, Whitefield claimed, was the only message worth hearing, and the beauty of Christ was the only treasure to be sought in the world.[7] In another sermon, he examined how Jesus conducted himself as the "faithful physician" and spoke only to expose the hidden secrets of the human heart and edify his listeners with the nature of "real Christianity," so that their daily behavior might be transformed.[8] Whitefield followed this same pattern of speaking the truth of Scripture to direct souls only to Jesus.

---

[5] George Whitefield, *The Balm of Gilead Displayed, or, Christ the Physician of Souls* (Edinburgh: R. Drummond, 1742; repr., Oswestry, UK: Quinta, 2008), 3–15, quotation at p. 13. Whitefield echoed the same message in correspondence to a person in Boston. Whitefield to Rev. Mr. C—, January 1, 1741, in *Letters*, 230. We are aware of Whitefield's criticism of the inaccuracy of Joseph Gurney's shorthand record of this sermon. *Works*, 3:406.

[6] Whitefield to Dr. S—, June 14, 1749, in *Works*, 2:264.

[7] Whitefield to Lady —, August 9, 1755, in *Works*, 3:132–33, quotation at p. 133.

[8] Whitefield, "The Gospel Supper," in *Works*, 6:22.

Whitefield's Experience of Receiving Spiritual Direction

Chapter 1 recounted Whitefield's spiritual battles during his student days at Oxford, in which both Charles and John Wesley provided frequent spiritual direction as young George struggled to experience the new birth. Charles served as Whitefield's first guide, offering him numerous books and counsel. But when Charles grasped the deep anguish of his young friend's searching soul, he referred Whitefield to his more experienced brother, John, who was the recognized leader of the Oxford Methodists. Whitefield was receptive to John's wisdom and appreciatively called him "my spiritual father in Christ."[9] This paralleled Paul's language when he described himself as the father of the Corinthian church (1 Cor. 4:15). Spiritual parenthood had the same dual focus as the physician's care of the soul: both the birthing of believers and guiding them toward spiritual maturity in Christ.

During this period, Whitefield kept Wesley apprised of the recent events of his life, and as might be expected of a new believer, he narrated the early progress of his soul, including his fledging ministry. Whitefield continued the practice that the Wesleys had first instituted of reading Scripture to the prisoners at Oxford. The Holy Spirit was blessing the young evangelist's efforts, and many listeners felt the initial awakenings of the Spirit as they heard the biblical teaching on the new birth. Most revealingly, Whitefield confessed his disturbing awareness of pride in desiring to be a bishop in the Anglican Church. This echoed what he had called "my greatest affliction" from the previous Lent. Convicted of his great need for humility, he confessed that he was but a "worm." He struggled over whether to seek holy orders in the Church of England, and while he initially resisted the calling, his friends strongly encouraged him to pursue it.[10] Another letter to John Wesley reported on the "mercies [of] God" that Whitefield had recently experienced, which motivated his formation of a religious society, mimicking their earlier shared experience at Oxford. Eager to follow his spiritual father, Whitefield claimed with excitement, "I preach every Sunday to the prisoners, and follow your steps as close as possible."[11]

Spiritual guidance was not an isolated concern for John Wesley but, rather, a significant component of his ministry. Writing to a group of fellow clergymen, he reiterated the importance of being a physician (or in his

---

[9] Whitefield to Rev. John Wesley, approx. Summer 1735, in *Letters*, 484; Whitefield to Rev. John Wesley, September 2, 1736, in *Letters*, 486.
[10] Whitefield to Rev. John Wesley, approx. Summer 1735, in *Letters*, 484–85.
[11] Whitefield to Rev. John Wesley, September 2, 1736, in *Letters*, 486.

term, *shepherd*) of souls. Essential to this practice, according to Wesley, was the necessity of the "discernment of spirits" to guide the souls of others.[12] But by the later part of 1739, when the relationship between Whitefield and Wesley soured over the "Free Grace" controversy, Whitefield discontinued calling Wesley his spiritual father.[13] This language was both more relational and more personal than that of a soul physician. Nonetheless, this early spiritual tutelage had formed Whitefield significantly to build on and to expand his soul care in his distinctive Calvinist ways.

Whitefield's Perception of Being a Physician of the Soul

Being a soul physician reinforced Whitefield's lifelong desire to guide people to Jesus. His preaching never strayed far from the bedrock of the new birth in Christ. But he was never satisfied with only introducing people to Jesus; he wanted them to know and love Jesus deeply and enjoy the same sweet communion he did. This was confirmed in a 1739 letter where he emphasized to a minister, "The care of souls I find to be a matter of the greatest importance."[14] He reminded his colleague of his spiritual responsibility for all the people in his church and that it would be a "dreadful thing" if any of them would "perish through [his] neglect." The tone of the letter changed when Whitefield acknowledged that he had received news that the inconsistent behavior of this minister was contradictory to the gospel of Jesus Christ. Amazingly, Whitefield had not yet reached his twenty-fifth birthday when he penned this critical letter. Eventually, he repented of this and other brash intrusiveness, but it demonstrates the high value he placed on the care of souls.

In "The Indwelling of the Spirit, the Common Privilege of All Believers," Whitefield called himself a physician of the soul. Through this language, he justified confronting people with their sins. His intention was never to inflict pain but to awaken his listeners to the danger of living without the indwelling presence and guidance of the Holy Spirit. As a spiritual father, he understood that he must first wound his auditors before his "attempt to heal" them.[15] This reflects the Puritan practice of "law work" to convict the

---

[12] John Wesley, "An Address to the Clergy," in John Wesley, *The Works of John Wesley*, ed. Thomas Jackson, 3rd ed., 14 vols. (Grand Rapids, MI: Baker, 1996), 10:480–500.
[13] Geordan Hammond, "Whitefield, John Wesley, and Revival Leadership," in *George Whitefield: Life, Context and Legacy*, ed. Geordan Hammond and David Ceri Jones (Oxford: Oxford University Press, 2016), 105.
[14] Whitefield to Rev. Sir —, November 28, 1739, in *Letters*, 131.
[15] Whitefield, "The Indwelling of the Spirit, the Common Privilege of All Believers," in *Works*, 6:99.

lost of their need for Christ before they were able to receive the good news of salvation. Love was Whitefield's primary motivation for being a spiritual guide, and it inspired his careful watch over their souls. On one occasion, he spoke to someone whose father had just died and counseled him to live faithfully so that he too would inherit the heavenly reward, because only "a living faith in Jesus Christ can support us in a dying hour." However, this was complicated, since this correspondent's family were not believers and had already ridiculed this man's faith. Whitefield recognized his delicate context and encouraged him to continue to worship God and, above all, not to be "ashamed of the cross of Christ."[16] Consistent with this, John Gillies observed in his memoir of Whitefield that "sincere love in dealing so plainly with his correspondents about the interest of their souls" motivated his careful prayers for friends and enemies alike.[17]

To be a physician of the soul required a sensitive balance between conviction of sin and comfort of the sinner. Whitefield demonstrated this critical stance in a letter to a fellow clergyman, switching to the third person in this instance: "Do his parishioners fear, yet love him? Is he a *Boanerges*, and yet a *Barnabas* in the church of God?"[18] In Whitefield's estimation, a wise spiritual physician needs to be both. If a soul guide only rebukes others, they will soon become demoralized. Alternatively, if he only speak words of affirmation, they will develop a distorted impression and lack both critical self-awareness and resilience.[19] Elsewhere, Whitefield revealed his vulnerability and confessed his early tendency to overemphasize the compassion of Barnabas until he learned the danger of offering comfort too quickly before a person experienced the necessary conviction of sin.[20]

A central purpose of a spiritual guide is to encourage soul prosperity. As a result, Whitefield frequently wrote to others to deepen their intimacy with Jesus Christ. He reassured a wealthy man that he had "an extraordinary power" to pray for the man. While the context is not known, it is evident that this man was caught in a "cruel, but glorious [spiritual] warfare." In response, Whitefield wrestled in prayer like Jacob (Gen. 32:24) for his friend and wrote, "There is no need to despair when we are under Christ's leadership and auspices." The embattled correspondent was also instructed to "go

16 Whitefield to Ebenezer Blackwell, August 16, 1739, in *Letters*, 503–4.
17 *Memoirs*, 285.
18 Whitefield to Rev. Mr. K—, November 10, 1739, in *Letters*, 96 (italics in the original).
19 This distinction was common in Puritanism. See Tom Schwanda, *Soul Recreation: The Contemplative-Mystical Piety of Puritanism* (Eugene, OR: Pickwick, 2012), 102–5.
20 Whitefield to Mr. J— H—, June 25, 1740, in *Letters*, 190–91.

on; though faint, yet still pursue," which echoes Paul's counsel to Timothy to "fight the good fight of faith" (1 Tim. 6:12).[21] This letter also unveiled the necessary heart of a spiritual guide for a needy person and the practical support that can be received through Scripture, prayer, and the reminder that Christ will guide the way to victory. Fifteen years later, Whitefield updated a lady of nobility on his preaching and concluded with a similar desire that her "soul may always prosper, and that [she] may increase with all the increase of God."[22] This combination of letter writing and preaching suggests that being a physician of the soul can occur both one-on-one and in group settings.

At various times Whitefield referred to himself as a spiritual father.[23] Central to this practice was the expression of deep love and concern for people's lives and faith. Once he was deeply pained by a doctrinal error that had affected many of his London congregation. He took up his pen to one correspondent in particular regarding how the error had restricted this person's communion with God. After he examined the theological dimensions that had misled his friend, Whitefield pointedly asked, "Have you returned home with Christ in your heart?"[24] Later he revisited this same situation, observing that this theological controversy had splintered his congregation and produced great pain for him as their spiritual father, who suffered the desertion of his children in the faith.[25] Not only was love crucial to his practice of being a soul guide, but so too was a strong dependence upon the Holy Spirit, who lavished his love into Whitefield's heart. This in turn inspired his prayers that this recipient would be bathed in the love of Christ through the Spirit. Further, to increase this individual's faith, Whitefield counseled him to seek to be "humble, kind, and courteous" and confessed that the "desire of [his] soul" was for this man to live before the Lord. Whitefield concluded, "O my dear brother, love a precious Christ, and show it by adorning his gospel in all things."[26]

Whitefield's Methods for Guiding Souls

While the previous section revealed some of Whitefield's methods in general, we will now focus specifically on three of the most significant tools

21 Whitefield to Earl of L—, November 24, 1741, in *Letters*, 340–41, 546.

22 Whitefield to Lady —, November 17, 1756, in *Works*, 3:193.

23 See, for example, Whitefield to Dear Brother C—, December 11, 1740, in *Letters*, 229; Whitefield to Mr. Wm. G—, February 8, 1741, in *Letters*, 234.

24 Whitefield to Mr. G— C—, December 11, 1740, in *Letters*, 227–29, quotation at p. 229.

25 Whitefield to Doctor D—, December 21, 1748, in *Works*, 2:215.

26 Whitefield to Wm. G—, February 8, 1741, in *Letters*, 234. For another example of Whitefield's reference to being a spiritual father, see Whitefield to Lady H—, February 16, 1749, in *Works*, 2:231.

of a soul physician that he employed in guiding others to Jesus: the use of questions, cases of conscience, and spiritual counsel. There is overlap and dynamic interaction between these three dimensions, which will soon become evident.

Guiding Souls through Questions

Questions have long been used to awaken and invite people into greater awareness of Jesus. Christ himself was a master of this practice and frequently used it to teach others to discover the good news of God.[27] For example, he asked his listeners, "What do you want me to do for you?" (Mark 10:51); "Who do you say that I am?" (Matt. 16:15); "Where is your faith?" (Luke 8:25); "Do you love me more than these?" (John 21:15).[28] Following Jesus's example, Whitefield utilized questions for self-examination as a soul physician seeking to motivate his listeners and encourage greater growth in their relationship with God and others. This was vividly on display in his sermon titled "Self-Enquiry concerning the Work of God," when repeatedly he asked, "What hath God wrought?" As a spiritual father, he was most interested in what God had wrought in his hearers' souls. He confessed that he had learned this art of spiritual guidance over thirty years of listening to thousands of people tell their stories "about their hearts." Whitefield credited the Holy Spirit, who had enabled him to develop this spiritual sensitivity as he skillfully connected the question with different dimensions of the spiritual life according to the various situations of his audience. What has God wrought in convincing people of their sins? What has God wrought by the internal teaching of the Holy Spirit? What has God wrought to enable us to love God more deeply?[29] On another occasion, he urged a man seeking to enter the ministry to follow Whitefield's regular pattern of recognizing that "the Holy Ghost is the best director and support in all circumstances."[30] Without complete dependency upon the Spirit, Whitefield would have been ineffective as a physician of the soul and in every other aspect of his life. As a result, he instructed his listeners to cultivate an awareness of "the motions of God's blessed Spirit in your souls."[31]

---

[27] Roy Zuck claims that Jesus used 304 questions, while Don Everts counts 307. Roy B. Zuck, *Teaching as Jesus Taught* (Grand Rapids, MI: Baker, 1995), 237; Don Everts and Doug Schaupp, *I Once Was Lost: What Postmodern Skeptics Taught Us about Their Path to Jesus* (Downers Grove, IL: InterVarsity Press, 2008), 54. The actual number of questions varies, depending on which translation of the Greek text is used.
[28] Scripture quotations from the ESV.
[29] Whitefield, "Self-Enquiry concerning the Work of God," in *Eighteen Sermons*, 230, 233–234, 237.
[30] Whitefield to Mr. X— Y—, January 15, 1751, in *Works*, 2:393.
[31] Whitefield, "Walking with God," in *Works*, 5:30.

Sermons are directed to a broad public, which, for Whitefield, typically exceeded thousands of listeners, but a letter is specific, like a laser beam piercing the soul of an individual's need. Curious about the spiritual health of a couple living at Bethesda, his Georgian orphanage, he asked: "Do you live in love? Do you strive together with me in your prayers? . . . Is your heart enlarged? Is your soul swallowed up in God?"[32] These inquiries both focused on the couple's relationships with each other and God, and challenged them to review their partnership with Whitefield in the operation of Bethesda. In another epistle, he employed a cluster of prompts reflective of a spiritual guide: "Is your [heart] grown sick of original and actual sin? Is it grown sick of unbelief and self-righteousness? Is it closely united to the holy Jesus? Do you feed on him in your heart by faith? And do you receive of his fulness day by day?" These probes illustrate Whitefield's persistent concern for the necessity of growing in holiness with Jesus and the continual efforts to mortify sin. The result of these labors would produce an enlarged awareness of Christ's presence and provisions.[33] While the rapid and cumulative nature of these questions could be overwhelming, we need to recognize that Whitefield was not sitting across from individuals to pause and receive their responses. Rather, in light of his infrequent and delayed communication with his spiritual children through the mail, we can appreciate the benefit of written questions over those asked in person to challenge the recipients.

He justified asking personal questions because he was concerned for the recipients' "inward life" and expected that they would update Whitefield on their experiences of "having a feeling possession" of God.[34] In a letter to James Habersham, Whitefield's friend who managed the Georgian orphanage, he reinforced the importance of a vital relationship with Jesus Christ for the successful operation of Bethesda. Whitefield reminded him of the importance of holiness and walking closely with Jesus as a faithful disciple, and he posed these "daily questions" to Habersham: "Am I more like Christ? Am I more meek and patient? Does my practice correspond with my knowledge, and am I a light to enlighten and enflame all that are around me?" Once again Whitefield's keen interest in the interior life of his friend was evident, and he was concerned to see Habersham's knowledge of Jesus radiate to others and confirm his commitment to Christ. This

---

[32] Whitefield to Mr. B—, and his wife, February 17, 1741, in *Letters*, 244.
[33] Whitefield to Mr. W—, March 26, 1740, in *Letters*, 157.
[34] Whitefield to Mr. W—, March 26, 1740, in *Letters*, 157.

sampling of spiritual queries demonstrates Whitefield's care for the souls of others and his skillful use of questions to guide others in growing to maturity with Jesus Christ.[35]

Cases of Conscience

The second dimension of Whitefield's soul guidance dealt with cases of conscience or casuistry, which he learned from the Puritans.[36] This practice of directing troubled and inquiring souls was not developed in a vacuum but, rather, was derived from both a resistance to and reform of the larger reservoir of Roman Catholic literature.[37] It pertained not only to the sins individuals wrestled with before their conversion but also to the residual effect on them throughout life as they sought to grow into greater holiness.

Casuistry has been defined as "practical theology, training Christians to live uprightly, humbly, and gladly in the presence of God every day of their lives."[38] Puritan Richard Baxter's exhaustive treatment of Christian ethics in his *Christian Directory* ran to over nine hundred pages and included cases for the unconverted and those resistant to the gospel, as well as extensive guidance for walking with God and mortification of residual sins that restricted the progress of sanctification.[39] One historian observes that "strenuous, casuistical piety was clearly a very broadly based phenomenon among Anglican and Dissenting devotional writers by the early eighteenth century."[40] Whitefield demonstrated the importance of this in a letter to a friend by reiterating what he had learned from Henry Scougal's *The Life of God in the Soul of Man*: that true religion is not based merely on the external practices of piety. Jesus required his disciples to deny themselves, take up their cross daily, and follow him (Luke 9:23). Given the tenacity of sin, the Grand Itinerant stressed the importance of "acts of self-denial, and mortification," without which prayers would be of little value.[41] He also

---

[35] Whitefield to Mr. J— H—, February 18, 1741, in *Letters*, 247–48.
[36] See, for example, Gordon Stevens Wakefield, *Puritan Devotion: Its Place in the Development of Christian Piety* (London: Epworth, 1957), 113–29; Timothy Dwight Bozeman, *The Precisianist Strain: Disciplinary Religion and Antinomian Backlash in Puritanism to 1638* (Chapel Hill: University of North Carolina Press, 2004), 121–44; Keller, "Puritan Resources for Biblical Counseling."
[37] Bozeman, *Precisianist Strain*, 78–83, 121–29.
[38] Joel R. Beeke and Mark Jones, "Puritan Casuistry," in *A Puritan Theology: Doctrine for Life* (Grand Rapids, MI: Reformation Heritage, 2012), 927.
[39] Keller, "Puritan Resources for Biblical Counseling," 14–15.
[40] D. Bruce Hindmarsh, *The Spirit of Early Evangelicalism: True Religion in a Modern World* (New York: Oxford University Press, 2018), 19.
[41] Whitefield to Mr. H—, February 20, 1735, in *Letters*, 6.

alerted the same friend of the devil's attempt to deceive him with the supposed unreasonableness of practicing self-denial.[42] This cautionary word
was imperative, since Whitefield believed that whenever God is at work in
a person's soul, the devil seeks to sow seeds of despair and doubt.[43]

Cases of conscience normally involve three specific steps, as illustrated in a 1740 letter in which Whitefield identified the spiritual problem, examined the possible causes, and prescribed the solution to bring
healing to an individual. This particular person was struggling with the
apparent absence of God, often called spiritual darkness or desolation.
Whitefield described it to him as God no longer "manifest[ing] himself
to your soul." Truly, any person who intentionally seeks to mature in the
Christian life will experience periods when God seems absent; the critical
word is *seems*. It is a theological impossibility for God to be entirely absent
from a believer's life. Scripture abounds with the reassurance that God is in
our midst (Pss. 46:4–7; 139:7–10; Matt. 28:20) and that he will never leave
us or forsake us (Deut. 31:8; Josh. 1:5; Heb. 13:5). However, for Whitefield's
friend, God appeared absent, because the man could not sense God's felt
presence. To comfort this troubled soul, Whitefield expressed his gratitude
that this spiritual aridity could bring renewed clarity and joy to his friend.[44]
God, Whitefield wrote, would "never leave me nor forsake me. . . . He loved
me freely . . . he chose me from eternity, he called me in time, and I am
persuaded will keep me till time shall be no more." This biblical promise
renewed Whitefield's faith, and he trusted the same for his correspondent,
even amid times of affliction and doubt.[45]

After examining this situation, Whitefield rehearsed a few possible
causes. He discerned that his friend had probably lost a sense of his first
love, which must always be directed to Jesus (Rev. 2:4). As a spiritual father, Whitefield perceived that this individual had focused on his good
deeds in a self-righteous way and that he had not renounced the world suf-
ficiently. God may indeed intentionally withdraw his felt presence to wean
people from relying too much on their efforts, even in cultivating spiritual
disciplines. Clarity is important; God does not want believers to neglect
spiritual practices, but Whitefield cautioned his friend not to develop
a "self-complacence" in the means of grace, which can be dangerous in

---

[42] Whitefield to Mr. H—, March 6, 1735, in *Letters*, 7.
[43] Whitefield, "Self-Enquiry concerning God's Work," 233.
[44] Whitefield to Mr. M—, June 11, 1740, in *Letters*, 186–87.
[45] Whitefield to My Dear Sister —, January 31, 1740, in *Letters*, 145.

the Christian life. Perhaps this individual assumed that because he prayed or read Scripture or engaged in some other devotional activity, God would automatically respond to him. Instead, Whitefield directed this frustrated believer to dedicate more time to studying his heart. This would better attune him to his motivations and perhaps, with sufficient honesty, reveal areas of disobedience that further restricted his experience of God. Therefore, Whitefield encouraged him to recognize that his spiritual darkness was due to the indwelling sin within his heart. As his correspondent wrestled with God, Whitefield instructed him to renew his awareness of Jesus and reclaim him as his first love. This does not happen instantly, so Whitefield urged him to patiently wait for God's timing until he again sensed God's felt presence. Conscious of the potential danger of spiritual darkness, Whitefield concluded by urging his friend to continually seek Jesus and strive with all of his might until God's countenance again shined on him.[46]

Spiritual leaders today often focus on similar experiences of desolation, or the lack of the felt presence of God, and seek through the guidance of the Spirit to help people recover a sense of consolation. In a related case, Whitefield demonstrated this desired transformation through the life of Peter, who moved from a position of a "disconsolate soul," when Jesus rebuked him for his insistence that Christ would not die upon the cross (Mark 8:32–33), to the hopeful news when the angels on Easter morning specifically reported that Peter would experience the risen Christ (Mark 16:7).[47] Whitefield's optimism—that God always brings good out of painful situations—led him to consistently believe that Christ had triumphed over sin and the powers of darkness. He constantly sought to impart this message of hope to all of his spiritual children.

Almost a decade later, Whitefield gave spiritual counsel to a woman of nobility by following the same threefold pattern. She had just experienced the new birth and wondered about her assurance of salvation. He initially celebrated the news of her conversion and proceeded to assist her in the confirmation of this liberating discovery. Next, he instructed her that the righteousness of Jesus, who first brought her into this relationship, would be her faithful friend until she reached heaven. The initial discovery that she knew Jesus would continue through the promised presence of the Spirit. Whitefield addressed what must have been her original question

---

[46] Whitefield to Mr. M—, June 11, 1740, in Letters, 186–87.
[47] Whitefield to Mr. J— S—, July 25, 1741, in Letters, 287.

about the Holy Spirit. He affirmed that the Spirit was proof of her new birth and emphasized the need "to get a constant abiding witness and indwelling of the blessed Spirit of God in your heart." This echoed Jesus's teaching of the Spirit's indwelling presence (John 7:37–39), which confirms that a person belongs to God. Further counseling her to deepen her new life, Whitefield paraphrased Colossians 2:6, "As you have, therefore, honoured Madam, received the Lord Jesus, so walk in him even by faith." Additionally, he instructed her that the Christian life includes challenges and that the best way to travel through the "howling wilderness" of this world is to "lean on your beloved [Jesus]."[48] Unlike a sermon, which broadly covers a large group of listeners, casuistry requires a personal and tailored response for each inquiring soul.

Spiritual Counsel for Overcoming Barriers

The careful application of spiritual wisdom is a third means of guiding souls to Jesus. A recent study of Whitefield's and John Wesley's practice of spiritual guidance concludes that they relied more on exhorting than nurturing in their care of souls. No doubt the frenetic pace of their itinerant ministries shaped this and contributed to what has been called Whitefield's "exhortative default" approach to mentoring.[49] Within the broader context of spiritual direction during the seventeenth and eighteenth centuries, spiritual guidance was typically more directive than contemplative. This was equally true in the more authoritarian Roman Catholic practice of spiritual direction.

Given that exhortation is common for a soul physician, it is instructive to examine Whitefield's practice of exhorting others. A primary goal of spiritual direction has always been to assist individuals in recognizing the obstacles that prevent them from experiencing God more fully in their lives. While the range of Whitefield's counsel was extensive, we will limit our review to his consideration of some of the common hindrances to spiritual maturity. Whitefield's lifelong dependency upon the Spirit inspired much of his "sanctified advice" to others. His writings reveal numerous examples where people were stuck. They were busy and in a hurry. They seemed unable to surrender themselves to Jesus. They ignored the use of

48 Whitefield to Countess D—, February 22, 1749, in *Works*, 2:236–37.
49 Rhys S. Bezzant, "'Companions in the Way': Mentoring in the Ministry of Wesley and Whitefield," in *Wesley and Whitefield? Wesley versus Whitefield?*, ed. Ian J. Maddock (Eugene, OR: Pickwick, 2018), 215–17.

spiritual disciplines, they practiced worldliness and idolatry, and they experienced spiritual dryness.

The biblical witness that there is nothing new under the sun (Eccl. 1:9) is true in the Christian life. One of the most perennial barriers restricting deeper friendship with Jesus is hurry. People often complained then, as we do now, that their lives were too busy and that they were overwhelmed with too many obligations to devote adequate time to cultivating a relationship with Christ. In a letter to a close friend, Whitefield reminded him that it is the "Christian's privilege to keep holy day all the year round" with God. "Holy day" was a reference to Sunday and the expectation that even people with busy schedules during the week could devote more time to God on the seventh day. Whitefield acknowledged that the "noise and hurry of business" can easily "rob us of one moment's communion and fellowship with the ever-blessed God." The best solution to this barrier is to "keep close to our loving Lord," which Whitefield strongly urged his friend to do. Additionally, he counseled him to discover what it meant for him to "banquet on the love of Jesus." Embedded in this letter was the practical advice that Jesus Christ had died for him and that he should never forget Christ's sacrifice for him. Whitefield prayed that remembrance of Christ's life, death, and resurrection would create gratitude and inspire him to seek intimacy with Christ.[50]

Whitefield also addressed preoccupation with the self, which is related to a misunderstanding of the nature and dynamics of sin. Writing to a long-time friend from his hometown of Gloucester, he examined this person's refusal to submit his life to Jesus's basic call to deny himself, take up his cross, and follow Christ (Luke 9:23). Given the fundamental nature of this obstacle, Whitefield sought several different angles to guide this struggling friend. He first acknowledged that the devil distorts self-denial into something more complicated than it is; this is clear from the simple petition in the Lord's Prayer "Thy will be done" (Matt. 6:10). It was important for Whitefield's friend to recognize that denial is not a single act but, rather, a continuous and lifelong pursuit. While initially it might seem demanding, walking with Jesus is expected of all his disciples. Once the first step is taken, it becomes increasingly more realistic. Whitefield also perceived that his correspondent's faith had become stagnant because he depended more upon the world than Scripture as his guide. Reading and obeying

---

[50] Whitefield to Mr. R— K—, April 18, 1753, in *Works*, 3:11.

God's revelation would open his eyes to self-denial. Finally, practicing fervent prayer would greatly aid in his submission to God.[51]

To his same friend, Whitefield declared that another major obstacle is engaging the spiritual disciplines merely as an "outward performance." Whitefield's experience during his Oxford days was still fresh in his memory, and he continued to view true religion as a matter of the heart. To reinforce this truth, he included a copy of Scougal's *The Life of God in the Soul of Man*, challenging his friend to develop daily morning prayer and frequent reception of the Lord's Supper. Whitefield pointedly warned his colleague that nothing "so much be-dwarfs us in religion, and hinders our progress towards the heavenly Canaan, as starving our souls by keeping away from the heavenly banquet." Consequently, neglecting the spiritual disciplines not only robs a person of communion with God through ignoring Scripture, worship, prayer, the Lord's Supper, fasting, and service but also creates a strong resistance to knowing and loving God more fully. In his sermon "Walking with God," Whitefield further reinforced the importance of the means of grace as essential for those who desire spiritual maturity and as the primary means for "believers [to] keep up and maintain their walk with God."[52]

Another common barrier to the spiritual life is the competition of the world. Because of his celebrity status, Whitefield comprehended firsthand the temptation of worldly adulation and confessed the danger of having one's "heart drawn away by earthly objects." More specifically, he cautioned a woman regarding her similar risk of idolatry and the devil's deceitful schemes to turn her soul's focus away from its proper devotion to Jesus. Amid these challenges, he advised her "to keep up a close walk and communion with God," since God accepts no rivals and there is only room for Jesus to dwell within the believer. Further, Whitefield affirmed the gravity of guarding one's heart through using devotional books that are "truly evangelical and afford sweet nourishment" to a believer. Soul-searching books can penetrate a reader's heart and strengthen his or her love and commitment to Jesus Christ.[53]

On another occasion, Whitefield sent advice to a woman in Charleston, South Carolina. Following his normal practice, he distilled insights from his encounters with God. After an update on his own spiritual life and

---

[51] Whitefield to Mr. H—, March 6, 1735, in *Letters*, 7–9.
[52] Whitefield to Mr. H—, February 20, 1735, in *Letters*, 7. Whitefield, "Walking with God," 27–31.
[53] Whitefield to Mrs. Elizabeth D—, February 1, 1740, in *Letters*, 148.

activities, he turned his focus to her: "I shall be glad to hear how it is with your soul. I beseech you to live near to Christ, and to keep up a holy walk with God. Be inward with God in your duties," and always "trust and hang on God, even when he hides himself from you. He will be your guide unto death. Hunger and thirst daily after the righteousness of Christ. Be content with no degree of sanctification."[54]

The value of this spiritual counsel is accentuated once we grasp its context. Whitefield began this letter by confessing that he was in a "heavenly frame, swallowed up in God, and melted down by the love of [his] dear Lord Jesus." This heightened spiritual sensitivity impacted his guidance for this woman. While this letter contains much rich spiritual counsel, it is important to recognize, as Whitefield did in one of his cases of conscience, that God occasionally withdraws his presence from believers. Bouts of spiritual dryness (Pss. 13:1; 22:1; 89:46) should remind disciples that periods of desolation should not cause despair, because Jesus is always with his followers, even though he cannot be always felt. Additionally, a Christian should never be content with a partial experience of sanctification but always press onward for the fullness in Christ (Phil. 3:14). An obvious principle that can be missed amid Whitefield's spiritual guidance is that growing in deeper intimacy with Jesus is never automatic but always requires intentional efforts.

Guidance for Measuring Spiritual Growth

People naturally ask each other how they are doing: Are they making progress and advancing in whatever they are engaged in? Are they growing mentally, physically, relationally, and spiritually? Invariably questions arise about the merits of quantitative versus qualitative measurement of growth. While it is simple to measure, for example, a person's height and weight, it is far more difficult to assess spiritual growth. However, Scripture provides several markers of qualitative progress. Jesus grew in wisdom and stature with God and humanity (Luke 2:52), and John captured three levels of maturity when he spoke of children, young men, and fathers (1 John 2:12–14). Additionally, Paul distinguished between those who were worldly or infants in Christ and those who were spiritual (1 Cor. 3:1–3).

Whitefield recognized this same need and provided qualitative indicators that could encourage believers in their growth in Christ. First was the

---

[54] Whitefield to Mrs. S—, February 17, 1741, in *Letters*, 245.

helpful question about spiritual direction, "How is it between you and God, with respect to secret prayer?" Another revealing sign was growth in self-awareness, which he called "growing downward." This reflected Augustine's principle of double knowledge.[55] It was Whitefield's regular practice to teach only what he had learned, and he asked a friend to pray for him that, in his words, "I may know myself even as I am known."[56] This paralleled the Grand Itinerant's advice to know one's own heart. Writing to a man entering the ministry, he urged him to study "your own heart."[57] He counseled another person, "Study your heart and the Scriptures, get nearer and nearer to Christ, and he will lead you into all truth."[58]

As people grew in self-awareness, they would more accurately recognize the seriousness of sin and rebellion in their lives. For Whitefield, greater self-awareness produced a maturing love for Jesus as the "glorious Redeemer." Other signs of spiritual growth included the integration of knowing Jesus both cognitively and affectively, and a greater detachment from the things of the world.[59] Conversing with a minister friend from New York, Whitefield stressed the importance of fostering a catholic spirit that welcomed new believers from any tradition or background. The key to this was relying on the Spirit. Whitefield counseled, "There needs [to be] a close adherence to the motions of the Holy Spirit, and a constant watching over the corruptions of our own hearts, so that we may walk before God as very little children."[60]

Soul Prosperity

Whitefield's continual concern was to encourage soul prosperity and assist people in their growth in sanctification. He turned to 3 John 2, "Beloved, I wish above all things that thou mayest prosper and be in health, even as thy soul prospereth," as the text for his sermon "Soul Prosperity." While he acknowledged that some of his listeners were consumed with pursuing financial gain, he trusted that those who had become "acquainted with Jesus Christ" were more committed to seeing that their souls would prosper than that their bodies would. One authentic means of discerning this maturity in Christ was prayer in the individual's life. With deep appreciation for the

---

[55] Whitefield, "Soul Prosperity," in *Eighteen Sermons*, 63, 67.
[56] Whitefield to Mr. W— D—, June 28, 1740, in *Letters*, 195.
[57] Whitefield to Mr. J— E—, November 23, 1742, in *Letters*, 466.
[58] Whitefield to Mr. G— L—, September 26, 1740, in *Letters*, 213.
[59] Whitefield, "Soul Prosperity," 68–70.
[60] Whitefield to Mr. Thomas N—, February 26, 1742, in *Letters*, 372.

legacy of the Puritans, he validated Bunyan's claim that "if we are prayerless, we are Christless." Repeatedly we have seen Whitefield's emphasis on using the means of grace. One of his admirable traits was his realism; he understood both in his life and others' the intentional discipline required to experience and maintain soul prosperity. In what his listeners must have received as welcome words of encouragement, he proclaimed, "I don't say you will always have the same fervour as when you first set out; I don't say you will always be carried up into the third heavens," while urging them to be always conscious of their communion with Christ.[61]

The thread woven through these last three chapters is that the spiritual life is not about external behavior or posturing but about the inner life of heart religion. Jesus's critique of the Pharisees, who were more insistent in observing their human traditions than in following the liberating truth of divinely inspired Scripture (Matt. 22:29; Mark 7:9) found deep resonance in Whitefield's experience and teaching about the spiritual life and guiding others, that their souls might prosper. Simply stated, his goal as a physician of the soul was to guide them into soul prosperity so that they would "fall in [greater] love with the glorious Redeemer."[62]

---

[61] Whitefield, "Soul Prosperity," 61, 63, 65.
[62] Whitefield, "Soul Prosperity," 69.

CHAPTER 7

PREACHER OF ONE BOOK

It is not at all an exaggeration to say that preaching—and, more specifically, itinerant extemporaneous preaching—lay at the heart of Whitefield's life as a Christian. His vocation and self-identity were tightly bound together. Whitefield did not simply preach for a living. He lived to preach: by most reckonings, eighteen thousand sermons throughout a public ministry that spanned more than three decades. His voice was heard across the full spectrum of society. His sermons "were fit for the field, for the town, for the pulpit, . . . for the private chapel and drawing room," and, as part of a deliberate "preach and print" strategy, fit to be read.[1] On the verge of embarking on his first tour of the American colonies in 1739, and fresh off a series of highly successful field-preaching events in England throughout the previous six months, he reflected: "Everyone hath his proper gift. Field preaching is my plan. In this I am carried as on eagles' wings."[2] Decades later, his zeal had not abated in the slightest. "This itch after itinerating, I hope will never be cured till we come to heaven," he wrote.[3]

We have seen previously that Whitefield's extensive published writings reveal him to be a more subtle and astute theologian than he is sometimes given credit for. And yet Harry Stout's contention that, "for all intents and purposes, Whitefield's ministry was exclusively oral" nonetheless captures how his celebrity status during the eighteenth-century transatlantic

---

[1] Emma Salgård Cunha, "Whitefield and Literary Affect," in *George Whitefield: Life, Context and Legacy*, ed. Geordan Hammond and David Ceri Jones (Oxford: Oxford University Press, 2016), 193.
[2] Quoted in Robert Philip, *The Life and Times of the Reverend George Whitefield* (Edinburgh: Banner of Truth, 2007), 385.
[3] Whitefield to Mr. A—, August 14, 1767, in *Works*, 3:351.

revivals was founded largely upon his reputation as a remarkably talented preacher. His unscripted (though by no means unprepared) approach toward preaching "had the immense advantage of channeling the full heart and soul of the speaker into the actual moment of delivery and fusing a unique bond between speaker, audience and the immediate situation," suggests Stout. "Proper method and sequence were secondary to zeal; and zeal depended on the minister's ability to speak from the heart without the proper constraints of prepared notes."[4]

Not that Whitefield considered there to be anything in the least bit improper about his chosen homiletical method. Indeed, while he might have been temperamentally inclined toward a preaching style that quickly established him as a sensation in London, as a recently ordained twenty-one-year-old ("I began to grow a little popular," he noted with barely disguised satisfaction), it is not accidental that Whitefield's rationale for delivering dramatic sermons outside the confines of consecrated ground at mass outdoor gatherings explicitly emerged from his commitment to the Bible.[5]

And so if the colorful descriptions bestowed upon Whitefield by his contemporaries ("the Grand Itinerant" and "the Prince of Pulpit Orators"[6]) and recent generations ("the Divine Dramatist"[7]) emphasize the peripatetic and flamboyant character of his speaking ministry, our approach in this chapter will focus on these elements of Whitefield's preaching through an underemphasized lens: the influence Scripture exerted on the sermons he preached and subsequently printed. As a preacher of one book, Whitefield did not regard the Bible as simply providing the raw material or content for his sermons: as a founding father of the evangelical movement, he let Scripture shape both *where* and *how* he urged his listeners to experience the new birth.

Whitefield the Itinerant Field Preacher

Whitefield was well aware of how contentious and unusual his decision to pursue an itinerant field-preaching ministry was. At times he made conscious efforts to demonstrate that it did not contravene Church of England

---

[4] Harry S. Stout, *The New England Soul: Preaching and Religious Culture in Colonial New England* (New York: Oxford University Press, 2012), 198–99.
[5] *Journals*, 81.
[6] Joseph B. Wakeley, *Anecdotes of the Rev. George Whitefield, with a Biographical Sketch* (1879; repr., Oswestry, UK: Quinta, 2000), 7.
[7] Harry S. Stout, *The Divine Dramatist: George Whitefield and the Rise of Modern Evangelicalism* (Grand Rapids, MI: Eerdmans, 1991).

canon law.[8] He made sure that when he preached on Sundays, it did not coincide with the stated times of regular worship, and he also claimed, "We went not into the fields till we were excluded from the churches."[9] These conciliatory and defensive gestures notwithstanding, when it came to constructively justifying his decision to make the "mad trick" of field preaching his homiletical signature, it was the narrative world of the Bible that supplied Whitefield with the vocabulary and examples to buttress his pursuit of a ministry as innovative as it was controversial.[10]

It is also worth observing that by the time Whitefield first began preaching outdoors in early 1739, field-preaching role models already existed for him to copy. Indeed, he readily acknowledged his indebtedness to them. As an ordained Church of England clergyman, William Morgan had previously made a significant impression on Whitefield when he began preaching in England's West Country, motivated by his heart for "the rude and ignorant condition of the Kingswood colliers."[11] Further afield, in Wales, Howell Harris had already been field preaching since 1735. Whitefield saw in him a field-preaching kindred spirit, reflecting that "a divine and strong sympathy seemed to be between us."[12] He longed to "catch some of Harris's fire" and took careful notes on his creative preaching postures: "He discourses generally in a field, but at other times in a house, from a wall, a table, or anything else."[13]

Over time, Whitefield would become a keen student of the "science" of open-air public speaking. He wrote, "I am content to take the field, and when the weather will permit, with a table for my pulpit, and the heavens for my sounding-board, I proclaim to all, the unsearchable riches of Jesus Christ."[14] He looked to exploit topographical features in the natural landscape to amplify his already commanding voice. Typically that included preaching from raised areas; in the absence of a mound or hill, he often preached from a portable and demountable scaffold. On other occasions, such as at Cambuslang in 1742, he took advantage of a natural amphitheater to maximize his auditory range.[15] Preaching outdoors was an unpredictable

---

8 *Journals*, 249ff., 259.
9 *Journals*, 293.
10 *Journals*, 49.
11 John Cennick, "An Account of the Most Remarkable Occurrences in the Awakenings at Bristol and Kingswood (1750)," *Proceedings of the Wesley Historical Society* 6 (1907): 102–3.
12 *Journals*, 230.
13 *Journals*, 229.
14 Whitefield, "To the Bishop of B—, February 16, 1756, in *Works*, 3:162.
15 See Arthur Fawcett, *The Cambuslang Revival* (London: Banner of Truth, 1971).

business and involved contending with all manner of distractions. Weather conditions were not always favorable, but when they were, it helped extend his range. After preaching to a large crowd at Kennington Common on April 29, 1739, Whitefield observed that "the wind being for" him enabled his voice to carry "to the extremest part of the audience."[16]

Since contemporary open-air preaching role models were relatively few and far between, Whitefield appealed to historic precedents in support of his itinerant ministry. For instance, when in 1745 Harvard College publicly accused him of being "the first promoter . . . amongst us" of "that itinerant way of preaching," Whitefield vigorously defended himself against the charge of homiletical innovation. His preaching might have been unusual ("this strange way of preaching," as John Wesley put it[17]), but it was far from unprecedented.

> For itinerant preaching is certainly founded upon the word of God, and has been agreeably approved of, and practised by many good men, with great and happy success both in ancient and later times. Was not the reformation begun and carried on by itinerant preaching? Were not *Knox*, *Welch*, *Wishart*, and those holy men of God, several of the good old *puritans*, itinerant preachers? Are not itinerants sent forth by the societies for propagating the gospel and promoting Christian knowledge both in *England, Scotland* and *Denmark*?[18]

Precedent and Prescription in Scripture

As important as historical and contemporary examples of itinerant field preaching might have been for Whitefield, as the above quotation reflects, when it came to supplying his admirers and critics alike with a mandate for where and how he preached, he typically appealed first and foremost to Scripture. Any appeals to historic examples of field preaching came after Whitefield's initial and prime defense: namely, that the Bible is full of approving examples of itinerant preaching.

Throughout the period leading up to his conversion and ordination, Whitefield increasingly immersed himself in the world of the Bible, praying "over every line and word of both the English and Greek till the passage,

[16] *Journals*, 260–61.
[17] John Wesley, *The Works of John Wesley: Bicentennial Edition*, vols. 18–24, *Journals and Diaries I–VII*, ed. W. Reginald Ward and Richard P. Heitzenrater (Nashville: Abingdon, 1988–1997), 19:46.
[18] Whitefield, "A Letter to the Reverend the President, and Professors, Tutors, and Hebrew Instructors, of Harvard College in Cambridge," January 23, 1745, in *Works*, 4:218–19 (italics in the original).

in its essential meaning . . . [became] part of his soul."[19] As he imbibed Scripture's accounts of the lives of prominent evangelists and preachers, one lasting outcome was that his sermons became saturated with biblical vocabulary. James Downey contends that "because he was so entirely persuaded of the infallibility of scripture, he committed much of it to memory, and his sermons are rife with biblical allusions, quotations and idiom."[20]

But as Whitefield read the Bible, he also found its pages filled with authoritative precedents for his burgeoning ministry. If his Christian life was shaped by the normative authority of the Bible, then Whitefield discovered in Scripture not simply *descriptions* of the lives of saints in bygone times and places but also what he interpreted as *prescriptions* for subsequent generations to follow. He was convinced that "when the power of religion revives, the gospel must be propagated in the same manner as it was first established, 'itinerant preaching.'"[21] For example, Whitefield argued that the physical setting of many of the sermons Jesus preached outdoors established a clear paradigm for his ministry: like master, like eighteenth-century servant. Whitefield went so far as to envisage that were Jesus to appear then and there, "he would go about the streets, he would be a field-preacher, he would go out into the highways and hedges, he would invite, he would run after them."[22]

Another time, in his sermon "The Gospel, a Dying Saint's Triumph," Whitefield contended that Jesus had issued a "short but very extensive" command to his "vicegerents" to preach the gospel to "every creature"— a command that trumped the straitjacket of stifling and prudish ecclesiastical prohibitions. Continuing, Whitefield declared: "Did you ever hear Paul, or any of the apostles, send away a congregation without a sermon? No, no: when turned out of the temple they preached in the highways, hedges, streets and lanes of the city: they went to the waterside; there Lydia was catched."[23]

And yet Whitefield did not simply see himself as following Jesus's examples. In his *Journals*—spiritual autobiographies intended for mass distribution, characterized by "the exoticism of a foreign travelogue, the

---

[19] Arnold A. Dallimore, *George Whitefield: The Life and Times of the Great Evangelist of the Eighteenth-Century Revival*, 2 vols. (London: Banner of Truth, 1970, 1980), 1:83.
[20] James Downey, *The Eighteenth Century Pulpit: A Study of the Sermons of Butler, Berkeley, Secker, Sterne, Whitefield and Wesley* (Oxford: Clarendon, 1969), 179.
[21] Whitefield to Rev. Mr. S—, June 26, 1740, in *Letters*, 193.
[22] Whitefield, "Soul Dejection," in *Eighteen Sermons*, 282.
[23] Whitefield, "The Gospel, a Dying Saint's Triumph," in *Eighteen Sermons*, 79, 88.

didacticism of an apologetic tract and, best of all, the edifying tone of a miracle story"[24]—Whitefield unashamedly cast significant moments in his own life, including his birth[25] and conversion,[26] in terms that evoked the experiences of his Savior. The same was true in Whitefield's recounting of another momentous turning point in his ministry, when he made his first foray into field preaching, on February 17, 1739. Here he employed language and examples reminiscent of Mark 6, where Jesus extends compassion to the crowd (likened to shepherdless sheep) that had followed him into the Galilean wilderness, and Matthew 5, where Jesus made an ascent before delivering *the* Sermon on the Mount, prompting some to suggest that Whitefield effectively co-opted Kingswood Hill into "a veritable mount of the Lord."[27] In other words, Whitefield was very deliberate about memorializing this occasion by communicating that the physical setting of this pivotal sermon was not incidental and that he was not simply taking advantage of a prominent topographical landmark to be better seen and heard. He wrote: "My bowels have long since yearned toward the poor colliers, who are very numerous, and as sheep having no shepherd. After dinner, therefore, I went upon a mount, and spake to as many people as came unto me. There were upwards of two hundred. Blessed be God that I have now broken the ice!"[28]

Whitefield made a habit of closely aligning his ministry with that of Jesus, especially in the face of ecclesiastical opposition. In a journal entry in 1739, he insinuated that his detractors were spiritually akin to the Pharisees in Mark 8; demanding "to know by what authority we preach," his critics confirmed their calloused hearts. Responding to the rhetorical question "Has not God set His seal to our ministry in an extraordinary manner?" Whitefield defended his unorthodox preaching ministry with a choice of words that explicitly recalled the beginning of Jesus's public ministry in Luke chapter 4: "Have not many that were spiritually blind received their

24 Richard B. Steele, "John Wesley's Synthesis of the Revival Practices of Jonathan Edwards, George Whitefield, Nicholas von Zinzendorf," *Wesleyan Theological Journal* 30, no. 1 (1995): 159.
25 In the first edition of his *Journals*, a defense of his conviction that he had been called to a "public work," Whitefield highlighted the "circumstance of my being born in an inn," comparing himself with "the example of my dear Saviour, who was born in a manger belonging to an inn." *Journals*, 35, 37.
26 Whitefield described his conversion in terms reminiscent of Jesus's sufferings in John's Gospel: "One day, perceiving an uncommon drought and a disagreeable clamminess in my mouth and using things to allay my thirst, but in vain, it was suggested to me that when Jesus Christ cried out, 'I thirst,' His sufferings were near at an end. Upon which I cast myself down on the bed, crying out, 'I thirst! I thirst!' Soon after this, I found and felt in myself that I was delivered from the burden that had so heavily oppressed me." *Journals*, 58.
27 A. Skevington Wood, *The Inextinguishable Blaze: Spiritual Renewal and Advance in the Eighteenth Century* (Eugene, OR: Wipf and Stock, 2006), 91.
28 *Journals*, 215–16.

sight? Many that have been lame strengthened to run the way of God's commandments? Have not the deaf heard? The lepers been cleansed? The dead raised? And the poor had the Gospel preached unto them? . . . And yet they require a sign."[29]

Whitefield was not alone among fellow first-generation Methodists in evoking biblical language in this way and for this purpose. For example, John and Charles Wesley sought to vindicate their claims to authority by frequently using biblical quotations and allusions.[30] Similarly, Whitefield internalized the ministries of the apostles, appealing to Scripture to vindicate his unorthodox ministry. To one critic he wrote: "What do you think of *Jesus Christ* and his Apostles? Were they not field-preachers? Was not the best sermon that was ever delivered, delivered from a *Mount?* Was not another very excellent one preached from a place called *Mars-Hill?*" He continued: "These were the persons I had in view, when I began my *adventures* of field-preaching. Animated by their example, when causelessly thrust out, I took the field; and if this be my shame, I glory in it."[31]

"Speak Out, Paul"

When it came to Whitefield's fondness for imitating the lives of the apostles, one in particular stood out above all others: Paul. It is hard to overstate the effect of the life and ministry of the apostle upon Whitefield's self-identity. According to Stout, Whitefield did not simply utilize the Bible's descriptions of Paul's ministry; instead, "so ingrained was the influence of the apostle's language and peripatetic lifestyle on Whitefield's imagination that he virtually adopted Paul's persona for his own." Additionally, "biblical characters became 'types' or models that provided a pattern for his own image," to the extent that "he *became* the apostles he embodied. His actions were not mere 'act' but reality."[32]

Whether or not one agrees with this psychological assessment, it is clear that Whitefield nurtured and propagated a self-conception of his itinerant field-preaching ministry that was borne out of the events and characters described in the Scriptures. Indeed, the earliest editions of his *Journals* supplied ammunition for those who censured him for what they

---

[29] *Journals*, 293–94.
[30] See Brian Clark, "The Contentious Birth of Wesleyan Methodism, 1738–1741: Gender, Charism, and Sectarian Division" (PhD diss., Boston University, 2008).
[31] Whitefield, "Remarks on a Pamphlet Entitled, The Enthusiasm of Methodists and Papists Compared," in *Works*, 4:232 (italics in the original).
[32] Stout, *The Divine Dramatist*, 56 (italics in the original).

perceived to be his colossal self-regard in so closely aligning his own experiences with those of the apostle. For instance, he recounted that the day after his ordination he was struck by a lengthy and perplexing bout of indecision. "The next morning," he recollected, "waiting upon God in prayer to know what he would have me do, these words, 'Speak out, Paul,' came with great power to my soul. Immediately my heart was enlarged. God spake to me by His Spirit, and I was no longer dumb."[33] Based on excerpts such as this, Whitefield reflected with seeming pride and no hint of exegetical self-doubt how the faculty of Harvard rebuked him for applying "even the historical parts of Scripture particularly to himself, and his own affairs."[34]

At other times Whitefield appealed to the example of Paul's missionary journeys in Acts as precedents validating the adventurous scope of his preaching ministry. For example, in a response to detractors written in 1749, Whitefield rhetorically asked, "Was [Paul] not filled with a holy restless Impatience and insatiable Thirst of travelling, and undertaking dangerous Voyages for the Conversion of Infidels . . . ?"[35] Beyond identifying with Paul in his travels, he also identified with him in his trials, especially when his itinerant ministry was challenged by his authorities in the Church of England. Reflecting on these frequently testy interactions, Whitefield wrote, "Blessed be God, in most of the things there recorded, I have, in some small degree, had fellowship with the Apostle, and before I die, I doubt not but I shall sympathise with him in most other circles."[36]

Whether he actively sought conflict or conflict found him, Whitefield was undoubtedly a polarizing figure: "idolized" by some "and railed at by others."[37] If his critics found in his adoption of a Pauline persona evidence of high hubris, then his admirers saw evidence of divine anointing. Indeed, a willingness among the latter to baptize Whitefield's ministry in apostolic terms was well in place from the beginning of his itinerancy. An early instance of this trend, not to mention one of the most memorable firsthand reports of what it was like to experience the phenomenon that was a George Whitefield open-air preaching event, is found in *The Spiritual*

---

[33] *Journals*, 69.
[34] Whitefield, "A Letter to the Reverend the President," 207–8. Similarly, he reported that the bishop of London challenged Whitefield for "speaking of [himself] in the language, and under the character of *Apostles of Christ*, and even of *Christ* himself." Whitefield, "Answer to the Bishop of London's Last Pastoral Letter," in *Works*, 4:15 (italics in the original).
[35] Whitefield, "Remarks on a Pamphlet," 236.
[36] *Journals*, 215.
[37] This was Robert Blair's assessment of Whitefield's ministry in a letter written to Philip Doddridge on July 28, 1743. *The Correspondence and Diary of Philip Doddridge*, ed. J. D. Humphreys, 5 vols. (London: Henry Colburn and Richard Bentley, 1829–1831), 4:265.

Travels of Nathan Cole, the autobiography of an eighteenth-century Connecticut farmer. Cole provides a famously breathless account of the collective hysteria that overtook Middletown, Connecticut, on October 23, 1740,
as news spread that Whitefield was soon to preach on the banks of the
Connecticut River that morning. Cole's description of the events of that October morning begins, "Now it pleased God to send Mr Whitefield into this
land . . . like one of the old apostles, and many thousands [were] flocking to
hear him preach the Gospel, and great numbers were converted to Christ."[38]
Cole's report not only lends credence to the estimates that Whitefield was
heard by "perhaps eighty per cent of the American people"; it also affords
insight into the way many of Whitefield's admirers saw in his ministry a
return to the halcyon days of the primitive, apostolic church.[39]

Cole was not alone in casting Whitefield's field-preaching ministry in
apostolic labels. For instance, following Whitefield's pioneering foray into
field preaching, William Seward reported to James Hutton:

> We had yesterday the finest sight at Kingswood . . . our Dear Br . . .
> preached to such a Multitude as no man could Number, perhaps 4 or
> 5000 and all so quiet that all might hear. There was persons on Horse-
> back and several Coaches—The Hedges lined the Trees served for Scaf-
> fold as the Sycamore did to Zacchaeus—surely since the Apostles Days
> has not been the like.[40]

Meanwhile, on the other side of the Atlantic there was no less enthusiasm
for describing Whitefield as a virtual eighteenth-century iteration of the
apostle Paul. In November 1740, as Whitefield's preaching tour spanning
Georgia to Massachusetts drew to a close, William Cooper, a minister at
Brattle Street Church in Boston, enthused, "The apostolical times seem to
have returned upon us: such a display has there been of the power and
grace of the divine Spirit in the assemblies of his people, and such testimonies has he given to the word of the gospel."[41]

---

[38] Cited in Michael J. Crawford, "The Spiritual Travels of Nathan Cole," *The William and Mary Quarterly* 33, no. 1 (1976): 92.
[39] Mark A. Beliles, "The Christian Communities, Religious Revivals, and Political Culture of the Central Virginia Piedmont, 1737–1813," in *Religion and Political Culture in Jefferson's Virginia*, ed. Garrett Ward Sheldon and Daniel L. Dreisbach (Lanham, MD: Rowman and Littlefield, 2000), 5. See also J. I. Packer, "The Spirit with the Word: The Reformational Revivalism of George Whitefield," in *The Bible, the Reformation and the Church: Essays in Honour of James Atkinson*, ed. W. P. Stephens (Sheffield: Sheffield Academic Press, 1995), 167–68.
[40] Quoted in David A. Smith, "George Whitefield as Inter-Confessional Evangelist, 1714–1770" (DPhil. diss., Oxford University, 1992), 66.
[41] William Cowper, "Hope," quoted in Iain H. Murray, *Jonathan Edwards: A New Biography* (Edinburgh: Banner of Truth, 1987), 154.

Even in death, Whitefield the preacher was still being described in apostolic, and specifically Pauline, terms. News of his death on September 30, 1770, in Newburyport, Massachusetts, was met with a widespread outpouring of grief. Many of the eulogies and memorial sermons in the weeks and months that followed were notable in their use of apostolic superlatives, in an attempt to capture the essence of his life and ministry. For instance, despite his well-known theological disagreements with Whitefield, John Wesley preached at two memorial services for his fellow itinerant, one at Whitefield's chapel in Tottenham Court Road and another at his tabernacle near Moorfields. The rhetorical high point of Wesley's sermon came as he described Whitefield's preaching: "Have we ever heard of any person since the apostles, who testified the gospel of the grace of God . . . through so large a part of the habitable world?"[42]

Similarly, William Cowper (1731–1800) eulogized Whitefield as one who "copied close" the life experience of the apostle Paul. He accentuated Whitefield's ceaseless itinerant preaching ministry ("Like [Paul], cross'd cheerfully tempestuous seas, / Foresaking country, kindred, friends, and ease") and the physical discomfort and sufferings that accompanied his ministry ("Like [Paul] he labour'd, and, like him, content, / To bear it, suffer'd shame where'er he went"). He also depicted Whitefield as a remarkably dramatic preacher whose ministry was shaped by a singular commitment to advancing the gospel, free of disingenuous or ulterior motivations: "Paul's love for Christ, and steadiness unbrib'd, / Were copied close in him, and well transcrib'd."[43]

Whitefield was a quintessentially evangelical preacher: evangelical not simply in terms of the doctrines he preached but also in terms of the way his reverence for the Bible manifested itself in his appeals to Scripture to vindicate his itinerant field-preaching ministry. His commitment to the authority of the Bible and his commitment to field preaching went hand in hand. Scripture was decisive in buttressing and nurturing *where* Whitefield preached; and as we shall now see, it was no less crucial in informing *how* he preached.

Whitefield the Extemporaneous Preacher

Well before Whitefield began itinerant field preaching, he had already firmly established his reputation as a preacher of dramatic—and extempore—

---

42 John Wesley, *The Works of John Wesley: Bicentennial Edition*, vols. 1–4, *Sermons*, ed. Albert C. Outler (Nashville: Abingdon, 1984–1987), 2:340–41. Likewise, in his funeral sermon for the evangelist, Augustus Toplady memorialized Whitefield as "the apostle of the English empire." Augustus M. Toplady, "A Concise Character of the Late Rev. Mr. Whitefield," in *The Complete Works of Augustus Toplady* (Harrisonburg, VA: Sprinkle, 1987), 494.
43 Quoted in Downey, *The Eighteenth Century Pulpit*, 187.

sermons. Preparing in late 1737 to embark on a ministerial stint in the fledgling colony of Georgia as John Wesley's replacement, he reflected in his journal: "The tide of my popularity now began to run very high. In a short time, I could no longer walk on foot as usual, but was constrained to go in a coach, from place to place, to avoid the hosannas of the multitude."[44]

This celebrity status was built on his remarkable gift for public speaking without notes, a talent he identified and developed during his youth. Indeed, "frivolity and profanity aside, the theater taught Whitefield a great deal about how to perform in public."[45] Extempore preaching appears to have come naturally for Whitefield in a way that it did not for his Oxford mentor, John Wesley. If "Wesley's talents and temperament were those of a scholar," then "Whitefield's [were] those of an actor." In fact, "Wesley's triumph as a popular preacher may almost be said to have been in spite of his gifts; Whitefield's precisely because of them. Though Wesley was the more astute thinker, organizer, and teacher, Whitefield was supremely the finer orator."[46]

It is therefore no surprise that whereas Wesley gave no hint of seeking his first experience of preaching without notes in 1735 at All Hallows Church in London (much less that it was in any way premeditated), Whitefield actively prayed for an opportunity to preach in a way that liberated him from the prevailing—and staid—stylistic conventions that characterized English pulpits of his day.[47] Reflecting on the events of December 29, 1737, when he preached his first extemporaneous sermon, Whitefield recorded that despite his initial anxiety at entering the pulpit without any notes, he was "enabled to preach to a large congregation without the least hesitation." He added, "What gave me great comfort and made me more thankful was, that the opportunity, I believe, was granted in answer to prayer."[48]

The Pulpit as Whitefield's Sanctified Stage

Just as Whitefield was censured for *where* he preached, so too the *way* he preached aroused opposition. One "could go to any number of parishes

---

44 *Journals*, 89.

45 Thomas S. Kidd, *George Whitefield: America's Spiritual Founding Father* (New Haven, CT: Yale University Press, 2014), 14.

46 Downey, *The Eighteenth Century Pulpit*, 179.

47 Flavius Conrad comments that Whitefield "dared to crusade for extempore preaching in a day when almost every minister carried a full manuscript or a sheaf of notes into the pulpit with him." Flavius L. Conrad Jr., "The Preaching of George Whitefield, with Special Reference to the American Colonies: A Study of His Published Sermons" (PhD diss., Temple University, 1959), 42.

48 *Journals*, 98.

in England and hear dry recitations of traditional doctrine. [Whitefield's] background in the theater, the dramatic setting of the field sermon, and the freedom of the extemporaneous mode helped the young preacher shake people out of complacency."[49] His critics tended to equate extemporaneous preaching with sermons that were utterly unprepared. "It is impossible that any man should be able to manage any argument with that strength, or any instruction with clearness in an extempore manner, as he may with study and meditation," argued Harvard's president and faculty.[50] And yet, by and large, his extempore sermons were the furthest thing from completely spontaneous. He rehearsed and memorized his sermons just as he had once memorized his part in theater productions at school, preaching these discourses from pulpits—makeshift or otherwise—that became for him a form of sanctified stage.

And so, whereas some of his field-preaching contemporaries in New England, such as James Davenport, often eschewed preparation in favor of entering the pulpit "totally reliant upon immediate inspired utterance, allegedly from the Spirit,"[51] Whitefield clarified that his sermons were extemporaneous only "if you mean that they are not written down," and that he preached "without notes: but they are not extempore," he stressed, "if you think that I preach without study and meditation."[52] Indeed, as Stout elaborates, "Where other preachers recorded their notes and repeated favourite sermons three or four times in a pulpit career, the itinerant Whitefield repeated some favourite sermons thirty times or more, adapting the details . . . to suit immediate settings and circumstances."[53]

Benjamin Franklin observed this distinctive feature of his preaching firsthand. The Philadelphia-based publisher was a prolific distributor of Whitefield-related literature, including his sermons, his *Journals*, and publicity surrounding Whitefield's travels and itinerant preaching schedule. Franklin frequently found himself attending his famous and lucrative client's open-air preaching events. As such, he was well placed to be able to distinguish "between Sermons newly composed and those which

---

[49] Kidd, *George Whitefield*, 65.

[50] Whitefield, "A Letter to the Reverend the President," 216.

[51] Smith, "Inter-Confessional Evangelist," 302.

[52] Whitefield, "A Letter to the Reverend the President," 216.

[53] Stout, *The Divine Dramatist*, 79. As Cunha observes, "Whitefield's habit of perfecting his favourite sermons through multiple deliveries suggests that what is found in the printed collections might well be taken as a concentrated representative corpus." Cunha, "Whitefield and Literary Affect," 195–96. See also Ian J. Maddock, *Men of One Book: A Comparison of Two Methodist Preachers, John Wesley and George Whitefield* (Eugene, OR: Pickwick, 2011), 103–9.

[Whitefield] had often preached in the course of his travels." He offered this assessment:

> His delivery of the latter were so improved by frequent repetition that every accent, every emphasis, every modulation of voice, was so perfectly well-tuned and well-placed that, without being interested in the subject, one could not help being pleased with the discourse; a pleasure of much the same kind with that received from an excellent piece of music.

Franklin's appraisal affords an insight into not only the wide range of motivations that attracted people to hear Whitefield but also the "advantage itinerant preachers have over those who are stationary, as the latter cannot well improve their delivery of a sermon by so many rehearsals."[54]

Whitefield's understanding of the gospel conditioned the way he communicated its message. The gospel of God's passionate self-sacrificial love for lost sinners in turn demanded passionate preaching. In Whitefield's thinking, how could it not? Two hundred years before Marshall McLuhan coined the insight "the medium is the message," Whitefield intuitively recognized that not only is a dispassionate proclamation of the gospel unbefitting of the good news, but it threatens to undermine its very credibility. He often wept as he preached, though despite the apparent regularity of this occurrence, "there is no compelling reason to see such tears as inauthentic or simply theatrical."[55] Instead, these visceral emotional outpourings were expressions of the intense sadness he felt as he reflected on the prospective fate of unbelievers, or else the joy he felt as he preached on the depths of God's love for sinners in Christ. "I hardly ever knew him go through a sermon without weeping," observed Cornelius Winter; he was "frequently so overcome, that, for a few seconds you would suspect he never could recover."[56]

In Whitefield's estimation, the fervency with which a sermon is delivered is a strong indication of its spiritual potency and a barometer of the preacher's spiritual health. He speculated that sermons designed to "inform the understanding" alone are reasonable grounds for listeners "to suspect, that the preacher, let him be who he will, only deals in the false commerce of unfelt truths."[57] While he did not quite go so far as to draw a

---

[54] Wakeley, *Anecdotes of the Rev. George Whitefield*, 71.
[55] Kidd, *George Whitefield*, 65.
[56] William Jay, *Memoirs of the Life and Character of the Late Rev. Cornelius Winter* (New York, 1811), 27–28.
[57] Whitefield, "A Letter to the Reverend Dr. Durell," in *Works*, 4:338–39.

completely symmetrical correspondence between "preaching by note" and spiritual lifelessness, he considered extempore preaching to be an indication of, and conduit for, genuine, inward Christian vitality. "I think the ministers preaching almost universally by note, is a mark that they have, in a great measure, lost the old spirit of preaching," he wrote less than two weeks after visiting Jonathan Edwards and his family in western Massachusetts. "Though all are not to be condemned who use notes, yet it is a symptom of the decay of religion, when reading sermons becomes fashionable where *extempore* preaching did once almost universally prevail."[58]

His zeal for extempore preaching was no short-lived fad. Nor did he ever waver in his conviction that it is scriptural. After almost three decades of preaching without notes, in 1768 he offered an exegetical defense of extempore preaching in response to detractors who criticized his flamboyance in the pulpit. Whitefield stressed that the task of "true gospel Christian orators" is in many ways the same as that of lawyers and actors on a stage. They share a common ambition not simply to "calmly inform the understanding, but by persuasive pathetic address, [to] endeavour to move the affections, and warm the heart."[59]

After appealing variously to Christian antiquity and human experience to justify his dramatic preaching style, in a familiar move, Whitefield ultimately turned to examples of impassioned oratory in the Bible for vindication. "You have . . . heard of a Prophet who was commanded by the Lord God himself, to smite with his hand, and stamp with his foot [Ezek. 6:11]; and gospel-ministers in general are commanded to 'cry aloud, and spare not, and to lift up their voices like trumpets [2 Chron. 15:14],'" he declared. But as compelling as the examples of Old Testament luminaries might be, he interpreted the power and authority with which Jesus spoke to his disciples on the road to Emmaus in Luke 24 as a precedent for the normativity of the homiletical flair he exhibited:

> I believe we may venture to affirm, that if preachers in general spake and opened the Scriptures more under the influence and energy of his blessed Spirit, whether in consecrated or unconsecrated ground, within or without doors, they would find their hearers' hearts in a degree would burn within them too.[60]

---

[58] *Journals*, 483.
[59] Whitefield, "A Letter to the Reverend Dr. Durell," 338.
[60] Whitefield, "A Letter to the Reverend Dr. Durell," 338–40.

Whether these texts conclusively justify his chosen preaching style is debatable; skeptics might well question whether his argument amounts to an instinctive homiletical stylistic preference in search of biblical proof texts. What is apparent is that "Whitefield was utterly certain about the Christian gospel, the delights of divine grace, and the horrors of divine judgment" and that "these truths elicited strong feelings" that spilled over into his sermon delivery.[61] What is also unmistakable is that when it came to justifying *how* he preached, Whitefield was thoroughly evangelical: in his mind, the Bible supplied the clinching argument for any and every matter of ministry conjecture.

"Methinks I See"

The Bible also supplied the characters and events that he vividly embodied and reenacted during the retelling of memorable scenes that featured so prominently in his sermons. For example, in his sermon "The Resurrection of Lazarus," Whitefield appealed not just to the mind's eye of his audience but also to their sense of smell. He encouraged people to imagine themselves approaching the decomposing corpse of Lazarus and, in the process, gain a more pungent appreciation for the depths of their fallen state and need for spiritual regeneration:

> Come, ye dead, Christless, unconverted sinners, come and see the place where they laid the body of the deceased *Lazarus*; behold him laid out, bound hand and foot with grave-cloths, locked up and stinking in a dark cave, with a great stone placed on top of it! View him again and again; go nearer to him; be not afraid; smell him, ah! How he stinketh. Stop there now, pause a while; and while thou art gazing on the corpse of *Lazarus*, give me leave to tell thee with great plainness, but greater love, that this dead, bound, entombed, stinking carcase, is but a faint representation of thy poor soul in its natural state: for, whether thou believest it or not, thy spirit which thou bearest about with thee, sepulchred in flesh and blood, is as literally dead to God, and as truly dead in trespasses and sins, as the body of *Lazarus* was in the cave.[62]

Whitefield believed that, as God's word, the Bible is living and active, and through his preaching he strived to bring to life the scenes of this

---

61 Kidd, *George Whitefield*, 65.
62 Whitefield, "The Resurrection of Lazarus," in *Works*, 6:123 (italics in the original).

divinely inspired playscript. His oratory became a conduit through which he engaged "the heart, not just the head," helping his listeners (and readers) not simply to understand propositions but also to experience the truth of the gospel.[63] Oftentimes, his introductory formula "Methinks I see" signified that some degree of artistic and imaginative license lay ahead. For instance, in his sermon entitled "Abraham's Offering Up His Son Isaac," Whitefield mused:

> But who can tell what the aged patriarch felt during these three days? Strong as he was in faith, I am persuaded his bowels often yearned over his dear son *Isaac*. Methinks I see the good old man walking with his dear child in his hand, and now and then looking on him, loving him, and then turning aside to weep.[64]

As his creative and speculative conjecture continued, however, it became apparent that he employed it not just for dramatic effect or simply to engender greater empathy for the characters in Genesis 22. Instead, Whitefield's appeals to the emotions were profoundly theological, employing this oratorical technique to reinforce the crucicentrism that occupied such a cherished place in his evangelical theology. In particular, Whitefield's goal was to elicit thanksgiving toward God the Father for his willingness to offer his only begotten Son for the sins of the world and cast Isaac's experience as a prefiguring of Jesus's passive obedience in dying a substitutionary death in submission to his Father's will. With these theological motives in mind, and with head and heart going hand in hand, Whitefield continued:

> O what pious expressions passed now alternately between the father and the son! . . . Methinks I see the tears trickle down the Patriarch Abraham's cheeks; and out of the abundance of the heart, he cries . . . adieu, my Isaac, my only son. . . . I see Isaac at the same time meekly resigning himself into his heavenly Father's hands, and praying to the most High to strengthen his earthly parent to strike the stroke.[65]

"I Never Saw or Heard the Like"

As an open-air, extemporaneous preacher, Whitefield had a remarkably widespread and lifelong appeal: committed Christians; seekers; ecclesiastical critics; secular playwrights looking for raw material; those

---

[63] Kidd, *George Whitefield*, 65.
[64] Whitefield, "Abraham's Offering Up His Son Isaac," in *Works*, 5:43 (italics in the original).
[65] Whitefield, "Abraham's Offering Up His Son Isaac," 43–44, 46.

lurking on the periphery, "giggling, scoffing, talking . . . laughing," and otherwise intent on disruption—all were to be found at his open-air sermons.[66] Some of the more famous firsthand accounts of Whitefield's open-air sermons feature skeptical onlookers being won over by a combination of his eloquence and the message he preached.

One noteworthy instance, most likely the experience of Ebenezer Pemberton, minister of the Wall Street Church in New York, came after he heard Whitefield preach in late 1739. Pemberton had feared he would be subjected to a display of protracted and public religious enthusiasm, but his fears were soon replaced with a compelling endorsement: "He is a man of a middle stature, of a slender body, of a fair complexion and of a comely appearance. . . . He has a most ready memory, and I think, speaks entirely without notes," Pemberton reflected in the December 4, 1739, edition of the *New England Journal*.

> He has a clear and musical voice, and a wonderful command of it. He uses much gesture, but with great propriety; every accent of his voice, every motion of his body, speaks, and both are natural and unaffected. If his delivery is the product of art, 'tis certainly the perfection of it, for it is entirely concealed.

Pemberton's eventual verdict could not have been further removed from his initial reservations: "Every scruple vanished. I never saw or heard the like, and I said to myself, 'Surely God is with this man of a truth.'"[67]

Vast throngs agreed, and they flocked to hear Whitefield preach in their thousands and even tens of thousands. Indeed, his sermons even seem to have had the unrivaled capacity to single-handedly bring a region's economy to a halt. In England, one critic lamented:

> The Industry of the inferior People in a Society is the great Source of its Prosperity. But if one Man, like the Rev. Mr. Whitefield should have it in his Power, by his Preaching, to detain 5 or 6 thousands of the Vulgar from their daily Labour, what a Loss, in a little Time, may this bring to the Publick!

He speculated at the dire possibilities: "For my part, I shall expect to hear of a prodigious Rise in the Price of Coals, about the City of Bristol, if this

[66] *New England Journal*, December 4, 1739, 39, quoted in Dallimore, *George Whitefield*, 1:435.
[67] Dallimore, *George Whitefield*, 1:435.

Gentleman proceeds, as he has begun, with his charitable Lectures to the Colliers of Kingswood."[68] The temporary impact of Whitefield's sermons was no less visceral on the other side of the Atlantic, as Nathan Cole's description of his frantic efforts to reach Middletown, Connecticut, in time to hear Whitefield preach attests: *"The land and banks over the* [Connecticut] *river looked black with people and horses*[;] all along the 12 miles I saw no man at work in his field, but all seemed to be gone."[69]

Whitefield's Christian life was a life lived preaching. He expressed his love for God through preaching, and as a vocation, it brought him unmatched joy and satisfaction: "The open firmament above me . . . with the sight of thousands and thousands, some in coaches, some on horseback, and some in trees, and at times all affected and drenched in tears together . . . was almost too much for, and quite overcame me."[70] As he set sail for America in 1739, already established as "the sensation of the British Atlantic world," if any person could be said to be singularly fitted for so bold a venture as itinerant, extemporaneous field preaching, it was George Whitefield: young, precociously talented, and empowered by an unshakeable conviction that not only had God set him apart for such a ministry but God's word vindicated both where and how he preached.[71] As a founding father of evangelicalism, Whitefield took the Bible to be the supreme authority in matters of faith and practice—including preaching. The Whitefield we remember was first and foremost a preacher; and not simply a preacher, but a preacher of and shaped by one book.

---

[68] Anonymous, "Of Enthusiasm, and the Present Practices of the Methodists," *The London Magazine* 98 (May 1739): 239.

[69] Crawford, "The Spiritual Travels of Nathan Cole," 93 (italics in the original).

[70] *Memoirs*, 38.

[71] Kidd, *George Whitefield*, 91.

CHAPTER 8

THE RELATIONAL WHITEFIELD

Relationship with God and neighbor lay at the heart of Whitefield's experience of the Christian life. He expressed his love for God primarily, though not exclusively, by preaching the gospel to "neighbors" near and far. About as widely known a personality as existed throughout the eighteenth-century English-speaking world, Whitefield did not minister from a relational distance. Instead, he sought intimate relationships with others, pouring himself wholeheartedly into discipling individuals and exhorting small informal gatherings, just as he did famously preaching to mass outdoor audiences numbering in the thousands.

Indeed, Whitefield's relational generosity, "whether in public or private," was evident right to the very end of his earthly life.[1] By the fall of 1770, and having reached the northernmost extent of what would prove to be his last preaching tour of the American colonies, an ailing Whitefield resolved to turn south from the Portsmouth area and begin the long journey along the Eastern Seaboard toward Georgia. But by the time he reached Exeter (in modern-day New Hampshire) on September 29, it was clear to those who had expectantly assembled to hear him preach, not to mention Whitefield himself, that he was gravely ill. Still, despite great difficulty breathing, he could not bring himself to pass by what he (correctly)

---

[1] Luke Tyerman, *The Life of the Rev. George Whitefield*, 2 vols. (London: Hodder and Stoughton, 1876–1877), 2:616.

supposed might be a final opportunity to proclaim the gospel. Later that evening, having reached the home of his longtime friend and pastor of the Old South Church in Newburyport, Massachusetts, Jonathan Parsons, Whitefield acquiesced once more, this time exhorting a small gathering from the landing of the parsonage stairs until his candle literally burnt out. Come the early hours of September 30, he breathed his last.

But ever willing and able as Whitefield was as a preacher, his identity as one of the foremost leaders of the burgeoning evangelical movement—one who "best represents the Awakening's international orientation"—owed not simply to the prowess and geographic breadth of his preaching but also to his ability to connect fellow proponents of revival across the transatlantic world.[2] Whitefield was a natural-born networker. He functioned as the widespread evangelical community's relational hub, developing "a reliable system of contacts through which he circulated information about his revival success, solicited funds for his missionary work, and instructed ministers on the practice of revivalism."[3]

Just as Whitefield's evangelistic ministry intentionally spanned and transcended spatial, socioeconomic, theological, and denominational boundaries, the relationships he developed across more than three decades of public ministry were remarkably varied. In this chapter, we shall explore a sample of these relationships and, in the process, gain a glimpse into Whitefield's expansive vision of the Christian life as one to be lived in relationship not simply with God but also with fellow divine-image bearers in all of their diversity.

Whitefield and (or versus?) Wesley

Very few relationships in Whitefield's life were as formative as his thirty-eight-year-long association with John Wesley. While an undergraduate student at Oxford in 1732, Whitefield first met and was mentored in the way of holiness by the Wesley brothers, John (aged twenty-eight) and Charles (aged twenty-five). Though Charles proved instrumental in introducing Whitefield to the necessity of the new birth, his personal and theological journey with John proved no less enduring, if not without considerable friction along the way.

---

[2] Douglas A. Sweeney, *The American Evangelical Story: A History of the Movement* (Grand Rapids, MI: Baker, 2005), 40.

[3] Frank Lambert, *"Pedlar in Divinity": George Whitefield and the Transatlantic Revivals* (Princeton, NJ: Princeton University Press, 1994), 9.

In many respects, their biographies and beliefs illuminate one another: Whitefield's life and ministry stand in sharper relief in light of his relationship with Wesley, and vice versa. Each one blazed a vocational trail for the other in his distinct way. For instance, although they both expressed retrospective ambivalence about their experiences as Oxford Methodists and as members of the "Holy Club," the intensity of their time spent in this religious greenhouse was highly formative for both men: Wesley as the cofounder of the select group of proto-Methodists and Whitefield as his eager protégé. While Whitefield later followed Wesley as a missionary with the Society for the Propagation of the Gospel, succeeding him in Savannah, Georgia, in 1738, it was Wesley who followed Whitefield into the fields as an open-air preacher in April 1739. Further, while each sought to be, in Wesley's language, *homo unius libri* (a man of one book), it was ultimately as extemporaneous *preachers* of one book that Wesley and Whitefield both found their vocational homes. Both were ordained and remained clergy within the Church of England while, at the same time, exuding an evangelistic spirit that transcended national and denominational boundaries. Their parallel histories also included dramatic experiences of the new birth that became paradigmatic for their proclamation of the necessity of regeneration and of being justified by faith, not works.[4]

Given these resonances, it is perhaps not surprising that Wesley and Whitefield have served as emblems of an evangelical ecumenicity that had the potential to overcome their doctrinal differences. One anecdote, enshrined in evangelical folklore, that accentuates the symbolic triumph of their brotherly love over and against theological parochialism centers on a "possibly apocryphal" encounter between Wesley and one of his Arminian followers in the years immediately following Whitefield's death.[5] A contemporary of Wesley's, Edward Pease, overheard one of Wesley's followers ask him whether he thought he would see the Calvinist Whitefield in heaven. After a lengthy pause, no doubt designed to build dramatic tension, Wesley replied in the negative. But before the exchange came to an end, Wesley delivered a punchline that upended expectations: "Do not misunderstand me, madam; George Whitefield was so bright a star in the firmament of God's glory, and will stand so

---

[4] Ian J. Maddock, introduction to *Wesley and Whitefield? Wesley versus Whitefield?*, ed. Ian J. Maddock (Eugene, OR: Pickwick, 2018), 4.
[5] Kenneth J. Collins, *John Wesley: A Theological Journey* (Nashville: Abingdon, 2003), 117.

near the throne, that one like me, who am less than the least, will never catch a glimpse of him."[6]

In a delightful twist, an alternative version of the story follows an identical plotline—but now it is *Whitefield* who bestows a partisan-defying verdict on his Arminian co-revivalist, taking his Calvinistic conversation partner by surprise. In this version, described by Leslie Church, "One of [Wesley's] critics came to George Whitefield and said, 'Sir, do you think when we get to heaven we shall see John Wesley?' 'No, sir,' answered George Whitefield, 'I fear not, for he shall be so near the Eternal Throne and we shall be at such a distance, we shall hardly get a sight of him.'"[7] Charles Spurgeon (1834–1892) was particularly enamored with this iteration, rehearsing it from his pulpit as an example of evangelical unity in Christ. Siding with Whitefield both theologically and in his assessment of Wesley, he reflected, "In studying the life of Wesley, I believe Whitefield's opinion is abundantly confirmed—that Wesley is near the eternal throne, having served his Master, albeit with many mistakes and errors, yet from a pure heart, fervently desiring to glorify God upon earth."[8]

Spurgeon's comments nonetheless betray the undeniable: that Wesley and Whitefield held subtle but significant soteriological differences. Without doubt, their disagreement came to its most visible head in April 1739, when Wesley first preached his "Free Grace" sermon, an incendiary and impassioned critique of the Calvinist doctrine of unconditional election. Learning of Wesley's decision not simply to preach but also to print and distribute this sermon as a means of enhancing its exposure, Whitefield urged his former mentor to reconsider. His reasoning? Not that he considered their differences regarding the divine-human relationship in salvation to be unimportant but, instead, that he wanted to avoid the relational fallout that would surely ensue if their differences reached the public sphere. He wrote to Wesley: "I hear . . . you are about to print a sermon against predestination. It shocks me to think of it. What will be the consequence but controversy?" Wary of gifting those hostile to the growing Methodist movement with evidence of internal division, Whitefield continued: "If people ask me my opinion, what shall I do? I have a critical part to act. God enable

[6] John Fletcher Hurst, *John Wesley the Methodist: A Plain Account of His Life and Work* (New York: Eaton & Mains, 1903), 168.
[7] Leslie F. Church, *Knight of the Burning Heart: The Story of John Wesley* (London: Epworth, 1938), 126.
[8] Charles H. Spurgeon, "John Wesley," *Banner of Truth* 70 (1969): 58. On another occasion he declared, "If there were wanted two apostles to be added to the number of the twelve, I do not believe there could be found two men more fit to be so added than George Whitefield and John Wesley." Charles H. Spurgeon, *C. H. Spurgeon's Autobiography*, vol. 1, *1834–1854* (London: Passmore, 1899), 176.

me to behave aright. Silence on both sides will be best. It is noised abroad already that there is a division between you and me. Oh! My heart within me is grieved!"[9]

Despite Whitefield's pleas, multiple editions of Wesley's "Free Grace" appeared in the coming months and years. And to a large degree, Whitefield's fears about the relational repercussions were realized. Their brief but feisty dispute had a lasting ecclesiological legacy, resulting in the permanent division of the Methodist Societies along Whitefieldian-Calvinist and Wesleyan-Arminian lines. Frank Baker went so far as to describe the "Free Grace" episode as "one of the most pregnant events in English church history," implicitly acknowledging that although they managed to achieve a measure of personal reconciliation, the Wesley-Whitefield relationship would forever be tinged with the memory of this conflict: Wesley versus Whitefield.[10]

In the years that followed the "Free Grace" episode, Wesley would go on to quarrel with a host of Calvinists. Among others, he tussled with the Particular Baptist John Gill (1697–1771) and the hymn writer–theologian Augustus Toplady (1740–1778) over the doctrines of predestination and reprobation, and with fellow Anglican James Hervey (1714–1758) over the nature of imputation. For his part, Whitefield also continued to regularly champion both unconditional election and the imputation of Jesus's righteousness in his preaching about the nature of justification. But although Wesley and Whitefield were often willing to vigorously contend for their respective Arminian and Calvinistic theologies in the public arena, whether through sermons, letters, or treatises, following the "Free Grace" episode they largely shied away from conflict with one another.

Indeed, despite occasional flash points (in a 1753 sermon, Whitefield characterized Wesley's perfectionism as a "delusional dream"[11]), their relationship eventually began to heal, to the point that they were often found preaching in one another's pulpits. It prompted Charles Wesley to dub the restored ministry partnership between himself, his brother, and Whitefield a "threefold cord" that "will nevermore be broken"—the addition of the Countess of Huntingdon to this triplet forming "a sort of quadruple

---

[9] John Wesley, *The Works of John Wesley: Bicentennial Edition*, vols. 25–26, *Letters I–II*, ed. Frank Baker (Nashville: Abingdon, 1980–1982), 25:662.
[10] Frank Baker, "Whitefield's Break with the Wesleys," *Church Quarterly* 3, no. 2 (1970): 103.
[11] George Whitefield, *The True Nature of Beholding the Lamb of God, and Peter's Denial of His Lord, Opened and Explained, in Two Sermons* (London, 1753), 6.

alliance."[12] In 1767, Whitefield even accepted an invitation to attend one of Wesley's conference meetings. Rejoicing in their renewed evangelical unity, John Wesley wrote, "God has indeed effectually broken down the wall of partition which was between us. Thirty years ago we were one: then the sower of tares rent us asunder: but now a stronger [one] than him has made us one again."[13]

And yet, perhaps the most moving testament to the enduring nature of their relationship was that for all of their differences, John Wesley was given the honor, at Whitefield's request, of preaching at his fellow revivalist's memorial service at the Tottenham Court Road Chapel in London on November 18, 1770. It took almost six weeks for the news of Whitefield's death to filter back to England. Wesley was informed on November 10, leaving him with one week to fulfill a daunting challenge: amid his undoubted grief, to provide a fitting encapsulation of Whitefield's rich and celebrated life in a way that also honored his desire that the occasion would help foster intramural harmony within the evangelical movement.

As expected, Wesley celebrated Whitefield's pulpit oratory: "that torrent of eloquence, which frequently bore down all before it." He also accentuated the doctrines upon which he and Whitefield unequivocally agreed—though, much to the displeasure of Calvinistic critics, he chose to make no mention of the important place unconditional election held in Whitefield's theology. Less controversially, he emphasized the way Whitefield's love for God translated into a love for those created in his image from across all segments of society, including "women as well as men; and those from every age and condition." Wesley continued, "He feared not the faces of men, but used great plainness of speech to persons of every rank and condition, high and low, rich and poor; endeavouring only by manifestation of the truth to commend himself to every man's conscience in the sight of God."[14]

"Chaplain to the Right Honourable Countess of Huntingdon"

If Whitefield's first forays into itinerant preaching tended to focus on the "low" and "poor" within British society, then his segue into the world of the "high" and "rich" came largely via his relationship with the aristocratic

---

[12] Charles Wesley, *The Journal of Charles Wesley*, vol. 2 (London: Wesleyan Methodist Bookroom, n.d.), 247.
[13] John Wesley, *The Works of the Rev. John Wesley, A.M.*, vol. 12 (London: John Mason, 1830), 256.
[14] Tyerman, *George Whitefield*, 2:617.

patroness of the Methodist movement, Selina Hastings, the Countess of Huntingdon. Born in 1707 and born again in 1739, she was initially attracted to the Wesleys' teaching on Christian perfection, despite the concerted efforts of Whitefield and Howell Harris, who did their utmost to win the countess over to the Calvinistic branch of the Methodists.

By the mid-1740s, however, Selina began to find Whitefield's Calvinistic doctrine more compelling than Wesley's Arminianism. Amid long-standing struggles with indwelling sin and a fragile sense of assurance, she discovered great comfort in the doctrine of election she had once rejected. Whitefield's Tabernacle at Moorfields—and not Wesley's Foundry, a quarter of a mile away—thereafter became her preferred London congregation. From this point on, for all her affection for the Wesley brothers, her theological die was cast in a Whitefieldian mold. "Her religious principles were strictly Calvinistic," reflected one admirer in a funeral sermon preached two weeks after her death, "and the doctrines of grace were the marrow and life of her soul."[15]

When her husband, Theophilus, died suddenly in October 1746, the thirty-nine-year-old countess found herself widowed and at a crossroads in her life. Overwhelmed by grief, for the next four months she was a virtual recluse and even contemplated withdrawing from society permanently. In early 1747 she consulted Harris "about which was best, to live retired and give up all, or fill her place." In what would prove to be a pivotal conversation, Harris encouraged her toward the latter.[16] Selina was persuaded, and from this point onward, her mind was set. "I dread slack hands in the vineyard," she wrote to the congregational pastor Philip Doddridge. "We must all up and be doing."[17]

Selina instinctively recognized that she had access to a unique aristocratic mission field—and just the evangelist for the task of reaching them. In her role as a countess, she was entitled to appoint several personal chaplains and had Whitefield in mind as the larger-than-life personality to reach her wealthy and well-connected contemporaries. Over the summer of 1748, the countess hosted four events at her London residence to road test Whitefield's preaching before audiences, including, among others, Lord Bolingbroke, the former chief secretary of state, the Earl of

---

[15] William Aldridge, *A Funeral Sermon, Occasioned by the Death of the Late Countess Dowager of Huntingdon, 3rd of July, 1791* (London: Henry Teape, 1791), 22.

[16] Tom Beynon, ed., *Howell Harris's Visits to London* (Aberystwyth, UK: Cambrian News, 1960), 137.

[17] Aaron C. H. Seymour, *The Life and Times of Selina: Countess of Huntingdon*, vol. 1 (London: William Edward Painter, 1839), 79.

Chesterfield, and future prime ministers William Pitt (the elder) and Frederick North. They embodied her envisioned target audience: rich and famous—and unconverted.

The preaching of the Grand Itinerant was a hit. Bolingbroke offered this verdict: "Whitefield is the most extraordinary man of our times. He has the most commanding eloquence I have ever heard in any person." Chesterfield was no less enthusiastic: "Mr. Whitefield's eloquence is unrivalled—his zeal inexhaustible; and not to admire both would argue a total absence of taste."[18] Selina was delighted; if anything, her expectations were surpassed. She reported to Doddridge: "I must tell you that I have had two large assemblies at my house of the mighty, the noble, the wise & the rich to hear the Gospel by Mr Whitefield & I have great pleasure in telling you they all expressed a great deal in hearing of him. Sometimes I do hope for Lord Chesterfield."[19]

Whitefield was no less optimistic: "I went home never more surprised at any incident in my life. The prospect of doing good to the rich that attend her Ladyship's house is very encouraging. Who knows what God may do?"[20] He wrote to one fellow Methodist, "The prospect of catching some of the rich in the gospel net is very promising,"[21] while to John Wesley he wondered expectantly if "the hour is coming when some of the *Mighty* and *Noble* shall be called."[22] Even deists like Benjamin Franklin recognized the tremendous societal good that might transpire from the religious awakening of the upper classes: "If you can gain them to a good and exemplary life," Franklin encouraged, "wonderful changes will follow in the manner of the lower ranks."[23]

Neither Whitefield nor the countess needed any more convincing that they were a perfect ministry match. Soon afterward Selina offered Whitefield her scarf, indicating appointment as a personal chaplain, and he accepted. Always sure to adopt a posture of deference and humility toward his patroness, Whitefield was nonetheless dizzy with excitement over this unexpected upward social mobility. The son of a publican and a one-time lowly servitor at Oxford University, he had become, as he would hence-

---

[18] Quoted in Tyerman, *George Whitefield*, 2:194.

[19] Geoffrey F. Nuttall, *Calendar of the Correspondence of Philip Doddridge DD (1702–1751)* (London: Historical Manuscripts Commission, 1979), letter 1392.

[20] John Pollock, *George Whitefield and the Great Awakening* (Garden City, NY: Doubleday, 1972), 39.

[21] Whitefield to Lady B—, December 30, 1748, in *Works*, 2:220.

[22] Whitefield to Rev. Mr. J— W—, September 1, 1748, in *Works*, 2:170 (italics in the original).

[23] Leonard W. Labaree, ed., *The Papers of Benjamin Franklin*, vol. 3, *January 1, 1745 through June 30, 1750* (New Haven, CT: Yale University Press, 1961), 383.

forth always style himself, "Chaplain to the Right Honourable Countess of Huntingdon."

At Whitefield's urging, Selina adopted a prominent leadership role among the Calvinistic Methodists, one that he had declined in favor of pursuing "a moving life."[24] "Perhaps the Lord is fitting your Ladyship for some new work," Whitefield suggested in May 1749.[25] Six months later he was more direct: "A leader is wanting. This honour hath been put upon your Ladyship by the great head of the church."[26] Fashioned in her Calvinistic theological image, "Lady Huntingdon's Connexion" was the result of this encouragement, the functional counterpart to Wesley's Methodist Societies.

If Selina was "Empress of her new connexion," overseeing an array of itinerant preachers who serviced a constellation of private chapels, then "Whitefield was her prime minister."[27] In addition to their prolific ministry-related correspondence, for over two decades Whitefield would continue to preach regularly to audiences she had assembled, comprising the well-heeled, well-born, (oftentimes) incognito clergy, and politicians. During the twelve months before embarking on his final transatlantic journey, Whitefield was the keynote preacher at the opening of two of Selina's signature institutions: Trevecca College in Wales on the countess's sixty-first birthday, on August 24, 1768, and her Tunbridge Wells Chapel on July 23, 1769—the latter of these likely the last time they would experience one another's company in shared ministry.

When Whitefield died suddenly the following September, Selina was high on the list of those on the other side of the Atlantic to be informed. On October 1, 1770, a local minister in Massachusetts wrote to her, "Most Noble Lady, in God's providence an important and sorrowful event took place yesterday, in which I believe your Ladyship to be interested. I mean the death of that truly excellent and faithful servant of Christ, the Reverend Mr. Whitefield." He continued, "Being favoured with his acquaintance, I have heard him speak in the highest and most respectful manner of your Ladyship."[28] Leaving no heirs of his own, Whitefield bequeathed everything to Selina, a tribute to the depth of his ministry partnership with

---

[24] Whitefield to Mr. D—, May 27, 1749, in *Works*, 2:260.
[25] Gomer Morgan Roberts, ed., *Selected Trevecka Letters: 1747–1794* (Caernarvon, UK: Calvinistic Methodist Bookroom, 1962), 256.
[26] Whitefield to Lady H—, November 30, 1749, in *Works*, 2:294.
[27] Tyerman, *George Whitefield*, 2:21.
[28] John R. Tyson and Boyd Stanley Schlenther, *In the Midst of Early Methodism: Lady Huntingdon and Her Correspondence* (Lanham, MD: Scarecrow, 2006), 111.

his patroness. This included his orphanage in Bethesda and its inhabitants, including the slaves that Whitefield had declined to liberate. Indeed, over the next few years, the countess added to their number. They included, perversely, a "woman-slave" named Selina.[29]

In addition to managing her college and navigating the tricky ecclesial waters surrounding her "Connexion," Selina's final decades thus included long-distance oversight of Bethesda's facilities and human "property." No doubt meant as a way of honoring her, Whitefield's bequest of "buildings, lands, Negroes, books [and] furniture" had the unintended effect of implicating her in his moral failure. In the end, the orphanage proved to be as much of an administrative, financial—and moral—albatross around her neck as it had been for Whitefield throughout his lifetime. Bethesda eventually burned to the ground in 1773 after being struck by lightning, and Georgia state officials took custody of the derelict property following Selina's death in 1791.

Whitefield and Franklin: A Merely Civil Friendship

Whitefield's relational versatility not only extended across theological and socioeconomic boundaries but even included the publisher-scientist-entrepreneur Benjamin Franklin, one of the eventual founding fathers of the American republic. "On the face of it," suggests Stout, "there could have been no more unusual a combination for friendship than the creed-despising Franklin and the deist-despising Whitefield."[30] And yet, compared with the relational ruptures that Whitefield experienced over the years with certain high-profile evangelicals, including Count Nicolaus Zinzendorf, John Cennick, Ebenezer and Ralph Erskine, and even Howell Harris for a time, the affectionate bond he shared with the avowedly deistic Franklin proved to be remarkably resilient.

Nine years Whitefield's senior, Franklin was well underway in his first career as a publisher by the time Whitefield arrived in New England in late 1739 as a breakout preaching celebrity. Franklin immediately recognized that publishing Whitefield's sermons and *Journals* represented a lucrative opportunity. Their budding association was mutually beneficial, opening new vistas for Whitefield in his ability to promote

---

[29] Thomas S. Kidd, *George Whitefield: America's Spiritual Founding Father* (New Haven, CT: Yale University Press, 2014), 262.
[30] Harry S. Stout, *The Divine Dramatist: George Whitefield and the Rise of Modern Evangelicalism* (Grand Rapids, MI: Eerdmans, 1991), 222.

revival. "You may print my life, as you desire," he wrote to Franklin on November 26, 1740. "God willing, I shall correct my two volumes of sermons, and send them the very first opportunity."[31] Indeed, as an example of Franklin's early adoption of new forms of mass communication, "Franklin's effective use of the newspaper in Pennsylvania politics was a model for Whitefield in his pioneering work with religious magazines and letters to the press."[32]

And yet their relationship was the furthest thing from strictly business. They instinctively understood one another's peripatetic existences, both living "in a public world to a far greater extent than most of their contemporaries."[33] When Whitefield's itinerant preaching schedule took him through Philadelphia and their paths crossed, Franklin jumped at the opportunity to extend hospitality and make the most of their time together. "You know my house; if you can make shift with its scanty accommodations you will be most heartily welcome," he wrote.[34]

Their regular correspondence ranged freely across personal, financial, and spiritual concerns. Indeed, rather than proving to be a conversation stopper, a ready acknowledgment of religious differences seems to have liberated them to engage in candid, good-natured exchanges about the gospel. For instance, in 1752, when Franklin received acclaim in the scientific realm for his explanation of the phenomenon of the Leyden jar, Whitefield was quick to celebrate his friend's success—and remind him of eternity. He wrote: "I find that you grow more and more famous in the learned world. As you have made a pretty considerable progress in the mysteries of electricity, I now humbly recommend to your diligent unprejudiced pursuit and study the mystery of the new birth." Whitefield was no doubt confident that Franklin would not take offense at his evangelistic forwardness, but he nonetheless concluded his letter: "You will excuse this freedom. I must have *aliquid Christi* [some of Christ] in all my letters."[35]

But for all of Whitefield's encouragements to experience regeneration, Franklin was stubbornly resistant, reflecting, with evident satisfaction,

---

[31] Whitefield to Mr. F—, November 26, 1740, in *Letters*, 226. Franklin would eventually publish two volumes of Whitefield's sermons later that year, entitled *Sermons on Various Subjects. In Two Volumes. By George Whitefield, A.B. of Pembroke College, Oxford.*
[32] Stout, *The Divine Dramatist*, 223.
[33] Stout, *The Divine Dramatist*, 225.
[34] Leonard W. Labaree et al., eds., *The Autobiography of Benjamin Franklin*, 2nd ed. (New Haven, CT: Yale University Press, 2003), 178.
[35] Whitefield to Mr. F—, August 17, 1752, in *Works*, 2:440.

that Whitefield "us'd indeed sometimes to pray for my conversion, but never had the satisfaction of believing his prayers were heard."[36] By his admission, Franklin was not "without some religious Principles." He believed, for example, in "the Existence of the Deity, that he made the World, and govern'd it by his Providence." But compared with Whitefield's God, Franklin's deity was remote, and his religion largely demythologized and devoid of the supernatural. Franklin was a lifelong skeptic when it came to orthodox Christian beliefs (including Jesus's virgin birth, two natures, and bodily resurrection), eschewed affiliating with any one church, and was suspicious of preaching that he considered to be aimed at inculcating sectarian loyalties rather than helping congregations live as "good citizens." In Franklin's estimation, any religious organization's worth—Christian or otherwise—lay in its "tendency to inspire, promote or confirm Morality."[37]

Accordingly, it is not surprising that Franklin admired and endorsed Whitefield's ministry, not because of the doctrinal content of his sermons but because of his friend's integrity and what he perceived to be the wholesome influence of his transdenominational preaching upon collective societal morality and harmony. "The multitudes of all sects and denominations that attended his sermons were enormous," he marveled, after Whitefield had recently passed through Philadelphia.

> It was wonderful to see the change soon made in the manners of our inhabitants. From being thoughtless or indifferent about religion, it seem'd as if all the world were growing religious so that one could not walk thro' the town in the evening without hearing psalms sung in different families of every street.[38]

Similarly, in a 1740 edition of his *Pennsylvania Gazette*, Franklin observed approvingly how, "since Mr. Whitefield's preaching here, the Dancing School, Assembly and Concert Room have been shut up, as inconsistent with the Doctrine of the Gospel"—where "doctrine" was synonymous with tangible moral reformation rather than intangible theological beliefs.[39]

For one as ostensibly disinterested in the doctrinal content of Whitefield's sermons, Franklin nonetheless invested financially in Whitefield's

---

36 Labaree, *Autobiography of Benjamin Franklin*, 178.
37 Labaree, *Autobiography of Benjamin Franklin*, 179.
38 Labaree, *Autobiography of Benjamin Franklin*, 179.
39 Benjamin Franklin, *Pennsylvania Gazette*, May 1, 1740, 3.

public ministry and was a regular attendee at his high-profile preaching events. Ever the empiricist, on one occasion in 1739 Franklin conducted an experiment in downtown Philadelphia to gauge whether the reports of the enormous numbers reportedly attending Whitefield's preaching events were exaggerated. Franklin wrote:

> I had the curiosity to learn how far he could be heard, by retiring backwards down the street towards the River, and I found his voice distinct till I came near Front Street. Imagining then a semicircle, of which my distance should be the radius, and that it were filled with auditors, to each of whom I allowed two square feet; I computed that he might well be heard by more than thirty thousand.

Hypothesis satisfactorily tested, he continued, "This reconciled me to the newspaper accounts of his having preached to 25000 in the fields, and to the history of generals haranguing whole armies, of which I had sometimes doubted."[40]

Try as he might to maintain a professional distance from Whitefield's homiletical persuasion, Franklin occasionally succumbed. As one particularly meaningful sermon drew toward a close, Franklin reported:

> I had in my pocket a handful of copper money, three or four silver dollars, and five pistoles of gold. As he [Whitefield] proceeded I began to soften, and concluded to give the copper; another stroke of his oratory made me ashamed of that, and determined to give the silver; and he finished so admirably that I emptied my pocket into the collection dish, gold and all.[41]

In 1756, seeking a legacy-defining project with which he might "spend the remainder of life with pleasure," Franklin even floated before Whitefield the utopian-tinged vision of being "jointly employ'd by the Crown" and together spearheading a "Colony in the Ohio." He imagined a future outpost on the western frontier in which their respective business acumen and Christian piety might dovetail to the benefit of many. "What a glorious thing it would be to settle in that fine country a large strong body of religious and industrious people!" he mused. "I firmly believe God would bless us with success," he assured Whitefield, "if we undertook it with a sincere

---

40 Labaree, *Autobiography of Benjamin Franklin*, 179.
41 Quoted in Joseph B. Wakeley, *Anecdotes of the Rev. George Whitefield, with a Biographical Sketch* (1879; repr., Oswestry, UK: Quinta, 2000), 71–72.

regard to his honor, the service of our gracious King, and (which is the same thing) the public good."[42] Whatever Whitefield made of this adventurous and entrepreneurial proposal (no record of his response survives), it "stands as an unequalled testimony to the trust and friendship Franklin exhibited towards his itinerant friend."[43]

Franklin might have felt that he was nearing his "last act" when he put his proposition to Whitefield, but ultimately he outlived the evangelist by two decades. Whitefield's deteriorating health—his self-styled "frail tabernacle"[44] and "feeble carcase"[45] suffered under the strain of frequent preaching and his punishing travel schedule—had been a cause of much concern to his friends for many years. In a letter to Whitefield's brother John in 1747, Franklin enquired about George's fragile health before poignantly declaring, "He is a good man and I love him."[46] The deist polymath proved to be just as staunch a postmortem defender of Whitefield's character as he had been during his lifetime. When "some of Mr. Whitefield's enemies affected to suppose he applied the collections he took up to his own profit," Franklin did not hesitate to defend his evangelical friend's moral probity. He contended, "I, who was intimately acquainted with him, being employed in printing his sermons and journals, never had the least suspicion of his integrity and I am to this day decidedly of the opinion that he was, in all of his conduct, a perfectly honest man." Indeed, Franklin cited their lack of shared evangelical identity as further confirmation of the trustworthiness of his character witness: "Methinks, my testimony ought to have the more weight as we had no religious connection." In Franklin's estimation, their relationship was no less robust despite the absence of spiritual union: "Ours was a mere civil friendship, sincere on both sides, and lasted to the death."[47]

Whitefield and Elizabeth James: "I Believe It My Duty to Marry"

Whitefield pursued his vocation as an itinerant evangelist with a single-minded focus. But for the majority of his ministry, he also did so as a married man. In 1738, at the age of 23, he prayed that God would grant

---

42 Leonard W. Labaree, ed., *The Papers of Benjamin Franklin*, vol. 6, *April 1, 1755 through September 24, 1756* (New Haven, CT: Yale University Press, 1963), 468–69.

43 Stout, *The Divine Dramatist*, 232.

44 Whitefield to Mrs. C—, July 25, 1755, in *Works*, 3:131.

45 Whitefield to Lady H—, November 1, 1755, in *Works*, 3:147.

46 Labaree, *Papers of Benjamin Franklin*, 3:169.

47 Labaree, *Autobiography of Benjamin Franklin*, 118.

him "deep humility, a well-guided zeal, a burning love," and, most of all, "a single eye" for his interdenominational evangelistic ministry.[48] Whitefield might have been singularly focused on ministry, but on November 14, 1741, he also entered into another monogamous relationship: his marriage to Elizabeth James.

James was not the first woman to receive a marriage proposal from Whitefield—nor even the first Elizabeth. The previous year, on April 4, 1740, he wrote to Elizabeth Delamotte, declaring, "I have great reason to believe it is the divine will that I should alter my condition, and have often thought that you [are] the person appointed for me." Although from all accounts he was smitten with "Betsy," Whitefield was conflicted. So determined was he to reinforce—as much to himself as to Delamotte—the conviction that his first love was for God and his highest allegiance was to his ministry, Whitefield's ensuing proposal (communicated via letter) was conspicuously devoid of anything resembling romantic affection. Indeed, he explicitly eschewed "the passionate expressions which carnal courtiers use" as incompatible with those who "would marry in the Lord" (cf. 1 Cor. 7:39).

Instead, Whitefield listed an inventory of ministry-related hardships that would likely characterize a marriage union that, if realized, would entail his nonnegotiable itinerant lifestyle. He challenged her, "Do you think, you could undergo the fatigues" of accompanying him on his unrelenting travel schedule? Alternatively, "can you, when you have a husband, be as though you had none, and willingly part with him, even for a long season, when his Lord and master shall call him forth to preach the gospel and command him to leave you behind?" Could she withstand "the inclemencies of the air both as to cold and heat" in North America's varied climates? Most transactional of all, did she possess the requisite skill matrix to assist in the day-to-day running of the Bethesda orphanage? He concluded,

> If after seeking to God for direction, and searching your heart, you can say "I can do all those things through Christ strengthening me," what if you and I were joined together in the Lord, and you came with me at my return from England, to be a help-meet for me in the management of the orphan-house?[49]

---

[48] Whitefield to Mr. H—, January 9, 1738, in *Letters*, 33.
[49] Whitefield to Miss E—, April 4, 1740, in *Letters*, 160–61.

Clearly, if Delamotte had chosen to enter into marriage with Whitefield, it would not have been for lack of forewarning.

Perhaps not surprisingly, she declined his offer. Undeterred, Whitefield refused to stray from his belief that "he could both find a wife and remain true to his first love."[50] He believed that it was his "duty to marry," ideally to "a gracious woman that is dead to everything but Jesus."[51] Marriage would confer respectability and would put to an end the distraction of would-be female suitors. He was confident that God would not allow him to "fall by the hand of a woman"—if by "fall" he meant not so much that a prospective spouse might tempt him to deny his faith but that she might tempt him to deny his vocational calling.[52]

Not long after Whitefield opined that those in ministry "who have wives" should "be as tho' they had none," Howell Harris introduced him to Elizabeth James.[53] Almost a decade older than Whitefield, she was a widow, a Methodist stalwart—and from all accounts, romantically drawn to Harris. Nevertheless, the Welshman, whose relational self-denial seems even to have exceeded Whitefield's on this occasion, persuaded her to marry his revivalist colleague. Despite the issue of her affection for Harris, Whitefield considered James a perfect match. Shortly after his low-key wedding, he wrote to Gilbert Tennent itemizing her recommending qualities: "I married . . . one who was a widow, of about thirty-six years of age, and has been a housekeeper for many years; neither rich in fortune, nor beautiful as to her person, but, I believe, a true child of God, and would not, I think, attempt to hinder me in his work for the world."[54]

Whitefield struggled to reconcile his new vocation as a husband with his vocation as an itinerant preacher. He might have entered into an altered condition, but his ministry schedule barely altered at all. Harris, who not only attended the wedding but gave the bride away, reported that within hours he was back preaching. He considered "every day lost, that is not spent in field preaching" and prayed that he would never be in a situation where he was forced to concede, "I have married a wife, and therefore I cannot come."[55] Two months after his wedding day, Whitefield was opti-

[50] Stout, *The Divine Dramatist*, 166.
[51] Whitefield to Rev. Mr. Ralph Erskine, February 16, 1741, in *Letters*, 509.
[52] Whitefield to Wm. S—, June 26, 1740, in *Letters*, 194.
[53] Whitefield to Rev. Mr. T—, February 17, 1741, in *Letters*, 242.
[54] Whitefield to Rev. Mr. G— T—, February 2, 1742, in *Letters*, 363.
[55] Whitefield to Lady H—, March 21, 1750, in *Works*, 2:341; Whitefield to Rev. Mr. G— T—, February 2, 1742, in *Letters*, 363.

mistic that his ministry capacity was "just the same as before marriage." But tellingly, he was also pining after his single days. To one ministry colleague, he wrote: "O for that blessed time when we shall neither marry nor be given in marriage, but be as the angels of God. My soul longs for that glorious season."[56]

Many of the likely trials that Whitefield had rehearsed in his proposal letter to Delamotte were realized in his marriage to Elizabeth—as were still others. In 1743, the Whitefields were blessed with their only child, a son they named John (after John the Baptist). But the joy of baptizing John at Whitefield's Moorfields Tabernacle in late 1743 was quickly followed by the grief of burying him in early 1744 at the church of Whitefield's youth, Gloucester's St Mary de Crypt. "Last night I was called to sacrifice my Isaac; I mean bury my only child and son about four months old," Whitefield lamented.[57] During John's short life, Whitefield appeared relationally torn between his love for his son (whom he felt sure would follow in his preaching footsteps) and his love for God and evangelism. In one letter, a brief update on his young family's well-being was quickly followed with the disclaimer "But why talk I of wife and little one?" Rather, "let all be absorbed in the thoughts of the love, suffering, free and full salvation of the infinitely great and glorious Emmanuel."[58] Indeed, while he "shed many tears" when his son died, he was back preaching multiple times the following day. "Weeping must not hinder sowing," he wrote.[59]

Elizabeth would suffer a string of subsequent miscarriages and endure significant time apart from her "ever-rambling" husband as ill health prevented her from accompanying him much in his travels after 1749.[60] While their separations were not nearly as fractious, or permanent, as those experienced by John and Molly Wesley, they were not always consensual. For instance, when Whitefield traveled without Elizabeth to preach in Bermuda in February 1748, he did so having committed to return and fetch his "dear yoke-fellow," whom he had left behind in Charleston, before returning to England. Instead, he reneged on his agreement when an opportunity emerged for him to travel directly from Bermuda to England in June. Whitefield expected Elizabeth to practice what he prayed, having

[56] Whitefield to the Reverend Mr. O—, December 30, 1741, in *Letters*, 355.
[57] Whitefield to Mr. D— T—, February 9, 1744, in *Works*, 2:50–51.
[58] Whitefield to Mr. H—, January 18, 1744, in *Works*, 2:50.
[59] Whitefield to Mr. D— T—, February 9, 1744, in *Works*, 51.
[60] Kidd, *George Whitefield*, 245.

previously composed a model petition for a Christian wife that encouraged her to be "willing to part with" her husband whenever God might call him away for ministry.[61] By any measure, it was a breathtakingly insensitive decision, and it was not until mid-1749 that they were reunited. She would never accompany him on any lengthy ministry journeys again.

In her absence, Whitefield attempted some relational repair work and had a residence built on the property next to his London chapel. It would be Elizabeth's home for the next twenty years; given his frequent absences, however, it functioned more as George's "home base" when he was not traveling. In 1768, Whitefield's twenty-seven-year marriage came to an end when Elizabeth died suddenly. In life, he may have found it difficult to display much overt affection toward his wife, but in death, Whitefield was struck with grief at the loss of his "right hand."[62]

The Whitefields' marriage resists easy evaluation. Those who knew them well and observed their relationship firsthand tended to cast it in an ambivalent light. "He was not happy in his wife," wrote Cornelius Winter, who lived with the Whitefields for a time. While there was never any hint of impropriety on Whitefield's part, Winter observed that Whitefield "did not intentionally make his wife unhappy," an assessment that betrays an underlying, persistent sadness in their marriage.[63] James Davenport captured the complicated, and in many ways unique, nature of their relationship in a letter he wrote to Elizabeth in 1754: "Shall I now sympathize with you, under the frequent and sometimes long absence of your dear husband? . . . Or shall I not withal, congratulate you on his being about his Master's business, and his success therein."[64]

Whitefield: "One of the Best Companions in the World"

Whitefield enjoyed a prodigious number of diverse relationships across his relatively short but well-traveled and connected life. The overwhelming impression is that he relished the company of others and that others frequently enjoyed his company too. This was especially the experience of like-minded evangelicals who encouraged him in his trailblazing ministry.

---

[61] Whitefield, "A Prayer for a Woman Lately Married to a Believing Husband," in *Works*, 4:478.

[62] Whitefield to Mr. A—, March 11, 1769, in *Works*, 3:382.

[63] Cited in Arnold A. Dallimore, *George Whitefield: The Life and Times of the Great Evangelist of the Eighteenth-Century Revival*, 2 vols. (London: Banner of Truth, 1970, 1980), 2:471.

[64] James Davenport to Elizabeth Whitefield, October 10, 1754, Dr. Williams' Library (London); cited in Kidd, *George Whitefield*, 246.

Augustus Toplady spoke for many when he described Whitefield as "one of the best companions in the world."[65] He was often an emotionally effusive correspondent, though he tended to reserve his most overt displays of affection for other men, possibly because he felt they presented no romantic challenge to his single-minded pursuit of a transatlantic, interdenominational evangelistic ministry. "The agony I was in at your departure, and the many strong cryings and tears which I offered up to God afterwards, plainly show, that I love you in sincerity and truth," he once wrote—not to his wife but to a ministry colleague. By contrast, while he was unfailingly courteous in his interactions with women, he was typically far more emotionally distant.[66]

The gospel of divine reconciliation that he preached shaped his relationships with individuals created in the divine image. The sheer volume of people he interacted with afforded many opportunities for mutual blessing and encouragement, but also many opportunities for interpersonal friction brought about by rivalry, misunderstanding, conflicting ministry philosophies, and divergent theologies. And yet Whitefield was not one to hold grudges. Indeed, his gravitational pull was consistently toward seeking and extending forgiveness, with a view to restoring impaired fellowship. Wesley experienced this firsthand, to the point that, by 1769, he could refer to Whitefield as his "old friend and fellow-laborer."[67] The following year, in the published version of his memorial sermon for Whitefield, Wesley affirmed Whitefield's "unparalleled zeal, his indefatigable activity, his tender-heartedness to the afflicted, and charitableness toward the poor. But should we not likewise mention . . . that he had a heart susceptible of the most generous and most tender friendship?" Wesley went on: "I have frequently thought that this, of all others, was the distinguishing part of his character. . . . Was it not this, which, quick and penetrating as lightning, flew from heart to heart? Which gave life to his sermons, his conversations, his letters? Ye are witnesses."[68]

---

[65] Augustus M. Toplady, *The Works of A.M. Toplady*, 6 vols. (London: Ebenezer Palmer, 1828), 4:156.
[66] Whitefield to My Dear Brother, August 15, 1739, in *Letters*, 63.
[67] John Wesley, *The Works of John Wesley: Bicentennial Edition*, vols. 18–24, *Journals and Diaries I–VII*, ed. W. Reginald Ward and Richard P. Heitzenrater (Nashville: Abingdon, 1988–1997), 22:172.
[68] Tyerman, *George Whitefield*, 2:616.

CHAPTER 9

WHITEFIELD AND SLAVERY

In June 1919, an eight foot tall bronze statue, *The Reverend George White-field*, was dedicated on the campus of the University of Pennsylvania in Philadelphia, an institution Whitefield had indirectly helped create with Benjamin Franklin. Robert Tait McKenzie's sculpture visualized Whitefield preaching in full dramatic flow, "clutching a bible in his left hand and pointing to the heavens with his right, as his gown billowed in the wind."[1] The inscription emphasized his identity and vocation: a "Humble Disciple of Jesus Christ" and "Eloquent Preacher of the Gospel." When it came to his contribution to higher education, it continued, "The University of Pennsylvania held its first sessions in a building erected for his congregations and was aided by his collections, guided by his counsel and inspired by his life."

One significant aspect of Whitefield's life not included in this inscription was his enthusiastic support for the introduction of slavery into Georgia, along with his extensive personal ownership of slaves. Come June 2020, these elements of Whitefield's legacy were suddenly thrust into the spotlight when, in the wake of a wider national controversy surrounding the place of systemic racism in the United States, the University of Pennsylvania announced its intention to immediately remove Whitefield's statue.

In a public statement, the university's leadership offered the conjecture that his advocacy for slavery was "undeniably one of Whitefield's principal legacies." They concluded that "there is absolutely no justification for

---

[1] Andrew Atherstone, "Commemorating Whitefield in the Nineteenth and Twentieth Centuries," in *George Whitefield: Life, Context and Legacy*, ed. Geordan Hammond and David Ceri Jones (Oxford: Oxford University Press, 2016), 290–91.

having a statue honoring him at Penn."[2] Just a few months later, in September, the celebrations to commemorate Whitefield on the 250th anniversary of his death at the Old South Presbyterian Church in Newburyport, Massachusetts, were also recalibrated to acknowledge his role in perpetuating slavery throughout the British Empire. Rebranded as "The Great Awakening Meets a Just Awakening," the event sought to honor Whitefield's legacy as a "life-changing, history-making evangelist," but in such a way as to also acknowledge "that his advocacy of slavery was tragically inconsistent with his message of the gospel's radical inclusivity."[3]

Whitefield's Early Critique of Southern Slaveholders

But if his complicity in preserving—and even activity extending—the practice of slavery in the American colonies has attracted censure, it is worth observing that many Americans' first introduction to Whitefield was as a vocal critic of the inhumane treatment of slaves and not simply as a dramatic itinerant evangelist. By the time Whitefield briefly toured the southern colonies in late 1739, he had developed a reputation in England for being willing to speak fearless and often controversial truth to power, especially toward his Anglican ecclesiastical superiors. Now finding himself on the other side of the Atlantic, he also took aim at the ubiquitous maltreatment of slaves.

In the initial two letters out of a collection of three published in February 1740 by Benjamin Franklin, Whitefield challenged the perceived bankruptcy of the archbishop of Canterbury's theology. His third, addressed to "the Inhabitants of Maryland, Virginia, North and South Carolina, concerning their Negroes," was an indictment upon slave masters for the miserable condition of the slaves Whitefield had thus far encountered in his travels. Anticipating that his letter would elicit hostility—akin to that of "the master of the damsel" in Acts 16, who was irate "with Paul for casting the evil spirit out of her"—Whitefield risked the condemnation of his readers and declared, "God has a quarrel with you for your abuse of and cruelty to the poor negroes."[4]

---

[2] Amy Gutmann, president; Wendell Pritchett, provost; and Craig Carnaroli, executive vice president, "Penn Announces Plans to Remove Statue of George Whitefield and Forms Working Group to Study Campus Names and Iconography," Penn Today, July 2, 2020, https://penntoday.upenn.edu/.
[3] "The Great Awakening Meets a Just Awakening," Old South Presbyterian Church, August 15, 2022, https://www.oldsouthnbpt.org/.
[4] Whitefield, "A Letter to the Inhabitants of Maryland, Virginia, North and South Carolina," in Works, 4:37–41.

Produced relatively early in his ministry, it would be an isolated denunciation. Tellingly, it also fell conspicuously short of challenging the institution itself. In many ways, it proved to be the high-water mark of his prophetic outspokenness against the practice of slavery. Just over a decade later, whatever uncertainty he had about the biblical warrant for slavery had been replaced with a settled conviction that Scripture endorsed its practice. But for now, he demurred on the subject: "Whether it be lawful for Christians to buy slaves, and thereby encourage the nations from whence they are brought to be at perpetual war with each other, I shall not take upon me to determine."[5]

While Whitefield was unable, or unwilling, to pronounce judgment upon the immorality of slavery, he had no qualms at this point in his ministry about issuing a comprehensive moral indictment of slave masters for their physical cruelty toward slaves. "But sure I am it is sinful, when bought, to use them as bad as, nay worse than brutes," he contended, "and whatever particular exceptions there may be, (as I would charitably hope there are some) I fear the generality of you that own negroes, are liable to such a charge." In a society where slaves were typically viewed as possessing more worth than other creatures but less than White people, Whitefield accused his readers of oppressing those who "work as hard, if not harder, than the horses whereon you ride." He continued, "Your dogs are cared for and fondled at your tables; but your slaves, who are frequently styled dogs or beasts, have not an equal privilege: they are scarce permitted to pick up the crumbs which fall from their master's tables."[6]

He charged slave masters with compounding their physical neglect of slaves with physical abuse. "Some, as I have been informed by an eyewitness, have been, upon the most trifling provocation, cut with knives, and have had forks thrown into their flesh," while others, he wrote, "have been given up to the inhuman usage of cruel task-masters, who by their unrelenting scourges have ploughed upon their backs, and made long furrows, and at length brought them even to death." Given these horrific experiences, Whitefield poignantly "wondered that we have not more instances of self-murder among the negroes, or that they have not more frequently risen up in arms against their owners."[7]

---

[5] Whitefield, "A Letter to the Inhabitants," 37.
[6] Whitefield, "A Letter to the Inhabitants," 37.
[7] Whitefield, "A Letter to the Inhabitants," 38.

And yet there were limits to his recognition of the plight of slaves. Perhaps sensing at this juncture in his letter that he might be suspected of advancing a radical abolitionist agenda, Whitefield faltered in his courage—and sympathy—and explicitly reaffirmed his support for the institutional status quo. For all his strident criticism of slave masters, he nevertheless prayed that slaves "may never be permitted to get the upper hand." He did add—pointedly, given the recent slave rebellion in Stono, South Carolina, in September 1739—that "should such a thing be permitted by providence, all good men must acknowledge the judgment would be just."[8]

The injustice of the contrast between the "plantations, cleared and cultivated, many spacious houses built, and the owners of them faring sumptuously every day" and the experience of slaves, who "had neither convenient food to eat, nor proper raiment to put on," aroused righteous indignation within him. Whitefield looked forward to the time when God would vindicate slaves and judge slave masters, though not for their vocation per se as much as for the ungodly way they pursued it. Leaving unclear whether he expected this divine justice to be realized in the present age or in the eschaton, he warned slave masters,

> [God] does not reject the prayer of the poor and destitute, nor disregard the cry of the meanest negroes: their blood which has been spilt, for these many years in your respective provinces, will ascend up to heaven against you; I wish I could say, it would speak better things than the blood of Abel.

In fact, he interpreted a range of calamities that had recently befallen South Carolina—including a smallpox epidemic, the aforementioned slave uprising at Stono, and the threat of invasion by a "foreign [Spanish] Enemy" during the War of Jenkins' Ear—as evidence of God's righteous anger against not only their woeful treatment of slaves but also their "Impenitence and Unbelief."[9]

Even more serious in Whitefield's estimation was the spiritual neglect slave masters exhibited toward slaves. "Enslaving or misusing their bodies, comparatively speaking, would be an inconsiderable evil, was proper care taken of their souls," he rebuked. Whereas slave masters reputedly argued that exposing their slaves to the gospel would render them "unwilling to submit to slavery," Whitefield betrayed his default

---

8 Whitefield, "A Letter to the Inhabitants," 38.
9 Whitefield, "A Letter to the Inhabitants," 38–39, 41.

support for the institution of slavery in responding that it was actually in slaveholders' enlightened best interests to see their slaves converted. In an effort to allay slave masters' fears that slaves' experience of liberty in the spiritual realm might translate into an increased appetite for rebellion, he asked rhetorically:

> Do you find any one command in the gospel, that has the least tendency to make people forget their relative duties? Do you not read, that servants, and as many as are under the yoke of bondage, are required to be subject in all lawful things to their masters, and that not only to the good and gentle, but also to the froward?

He concluded, "I challenge the world to produce a single instance of a negroe's being made a thorough Christian, and thereby made a worse servant: it cannot be."[10]

But if he was adamant that the gospel posed no economic, social, or political threat to slave masters' way of life, Whitefield also added to these reassurances a challenge that urged them to view slaves as fellow bearers of God's image, and with that recognition, as having equal access to the gospel message. "Blacks are just as much, and no more, conceived and born in sin, as white men are: both, if born and bred up here, I am persuaded are naturally capable of the same improvement," he wrote. "I am apt to think," he continued, "whenever the gospel is preached with power amongst them, that many will be brought effectually home to God."[11]

Whitefield the Evangelist to America's Slaves

As Whitefield's preaching tour of 1740 unfolded, he had the opportunity to put into practice these aspirations for evangelizing America's slaves. For instance, as he drew his sermon "The Lord Our Righteousness" to a close, Whitefield offered specialized words of application to a variety of people: "young men," "young maidens," "you of a middle age" (including "busy merchants," and "cumbered Martha's"), "gray-headed sinners," "little children," and last, but not least, slaves. "Here then I could conclude; but I must not forget the poor negroes; no, I must not," he wrote. Lest anyone come away with the impression that Whitefield included this demographic as an afterthought, he went out of his way to clarify otherwise: "Nor do I mention

10 Whitefield, "A Letter to the Inhabitants," 39–40.
11 Whitefield, "A Letter to the Inhabitants," 40.

you last, because I despise your souls, but because I would have what I shall say, make the deeper impression upon your hearts." Not only did he reinforce that Jesus's atoning death was just as much for them "as for others," but Whitefield was adamant that they possessed the same inherent dignity and worth as those who were not enslaved. Referring to Galatians 3:28, he wrote, "For in Jesus Christ there is neither male nor female, bond nor free; even you may be the children of God, if you believe in Jesus." Further, citing the precedent of the "eunuch belonging to the queen of Candace" in Acts 8, who came to believe the gospel and was baptized, he implored slaves to follow the North African's first-century example and do likewise: "Do you also believe, and you shall be saved."[12]

It seems Whitefield's targeted applications made a significant impression, and many in turn did believe. Whitefield's *Journals* and correspondence reflect his sincere desire to bring the gospel to this largely unreached and spiritually overlooked segment of the population. On April 28, 1740, he wrote, "The Word hath run and been much glorified, and many Negroes also are in a fair way of being brought home to God."[13] Soon afterward, he reflected, "I doubt not, when the poor negroes are to be called, God will highly favour them to wipe off their reproach, and shew that He is no respecter of persons."[14]

His repeated visits to places like Philadelphia throughout the spring of 1740 appear to have elicited an especially positive response among the city's resident slaves. He described one occasion in mid-May: "Nearly fifty negroes came to my lodgings, to give thanks for what God had done for their souls. How heartily did those poor creatures throw in their mites for my poor orphans. Some of them have been effectually wrought upon, and in an uncommon manner."[15] A little over a week later, Whitefield's correspondence with the overseer of a Philadelphia-based society of "poor negro women and children" illustrated the way he often warmly reciprocated the affection that was extended toward him: "My love to the Negro Peggy, and all her black sisters . . . ," he wrote. Though without doubt there was frequently a condescending and paternalistic hue to his interactions with slaves (he suggested to the same overseer, "What if they [the aforementioned female slaves] were put into a Society by themselves, and you,

12 Whitefield, "The Lord Our Righteousness," in *Works*, 5:232–34.
13 Whitefield to Mr. M—, April 28, 1740, in *Letters*, 167.
14 *Journals*, 420.
15 *Journals*, 422.

or some white woman, meet with them?"[16]), Whitefield recoiled from "civilizing" slaves as a worthy goal of his ministry among them.[17] Instead, spiritual conversion was always his ultimate end.

That being so, in true Methodist fashion, Whitefield's heavenly-mindedness was complemented by a concern for the physical well-being of those to whom he ministered. Within two months of landing in the American colonies, he had already begun to envision establishing a school for the children of slaves. In late December 1739, he wrote in his journal: "I do not despair, if God spares my life, of seeing a school of young negroes singing the praise of Him Who made them, in a psalm of thanksgiving. Lord, Thou hast put into my heart a good design to educate them: I doubt not but Thou wilt enable me to bring it to good effect."[18] Four months later he took the first steps toward realizing his plan, purchasing five thousand acres in Pennsylvania "on the forks of the Delaware," with help supplied by William Seward, who advanced the sum needed to purchase the land.[19] Ordering the construction of a large building "for the instruction of these poor creatures," Whitefield named the property Nazareth.[20] In July, buoyed by the recent interest in the gospel among slaves in Charleston and the conversion of several slave masters who had "resolved to teach them Christianity," he was even musing about the possibility of creating another school in the southern colonies. He wrote, "Had I time or proper schoolmasters, I might immediately erect a negro school in South Carolina, as well as in Pennsylvania."[21]

In the end, it was left to others to pursue this particular southern venture. A self-aware Whitefield, in words he might also have used to describe his perennial struggles to manage the Bethesda orphanage from afar, acknowledged that this was probably for the best: "The time would fail me were I to relate to every particular," he conceded.[22] As for the Pennsylvania project, while construction did begin in June 1740, Whitefield and the Moravian missionaries he had recruited to erect the school experienced a theological falling out later that year, and building promptly stopped. Already in serious debt, Whitefield was unable to

---

16 Whitefield to Mr. R—, May 22, 1740, in *Letters*, 176–77.
17 Whitefield, "A Letter to the Inhabitants," 39.
18 *Journals*, 379.
19 Arnold A. Dallimore, *George Whitefield: The Life and Times of the Great Evangelist of the Eighteenth-Century Revival*, 2 vols. (London: Banner of Truth, 1970, 1980), 1:498.
20 *Journals*, 411.
21 *Journals*, 444.
22 *Journals*, 450.

continue funding the establishment of the school and eventually sold the site to the Moravians in 1743.

Whitefield, Slavery, and His Bethesda Orphanage

Meanwhile, construction of Whitefield's Bethesda orphanage, ten miles to the south of Savannah, had begun in earnest on March 25, 1740. There were some early setbacks: Whitefield recounted that "a Schooner loaded with ten thousand Bricks, and a great deal of Provision" intended for the property was lost to a Spanish ship. But despite these losses, by and large progress during the first year was significant.[23] On December 23, 1740, he reported that "the Work has been carried on with great Success and Speed. There are no less than 4 framed Houses, a large Stable and Cart-house, beside the great House." As for the orphans themselves, Whitefield had gathered forty-nine "Objects of Charity" under his care, including English, Scottish, Dutch, French, and American-born children. In addition, he described the way almost "20 Acres of Land are cleared round about it, and a large Road made from Savannah to the Orphan-House, 12 Miles in Length."[24]

These positives notwithstanding, Whitefield was "several hundred pounds in Debt" and adamant that, despite the material kindness of benefactors, Bethesda's future was economically fraught on its present trajectory. "None but those upon the Spot can tell the Expense, as well as ill conveniency, that attends building in Georgia," he complained. The cost of labor—especially White labor, he specifically pointed out—was prohibitively high: "The produce of the Land cultivated by white servants, will scarcely furnish them with ordinary Food and Raiment, exclusive of the Expenses of Sickness and Wages. I cannot see how it is possible for the Colony to subsist on its present Footing." In case readers missed his point, even at this early stage of his philanthropic American ministry, Whitefield was explicit about advocating the introduction of slave labor in Georgia: "As for manuring more Land than the hired Servants and great Boys can manage, I think it is impracticable without a few Negroes. It will in no wise answer the Expense."[25]

In contrast to their neighbors in South Carolina, Georgia had been established in the 1730s as a slave-free colony. Having secured a royal

---

[23] George Whitefield, *An Extract of the Preface to the Reverend Mr. Whitefield's Account of the Orphan-House in Georgia* (Edinburgh: T. Lunisden and J. Robertson, 1741), 5.
[24] Whitefield, *Preface to Orphan-House*, 4, 6.
[25] Whitefield, *Preface to Orphan-House*, 6, 8.

charter in 1732, three years later the trustees of the colony, including prominent British member of Parliament James Oglethorpe, sought the king's "approbation and allowance" for "An Act for rendering the Colony of Georgia more Defensible by prohibiting the Importation and use of Black Slaves or Negroes into the same." Far from emerging from enlightened abolitionist sentiments, this blanket prohibition issued from essentially pragmatic motives.

Banning slaves was deemed in the best interests of the survival of the fledgling colony for several reasons. First, the trustees contended that slaves jeopardized the colony's ability to defend itself: "Experience hath Shewn that the manner of Settling Colonys and Plantations with Black Slaves or Negroes hath obstructed the Increase of English and Christian Inhabitants therein who alone can in case of a War be relyed on for the Defence and Security of the same." Second, and foreshadowing the Stono rebellion in South Carolina four years later, the legislation argued that introducing slaves "hath Exposed the Colonys so settled to the Insurrections, Tumults and Rebellions of such Slaves and Negroes." Third, the trustees speculated that a slave population posed a risk, should the colony fall prey to invasion by a foreign state, which in turn might incite the resident slave population to rise against the colony's White population. In other words, slavery ought to be prohibited "in Case . . . a Rupture with any Foreign State who should Encourage and Support such Rebellions might Occasion the utter Ruin and loss of such Colonys." Any slaves discovered in the colony were subject to being seized and sold by the trustees, and those importing them were liable to a substantial fine of fifty pounds.[26]

From the outset, not only were Black slaves "smuggled in, at least in small numbers," but this legislation was met with opposition from many White settlers who argued that a labor crisis necessitated the usage of slaves.[27] For example, in 1738, 117 residents near Savannah collectively petitioned Georgia's officials, on primarily economic grounds, for "the Use of Negroes, with proper limitations." Professing themselves to be "very sensible of the Inconveniences and Mischiefs" that "do daily arise from an unlimited Use of Negroes," they nonetheless asserted that importing slave labor "would both occasion great Numbers of white People to come here,

[26] Elizabeth Donnan, ed., *Documents Illustrative of the History of the Slave Trade to America*, vol. 4, *The Border Colonies and the Southern Colonies* (Washington, DC: Carnegie Institution of Washington, 1935), 587–88.
[27] Darold D. Wax, "Georgia and the Negro before the American Revolution," *The Georgia Historical Quarterly* 51, no. 1 (1967): 67.

and also render us capable to subsist ourselves."[28] While this constituted the majority view, some dissenting voices sided with the trustees, though their motivations for doing so were mixed at best. For example, while the community of German Lutheran Salzburgers in Ebenezer, Georgia, considered slavery to be inconsistent with their reading of Scripture, race-based xenophobia lay at the forefront of their reasons for urging Georgia's officials to maintain their exclusionary policy in 1739, "knowing by experience that houses and gardens will be robbed always by them; and white people are in danger of life from them, besides other great inconveniences."[29]

Undeterred, in 1741 the trustees continued to preclude slaves on the grounds of maintaining the colony's safety, anxious that "the Spaniards at St. Augustine [in Florida] would be continually enticing away the Negroes, or encouraging them to Insurrection."[30] However, the trajectory of public opinion was always against the trustees' legislation. Between 1735 and 1750, "hundreds of petitions and reports crossed the Atlantic," to the point that the House of Commons began to lose patience with the trustees' management of the colony.[31] A heated parliamentary debate in 1742 resulted in a vote that upheld the decision to ban slaves, but for the first time rejected Georgia's annual application for funds to help ensure the financial stability of the colony.[32]

Throughout the 1740s, Whitefield would add his voice to the persistently shrill chorus advocating the reversal of the 1735 "Act for rendering the Colony of Georgia more Defensible." He had never been wholly averse to the practice of slavery—only its excesses and abuses. Now, as the decade progressed, and as Bethesda's financial fortunes hung in the balance, he became more convinced of its warrant and necessity. The evolution of his position and practice regarding slavery did not occur in a relational vacuum. Whitefield was instrumental in the conversion of two prominent South Carolina plantation owners, brothers Hugh and Jonathan Bryan, who in turn were instrumental in his eventual willingness to embrace the life of a plantation owner himself. In 1745 he was offered the gift of a slave by William Hutson, minister of Stoney Creek Church in Lowcountry South

---

28 Cited in Wax, "Georgia and the Negro," 70.
29 Benjamin Martyn, "An Impartial Inquiry into the State and Utility of the Province of Georgia," in *Collections of the Georgia Historical Society*, vol. 1 (Savannah: Georgia Historical Society, 1840), 190.
30 *An Account, Shewing the Progress of the Colony of Georgia in America, from its First Establishment* (London: Peter Force, 1741), 8.
31 Codrina Cozma, "John Martin Bolzius and the Early Christian Opposition to Slavery," *The Georgia Historical Quarterly* 88, no. 4 (2004): 464.
32 Wax, "Georgia and the Negro," 71–72.

Carolina, where the Bryan brothers served as deacons. Hutson had also experienced the new birth under Whitefield's preaching, and the itinerant preacher was especially impressed at the way Hutson included converted slaves as part of his church community. In a letter to him, Whitefield was initially inclined to accept the gift but had second thoughts and in a post-script balked at the offer.[33]

"One Negroe Has Been Given Me": Whitefield the Slave Master

Two years later, in 1747, whatever reservations Whitefield might have har-bored regarding the propriety of slave owning had all but evaporated. Aided by the financial backing of James Habersham and Hugh Bryan, Whitefield purchased a plantation in South Carolina, which he named Providence, possibly in an effort to baptize his decision with divine imprimatur. Se-curing the long-term economic stability of Bethesda was influential in his decision-making. Justifying his momentous choice as the product of Geor-gia's "very bad" constitution ("it is impossible for the inhabitants to subsist themselves without the use of slaves"), he wrote to "a Generous Benefactor Unknown," "God has put it into the hearts of my South-Carolina friends, to contribute liberally towards purchasing a plantation and slaves in this province, which I purpose to devote to the support of Bethesda." Bought "at a very cheap rate," the plantation consisted of "six hundred and forty acres of excellent land." In almost an aside, he added, fatefully, "One negroe has been given me."[34] This time, he did not refuse the offer.

And yet Whitefield's seemingly inexorable journey toward adding "plantation owner" and "slave master" to his resume did not go unchal-lenged during the 1740s. Those prepared to oppose the practice of slavery during the first half of the eighteenth century were rare, but not unknown. Indeed, there were a number within Whitefield's relational orbit who at-tempted to steer him away from his increasing acceptance of slavery. For example, the German Lutheran Johann Martin Boltzius, pastor of the Salz-burger community situated near his orphanage, expressed skepticism about one of Whitefield's primary ostensible arguments for participating in the institution: namely, that it afforded opportunities to evangelize slaves. A far more likely outcome, argued Boltzius, was that slave masters would

---

[33] Thomas S. Kidd, *George Whitefield: America's Spiritual Founding Father* (New Haven, CT: Yale University Press, 2014), 190.
[34] Whitefield to a generous benefactor unknown, March 15, 1747, in *Works*, 2:90.

"take advantage of the Poor Black Slaves" and thus "increase the Sins of the Land to a great Height."[35] His firsthand observations in Charleston confirmed this conviction: slaves were "very much urged to work but never urged to become Christians."[36] Years of contending against slavery wore Boltzius down to the point that he eventually came to see his efforts as futile. While he never renounced his personal opposition to the practice, in 1748 he acquiesced to the idea of introducing slaves in Georgia.

Another vocal critic of Whitefield's proslavery trajectory was the Philadelphia-based French-American Quaker and abolitionist Anthony Benezet. On March 4, 1775, Benezet wrote to Selina, Countess of Huntingdon, offering her a candid explanation for the discernible migration in Whitefield's attitude toward slavery, evident over several decades. "He at first clearly saw the iniquity of this horrible abuse of the human race, as manifestly appears in the letter he published on that subject," Benezet observed, referring to Whitefield's excoriating attack on southern slave masters in 1740. But the (relative) clarity of moral vision Whitefield then possessed had become dulled over time, suggested Benezet: "Yet after residing in Georgia & being habituated to the sight & use of Slaves, his judgement became so much influenced as to palliate, & in some measure, defend the use of Slaves, [which] was a matter of much concern to me, and which I repeatedly, with brotherly freedom, expressed to him."[37] In other words, if proximity to slavery would eventually motivate later generations of evangelicals to pursue abolition, the more Whitefield experienced the peculiar institution firsthand and became dependent on its fruits, the more he appeared to become "attenuated to this moral evil."[38]

Although his indictment of slavery would begin to gain traction among a broad swathe of evangelicals in the decade after Whitefield's death, for the time being, most, including Whitefield, "did not share Benezet's outrage against the slave trade."[39] Brushing off his entreaties, Whitefield continued to lobby for the overturn of Georgia's ban on slavery in his quest to

[35] Allen D. Candler, *The Colonial Records of the State of Georgia*, vol. 24 (Atlanta: C. P. Byrd, 1915), 442.

[36] George Fenwick Jones, ed., *Detailed Reports on the Salzburger Emigrants Who Settled in America*, ed. Samuel Urlsperger, 8 vols. (Athens, GA: University of Georgia Press, 1968–1985), 1:57.

[37] Quoted in Irv A. Brendlinger, *To Be Silent . . . Would Be Criminal: The Antislavery Influence and Writings of Anthony Benezet* (Lanham, MD: Scarecrow, 2007), 101.

[38] Irv. A. Brendlinger, "Wesley, Whitefield, a Philadelphia Quaker, and Slavery," *Faculty Publications— George Fox School of Theology* (Fall 2001): 170.

[39] John Coffey, "Evangelicals, Slavery and the Slave Trade: From Whitefield to Wilberforce," *Anvil* 24, no. 2 (2007): 99.

ensure the financial liberty of Bethesda. On December 6, 1748, he appealed to the trustees, no doubt aware of the significant political clout he exerted: by this stage, the orphanage was "the colony's largest civil employer," providing "jobs, education, and religious services for Georgians."[40] "I need not inform you, honoured gentlemen," he observed, "how the colony of Georgia has been declining for these many years last past, and at what great disadvantages I have maintained a large family in that wilderness." Once more he reiterated not only his allegiance to the colony, manifested through his considerable investment in its betterment over the previous eight years, but also what he perceived to be the needlessly burdensome bureaucratic and legislative obstacles that prevented his endeavors from flourishing as they otherwise might have: "Upwards of five thousand pounds have been expended in that undertaking, and yet very little proficiency made in the cultivation of my tract of land, and that entirely owing to the necessity I lay under of making use of white hands." Whitefield's proposed solution was simple. "Had a negroe been allowed, I should now have had a sufficiency to support a great many orphans, without expending above half the sum which hath been laid out," he contended.[41]

He was quick to contrast Bethesda's perennial financial struggles with the success of his plantation in South Carolina, "where negroes are allowed." Even though "I have only eight working hands," he explained, "yet in all probability, there will be more raised in one year, and with a quarter the expense, than has been produced at Bethesda for several years last past." Despite his "private judgement" that the trustees ought to have long since opened the colony to slaves, Whitefield nonetheless declared himself willing to abide by the current legislation as long as it remained in place. "I am determined that not one of mine shall ever be allowed to work at the Orphan-house, till I can do it in a legal manner, and by the approbation of the honourable trustees," he wrote. For all his professed loyalty, Whitefield was nonetheless prepared to issue a scarcely veiled threat: that unless the trustees altered their legislation, he would be forced to seriously consider moving the orphanage to neighboring South Carolina:

> I am as willing as ever to do all I can for Georgia and the Orphan-house,
> if either a limited use of negroes is approved of, or some more indented

---

[40] Allan Gallay, "The Origins of Slaveholders' Paternalism: George Whitefield, the Bryan Family, and the Great Awakening in the South," *The Journal of Southern History* 53, no. 3 (1987): 379.
[41] Whitefield to the Honourable Trustees of Georgia, December 6, 1748, in *Works*, 2:208.

servants sent over. If not, I cannot promise to keep any large family, or cultivate the plantation in any considerable manner. My strength must necessarily be taken to the other side.[42]

It is impossible to ascertain just how decisive Whitefield's lobbying proved to be in the Georgia Trustees' decision two years later to request that the House of Commons repeal their 1735 act. What is clear is that when the legislation banning slavery was formally overturned on January 1, 1751, Whitefield celebrated the news as a mark of divine blessing:

Thanks be to God, that the time for favouring that Colony seems to be come. I think now is the season for us to exert our utmost for the good of the poor *Ethiopians*. We are told, that even they are soon to stretch out their hands unto God. And who knows but their being settled in *Georgia*, may be over-ruled for this great end?[43]

Preempting Georgia's decision to formally legalize slavery, it appears that by 1749 Whitefield had prematurely (and illegally) introduced slaves onto his Bethesda property to clear land for a plantation.[44] A decade earlier, he had deferred from passing judgment on whether he thought the Bible endorsed the institution of slavery, focusing his energy on redeeming its practice. But now—and coinciding with his freedom to introduce slaves onto his land with the blessing of Georgia's authorities—Whitefield was ready to declare his hand: "As for the lawfulness of keeping Slaves I have no doubt."[45]

As always, Whitefield's instinct was to appeal to Scripture to justify his actions. Citing instances of slavery in the Bible in a way that, as one historian notes, "anticipated proslavery thought in the antebellum American South," he interpreted these examples as proof that not only did the Scriptures describe the institution as it occurred in the ancient world, but also they prescribed its continuation in his own time and place.[46] "I hear of some that were bought with Abraham's money & some that were born in his house," he ventured, rehearsing possible evidence of slavery as far back as the era of the patriarchs. "I cannot help thinking that some of those

---

[42] Whitefield to the Honourable Trustees of Georgia, December 6, 1748, in *Works*, 2:208–9.
[43] Whitefield to Mr. B—, March 22, 1751, in *Works*, 2:404 (italics in the original).
[44] Kidd, *George Whitefield*, 209.
[45] Whitefield to Mr. B—, March 22, 1751, in *Works*, 2:404.
[46] Kidd, *George Whitefield*, 215.

servants mentioned by the Apostles in their Epistles, were or had been slaves," he added, before contending, speculatively, that "it is plain that the Gibeonites were doomed to perpetual Slavery."[47]

As contested and refutable as Whitefield's reading of Scripture on slavery would later appear to evangelicals like John Wesley, John Newton, and William Wilberforce (1759–1833), it was not unusual among his evangelical contemporaries. For example, in her 1743 "Letter to the Negroes," Whitefield's Calvinist Baptist ally Anne Dutton wrote on Whitefield's behalf to recent slave converts, "[God] doth not call you hereby from the Service of your Masters according to the Flesh; but to serve him in serving them, in obeying all their lawful commands, and submitting to the Yoke his Providence has placed you under." She even went on to appropriate Jesus's vicarious sacrifice as an example of the obedient suffering that slaves ought to imitate. Appealing to 1 Peter 2:18, she argued that Jesus called slaves "to be meek and patient in Sufferings" and that he gave them "himself for an Example of suffering Afflictions and of Patience."[48]

Jonathan Edwards (1703–1758) and Whitefield had much in common theologically—and also when it came to the practice of slavery. Both believed that while "the slave trade was immoral because it violated precepts such as the injunction against 'menstealers' in 1 Timothy 1," slave owning itself was not prohibited.[49] Conceding that "they are brought in a wrong way from their own country, and it is a trade not to be approved of," Whitefield deemed slavery a God-ordained fact of life in the eighteenth-century British world. "Let us reason no more about it, but diligently improve the present opportunity for their instruction," he wrote. As an evangelist, he envisaged his distinctive contribution would be to help redeem slavery, not abolish it. And what better way to do so, he figured, than as an active participant in the institution's practice itself and not a mere observer: "Yet as it will be carried on whether we will or not," he rationalized, "I should think myself highly favoured if I could purchase a good number of them, in order to make their lives comfortable, and lay a foundation for breeding up their posterity in the nurture and admonition of the Lord."[50]

---

[47] Whitefield to Mr. B—, March 22, 1751, in *Works*, 2:404.

[48] Joann Ford Watson, ed., *Selected Spiritual Writings of Anne Dutton: Eighteenth-Century British-Baptist, Woman Theologian*, vol. 5 (Macon, GA: Mercer University Press, 2003), 373–74.

[49] Kidd, *George Whitefield*, 215.

[50] Whitefield to Mr. B—, March 22, 1751, in *Works*, 2:404.

The prospect of evangelistic opportunities might have excited White-field, but it appears that pecuniary motives for embracing slavery were never far from his mind. Functionally, one outcome was that "the very eighteenth century evangelicalism that had opened his eyes to the spiritual needs of the slaves also blinded him to their inhuman temporal and cultural conditions."[51] With unintentional though breathtaking callousness, he casually speculated that "though liberty is a sweet thing to such as are born free, yet to those who never knew the sweets of it, slavery, perhaps, may not be so irksome." Confidently contending that "it is plain to a demonstration, that hot countries cannot be cultivated without Negroes," he lamented the profligate wastage of resources and (White) lives in a manner that unwittingly betrayed his default sense of racial superiority: "What a flourishing country might *Georgia* have been, had the use of them been permitted years ago? How many white people have been destroyed for want of them, and how many thousands of pounds spent to no purpose at all?"[52] Commenting on Whitefield's justification for pursuing slavery here, even one of Whitefield's earliest and most flattering biographers, Luke Tyerman, reflected that "his warmest admirer will find it difficult to defend his action," no matter how generously one might construe his intentions.[53]

"The First Great Friend of the American Negro"?

In many ways, Whitefield was a product of his eighteenth-century trans-atlantic time and place. Like all of us, he was unavoidably influenced, without being inevitably determined, by the prevailing attitudes and assumptions of the world in which he lived. Like all of us, he could exhibit sinful motivations and confounding contradictions. He embodied these especially vividly when it came to his involvement with slavery, one of the most ubiquitous features of life in the British Empire: "He endorsed it and indeed expanded it, while also working to improve it in keeping with his view that it could function as a Christian institution."[54] But while White-field devoted his life to proclaiming the good news of liberation from bondage to sin, death, and the devil in the spiritual realm for both Black and

---

51 Harry S. Stout, *The Divine Dramatist: George Whitefield and the Rise of Modern Evangelicalism* (Grand Rapids, MI: Eerdmans, 1991), 199.

52 Whitefield to Mr. B—, March 22, 1751, in *Works*, 2:404 (italics in the original).

53 Luke Tyerman, *The Life of the Rev. George Whitefield*, 2 vols. (London: Hodder and Stoughton, 1876–1877), 2:132.

54 Carla Gardina Pestana, "Whitefield and Empire," in Hammond and Jones, *George Whitefield*, 94.

White, this concern for the liberty of slaves' souls never translated into advocating their physical freedom.

On some level, and at certain moments, Whitefield seemed to grasp that extolling the former freedom without the latter entailed a measure of profound contradiction. For instance, in the spring of 1748, he made a two-month evangelistic side tour to Bermuda, with especially high hopes of preaching to the resident slaves. On May 1 he preached a sermon tailored especially to them, soon finding himself navigating ethical waters arguably more treacherous than the archipelago's shipwreck-filled coastline. Reflecting with satisfaction on his ability to communicate the gospel to the slaves, he wrote, "I believe the Lord enabled me so to discourse, as to touch the negroes." And yet, he quickly clarified, it was a gospel message calibrated in such a way so as "not to give them the least umbrage to slight, or behave imperiously to their masters." Possibly betraying a measure of internal dissonance at this unevenly applied good news, he continued, "If ever a minister in preaching, needs the wisdom of the serpent to be joined with the harmlessness of the dove, it must be when discoursing to negroes."[55]

But Bermuda's sizable slave population was not alone in gathering to listen to him preach that day. "A number of white people," apparently including some slave masters, also "came to hear what I had to say to them," he recounted. Affording a glimpse behind the curtain into his exegetical and homiletical method, Whitefield reflected on what he interpreted to be a providentially inspired omission in his sermon:

> Blessed be God, that I was directed not to say any thing, this first time, to the masters at all, though my text led me to it. It might have been of bad consequence, to tell them their duty, or charge them too roundly with the neglect of it, before their slaves. They would mind all I said to their masters, and, perhaps, nothing that I said to them.

He concluded, without irony, "Every thing is beautiful in its season"— everything that is, except presumably the physical emancipation of the majority of his audience. By his reporting, Whitefield's sermon aroused a measure of ill-feeling among some in the crowd of "nearly fifteen hundred people": not so much because of its lack of proabolition sentiment, but

---

[55] *Memoirs*, 165.

instead owing to the way he censured slaves for their "cursing, swearing, thieving, and lying," not to mention that he had also characterized them as possessing hearts as "black as their faces."[56]

These isolated responses notwithstanding, the overwhelming impression is that, for all of the shortcomings in his theology and practice, America's slaves responded to Whitefield with an "enduring adoration." At face value, his "love for the slaves was genuine and invariably reciprocated."[57] News of his death was met with genuine grief among the slave population. One of the most prominent eulogies came from the pen of an unlikely source: Phillis Wheatley, a seventeen-year-old Black servant and poet who had migrated to Boston from Africa nine years earlier. Her "Elegiac Poem" memorialized Whitefield as a British evangelist with a special affection for Americans in all of their diversity. She wrote,

He urg'd the need of Him to every one;
It was no less than God's co-equal Son!

Celebrating his lifelong commitment to America's slaves, she continued,

Take him, "my dear Americans," he said,
Be your complaints in his kind bosom laid:
Take him ye Africans, he longs for you;
Impartial Saviour, is his title due.[58]

But despite this effort to burnish Whitefield's image in the immediate aftermath of his death, there is little doubt his reputation in the ensuing years has suffered as a result of his engagement with slavery. This criticism has not been without considerable warrant. In many ways, he "shared in a racist culture that exploited the labor of a people considered to be inferior for its own commercial benefit," interpreting freedom to be a "matter contingent upon the circumstances of birth, race, and economic expediency."[59] And yet, if the president of the University of Pennsylvania in 2020 well might have raised an eyebrow at one historian's description of Whitefield as "the first great friend of the American

[56] Memoirs, 166.
[57] Stout, The Divine Dramatist, 108, 197.
[58] Phillis Wheatley, An Elegiac Poem, on the Death of That Celebrated Divine, and Eminent Servant of Jesus Christ, the Reverend and Learned George Whitefield (Boston: Ezekiel Russell, 1770), 7.
[59] Glen O'Brien, "Freedom in the Atlantic World: John Wesley and George Whitefield on Slavery," in Wesley and Whitefield? Wesley versus Whitefield?, ed. Ian J. Maddock (Eugene, OR: Pickwick, 2018), 182.

negro,"[60] we have also seen that many of Whitefield's eighteenth-century contemporaries—whether slave or free—would have looked askance at the university's decision to remove his statue.

In other words, there is little doubt that glossing over Whitefield's sins of commission and omission about slavery runs the risk of presenting him in an unjustifiably flattering light. But conversely, recasting his legacy exclusively in terms of a proslavery agenda in an effort to cancel his memory entirely runs the risk of falling victim to an anachronistic rendering of his life and ministry. Whitefield's failures, even more visible with the benefit of three centuries worth of hindsight, undoubtedly serve as a cautionary tale of the dangers of complicity with a prevailing culture's fallenness. They also force upon us the question Are there planks in our own spiritual eyes that threaten to impair the clarity of our own moral vision?[61]

Managing to successfully elude the university's censure was one-time slave owner Benjamin Franklin, on the grounds that, in contrast to Whitefield, he "changed course in his life and went on to become a leading abolitionist."[62] Naturally, this raises several final, if ultimately unanswerable, questions. Might Whitefield have embraced the abolitionist cause if he lived to experience the initial wave of antislavery activism that increasingly began to capture the evangelical community's hearts and minds from the mid-1770s onward? Might he have chosen to emancipate the slaves still residing at the Bethesda orphanage at the time of his death, including twenty-four men (one of whom was described as "so old as to be useless"), eleven women, and fifteen children?[63] Might he have followed in fellow revivalist John Wesley's footsteps, who in 1791, fully two decades after Whitefield's death, famously urged the evangelical parliamentarian William Wilberforce to pursue the end of "that execrable villainy, which is the scandal of religion, of England, and of human nature"?[64] Of course, as illuminating as answers to these questions would be, they remain tantalizingly out of reach. Rather than

---

60 Charles H. Maxson, *The Great Awakening in the Middle Colonies* (Gloucester, MA: Peter Smith, 1958), 57.
61 See Sean McGever, *Ownership: The Evangelical Legacy of Slavery in Edwards, Wesley, and Whitefield* (Downers Grove, IL: InterVarsity Press, 2024), esp. chap. 12, which encourages readers to examine their own lives today.
62 "Penn Announces Plans."
63 "Schedule of all the lands possessed by, and belonging to the late Reverend George Whitefield in Georgia," in *Works*, 3:496.
64 Quoted in Henry Moore, *The Life of John Wesley*, 2 vols. (New York: Methodist Episcopal Church, 1826), 2:257.

hypothesizing, perhaps there is wisdom in casting all speculation aside and opting for the approach Whitefield himself took in penning his own intended epitaph: "I am content to wait till the day of judgement for the clearing up of my character: and after I am dead I desire no other epitaph than this, 'Here lies G. W. What sort of a man he was the great day will discover.'"[65]

---

[65] Whitefield to Mr. J— D—, July 12, 1749, in *Works*, 2:268.

CHAPTER 10

WHITEFIELD'S LEGACY

Capturing the essence of George Whitefield's legacy, in the estimation of nineteenth-century American poet John Greenleaf Whittier, was a simple enough matter. In the title of Whittier's homage to the celebrated British itinerant, he was, succinctly, "The Preacher":

> a homeless pilgrim with dubious name
> blown about on the winds of fame.[1]

Many of Whitefield's contemporaries, not to mention generations of biographers, have followed suit in focusing on his reputation as a wayfaring evangelist. Artists commissioned to paint his portrait, including John Wollaston in 1742 and John Greenwood in 1768, depicted him as a theatrical preacher. The following century, Eyre Crowe's 1865 painting entitled *Whitefield Preaching in Moorfield's, A.D. 1742,* provided the visual template not only for Robert Tait McKenzie's now-removed sculpture at the University of Pennsylvania but also for the logo adopted by the Banner of Truth Trust. After all, given his theological commitments, who better than Whitefield to serve as the visual ambassador for that publishing house's brand of revival-oriented, experiential Calvinism?

While Whittier's poem celebrated Whitefield as an evangelist "on the errands of angels sent," the Quaker abolitionist's tribute did not shy away from acknowledging that Whitefield's legacy was complicated by his

---

[1] John Greenleaf Whittier, *The Complete Poetical Works of John Greenleaf Whittier* (Boston: Houghton, Mifflin, 1895), 69, 71.

unrepentant entanglements with slavery. It cast Whitefield as a flawed ambassador of a flawless gospel, akin to generations of God's people before him:

> He erred: shall we count His gifts as naught?
> Was the work of God in him unwrought? . . .
> Was the Hebrew temple less fair and good
> That Solomon bowed to gods of wood? . . .
> So in light and shadow the preacher went
> God's erring and human instrument.[2]

Whittier also drew attention to Whitefield's inauspicious final resting place: "under the church of Federal Street" in Newburyport, Massachusetts, a Presbyterian congregation he had helped establish a quarter of a century earlier. Whittier felt that the understated location, "walled about by its basement stones," was somehow unbefitting for one who achieved such unparalleled celebrity status during his lifetime.[3] Not that Whitefield himself would likely have complained. In fact, as one who routinely declared, "Let the name of Whitefield perish, but Christ be glorified,"[4] he might well have approved of his crypt's humble surroundings at the bottom of a rickety set of wooden stairs and adjacent to the Old South Church's furnace and an assortment of snow shovels and rakes.

But if Whitefield's burial place was, in the words of Phillis Wheatley's 1770 eulogy, a "tomb obscurely plac'd,"[5] it was not nearly remote or hidden enough to deter generations of admirers from making the pilgrimage to Newburyport to gaze upon his earthly remains—and in some cases, even extract souvenirs. One notable instance occurred in September 1775 when an entourage of American revolutionary soldiers, including the yet-to-become-infamous Benedict Arnold, stopped in Newburyport as they headed north on a military campaign to capture British-held Quebec. After marching into the Old South Church "with colors flying, and drums beating," they listened to a rousing sermon from their chaplain before descending to Whitefield's crypt, which lay immediately beneath them. Fearing the journey ahead through "the untrodden, mysterious wilderness" of what would eventually become the state of Maine, not to mention the armed conflict

---

2 Whittier, *Poetical Works*, 71–72.

3 Whittier, *Poetical Works*, 73.

4 Quoted in James C. Ryle, "George Whitefield and His Ministry," in *Select Sermons of George Whitefield* (Edinburgh: Banner of Truth, 1958), 42.

5 Phillis Wheatley, *An Elegiac Poem, on the Death of That Celebrated Divine, and Eminent Servant of Jesus Christ, the Reverend and Learned George Whitefield* (Boston: Ezekiel Russell, 1770), 7.

that awaited them in Canada, the soldiers "induced the sexton to take off the lid of the coffin," removed Whitefield's clerical "collar and wristbands," and proceeded to cut them up "in little pieces." These keepsakes from the "sainted sleeper" were then divided among them as virtual talismans— disappointingly ineffective, as it turned out, since they came off second best to the British shortly thereafter![6] While from this distance "we cannot divine the actual thoughts of the men present in the vault, their collective gesture may suggest a belief or superstition about relics," in effect communicating that if the spirit of Whitefield, patron saint of the American colonies, is for us, then who can be against us?[7]

In the years that followed, devotees and trophy hunters would remove more than Whitefield's clothing. In the mid-1820s a large bone from his right arm found its way into the possession of a Congregational minister in England. It was eventually restored to Whitefield's crypt in 1849. A fragment of his thumb still sits in the Methodist archives at Drew University in Madison, New Jersey, while one of his ribs is held at the Harvard Medical School. Even if we seek to interpret this "fascination with Whitefield's remains . . . within its own cultural milieu, not as a continuation of Catholic practice" and instead as "a form of nineteenth-century Christian antiquarianism,"[8] one cannot help but imagine Whitefield—or what remains of him—rolling over in his thankfully now-sealed-over grave.

And yet, if assessments of Whitefield's legacy have often focused on his reputation for famously affective and effective evangelistic preaching, then his ecclesiological impulses have arguably had just as significant an influence upon subsequent generations of evangelicals. As a "movement" theologically "rooted in classical Christian orthodoxy" and "shaped by a largely Protestant understanding of the gospel," evangelicalism is arguably unique in ecclesiological intuitions "shaped by the revivals of the so-called Great Awakening."[9] As we shall see, in several crucial ways Whitefield embodied and cultivated many of the distinctive practices that continue to find expression among professing evangelicals. These especially include (1) his evangelistic entrepreneurialism, (2) his willingness to embrace an

---

[6] J. T. Headley, *The Chaplains and Clergy of the Revolution* (New York: Charles Scribner, 1864), 92–93.

[7] Robert E. Cray, "Memorialization and Enshrinement: George Whitefield and Popular Religious Culture, 1770–1850," *Journal of the Early Republic* 10, no. 3 (1990): 350.

[8] Andrew Atherstone, "Commemorating Whitefield in the Nineteenth and Twentieth Centuries," in *George Whitefield: Life, Context and Legacy*, ed. Geordan Hammond and David Ceri Jones (Oxford: Oxford University Press, 2016), 282.

[9] Douglas A. Sweeney, *The American Evangelical Story: A History of the Movement* (Grand Rapids, MI: Baker, 2005), 23–24.

evangelical ecumenicity that transcended national and denominational boundaries, and, consequently, (3) his helping to normalize, wittingly or otherwise, evangelicalism's fondness for parachurch ministries and celebrity preachers. We shall also briefly observe (4) the major, if accidental, imprint Whitefield left on the American political landscape, along with his influence in helping to shape early Black evangelicalism.

Entrepreneurial Evangelist

As the preeminent evangelist of the transatlantic revivals, Whitefield left a legacy based largely on the phenomenal scope of his itinerant preaching ministry. Placing a premium on mobility, he chafed against geographic provincialism and denominational parochialism. In the process, he established a model for future generations of evangelicals to seek tangible unity with Christians from different denominations and regions, privileging matters of first importance over secondary theological concerns.

Despite all the dangers, difficulties, and slowness of travel during the eighteenth century, especially travel by sea, Whitefield was rarely sedentary. He visited Scotland fifteen times, Ireland twice, and the Netherlands, and seemed to have visited "almost every nook and cranny of England and Wales."[10] Perhaps most astonishing of all, he dared to cross the Atlantic thirteen times, spending a cumulative total of almost ten years of his life in the American colonies. If dual American-British citizenship could be posthumously bestowed, surely Whitefield would be eligible! When in America, he often lamented his inability to also be in Great Britain, and vice versa: "I find it is a trial to be thus divided between the work on this and the other side of the water," he wrote in 1749.[11] Within the orbit of the transatlantic world, this very English itinerant preacher was also very American—America's "first cultural hero," ventures Harry Stout. "Before Whitefield, there was no unifying intercolonial person or event. Indeed, before Whitefield, it is doubtful any name other than royalty was known equally well from Boston to Charleston."[12]

For those who knew Whitefield and followed his progress for any length of time, the sheer geographic scope of his ministry should not

---

10 A. Skevington Wood, *The Inextinguishable Blaze: Spiritual Renewal and Advance in the Eighteenth Century* (Eugene, OR: Wipf and Stock, 2006), 80.
11 Whitefield to the Reverend Mr. C—, February 20, 1749, in *Works*, 2:232.
12 Harry S. Stout, "Heavenly Comet," *Christian History* 38 (1993): 13–14.

have come as any surprise. After all, shortly after his first taste of field preaching in Kingswood near Bristol, he memorably declared to Daniel Abbot on March 3, 1739, "The whole world is now my parish."[13] Fusing apostolic Christianity, enlightenment bravado, and entrepreneurial boldness, it amounted to his virtual ecclesiological motto. Later that month, Whitefield's co-revivalist John Wesley uttered almost identical words to capture his own newfound sense of calling. That being said, they differed in what they meant by a slogan that was as aspirational as it was audacious.

Whitefield used the phrase to encapsulate his budding vision of an evangelistic ministry he hoped would transcend spatial, social, and denominational boundaries: the *whole world*, his parish. If Whitefield's ministry was expansive in a geographic and ecclesial sense, it was simultaneously quite narrow in its focus on evangelism. "My business seems to be, to evangelize, to be a Presbyter at large," he wrote to the Scottish Presbyterian seceder Ebenezer Erskine.[14]

But whereas Whitefield was content simply to "plant" the seed of God's word through evangelism, Wesley's ministry vision involved both evangelism and pouring his organizational energy into "watering" the seed of God's word through the ongoing spiritual nurture of those awakened under his preaching. Whitefield wrote to Wesley, "My business seems to be chiefly in planting; if God send you to water, I praise his name—I wish you a thousandfold increase."[15] In other words, if Whitefield's emphasis was primarily on evangelizing "the world," then Wesley was equally concerned with the ongoing discipleship of his far-flung "parish."

Given his visibility, popularity, and range, Whitefield was the obvious choice to assume the mantle of leadership over the Calvinistic branch of the Methodist movement. He nonetheless resisted overtures by Howell Harris in 1748 to diversify the scope of his ministry and take on this organizational role. Justifying his decision to Wesley, he wrote, "My attachment to America will not permit me to abide very long in England; consequently, I should but weave a *Penelope's* web if I formed societies; and if I should form them I have not proper assistants to take care of them." Expressing his awareness of just how differently he and Wesley envisaged their respective

---

[13] Whitefield to Daniel Abbot, March 3, 1738, quoted in Graham Thomas, ed., "George Whitefield and Friends," *National Library of Wales Journal* 26 (1990): 91. Whitefield used the phrase again the following year. See Whitefield to Rev. Mr. R— D—, November 10, 1739, in *Letters*, 105.

[14] Whitefield to Mr. E— E—, May 16, 1741, in *Letters*, 262.

[15] Whitefield to the Reverend Mr. J— W—, August 25, 1740, in *Letters*, 205.

ministries, Whitefield continued: "I intend therefore to go about preaching the gospel to every creature. You, I suppose, are for settling societies everywhere."[16]

Throughout their parallel ministries, Wesley was often critical of Whitefield's failure to consolidate the fruits of his itinerant ministry in the same way he had. Wesley lamented what he regarded as the sins of vocational omission committed by Whitefield and other Calvinistic Methodists: "How much preaching there has been for these twenty years all over Pembrokeshire! But no regular societies, no discipline, no order or connection. And the consequence is that nine in ten of the once awakened are now faster asleep than ever."[17]

For his part, although Whitefield never deviated from his dedicated focus on evangelism, there were times when he expressed retrospective remorse at the limitations he placed on the scope of his ministry. Comparing his legacy with Wesley's, Whitefield wrote: "My brother Wesley acted wisely. The souls that were awakened under his ministry he joined in class, and thus preserved the fruit of his labour. This I neglected, and my people are a rope of sand."[18] Gerald Cragg's memorable contrast between Wesley's and Whitefield's respective ministries, while verging on the hyperbolic and uncharitable, nonetheless captures this fundamental difference in their ministry philosophies: "Wherever Whitefield went he left an overwhelming impression of impassioned eloquence," he contended. By contrast, "wherever Wesley went, he left a company of men and women closely knit together in a common life."[19] Indeed, in terms of their respective legacies, one tangible consequence of "Whitefield's unconcern with organization" was that "English methodism would become almost entirely Arminian in its theology."[20]

But Whitefield was not simply an evangelist. "He was also an expert marketer of the gospel in the new, open spaces of British imperial commerce."[21] One of the most distinctive legacies of Whitefield's preaching ministry was his "breathtaking entrepreneurial spirit," especially

---

16 Whitefield to Rev. Mr. J— W—, September 1, 1748, in Works, 2:169–70 (italics in the original).

17 John Wesley, The Works of John Wesley: Bicentennial Edition. vols. 18–24, Journals and Diaries I–VII, ed. W. Reginald Ward and Richard P. Heitzenrater (Nashville: Abingdon, 1988–1997), 21:424.

18 Quoted in William L. Doughty, John Wesley: Preacher (London: Epworth, 1955), 57.

19 Gerald R. Cragg, The Church and the Age of Reason (Baltimore: Penguin, 1966), 145.

20 John Munsey Turner, John Wesley: The Evangelical Revival and the Rise of Methodism in England (London: Epworth, 2002), 13.

21 Mark A. Noll, The Rise of Evangelicalism: The Age of Edwards, Whitefield and the Wesleys (Downers Grove, IL: InterVarsity Press, 2003), 153.

his willingness to utilize innovative strategies that he borrowed from a quickly evolving commercial marketplace.[22] A tablet at St Mary de Crypt in Gloucester, the church of Whitefield's youth where he also preached his first sermon, memorializes him not simply as the "Prince of Preachers" but also as a "pioneer in evangelism." As an entrepreneurial evangelist, Whitefield blazed a trail for future generations of evangelicals in modeling the benefits to be had from exploiting new forms of mass communication and an emerging consumer culture to reach as wide an audience as possible.

His ministry coincided with the emergence of a transatlantic print culture, especially "the rise of British magazines and newspapers, media used by Christians both to advance the cause of revival and inform interested parties about God's work around the world."[23] To borrow Wordsworth's phrase, "Bliss it was in that dawn to be alive," and Whitefield made sure he capitalized on this blossoming promotional highway.[24] He "pioneered evangelicals' masterful use of media" and not only utilized his newspaper, *The Weekly History*, to communicate news of revival but also encouraged others to create their own publications, including Thomas Prince's *Christian History* and James Robe's *Christian Monthly History*.[25]

With their transatlantic coverage, newspapers provided "readers with a sense of identity . . . that transcended their own national and denominational ties."[26] These periodicals not only supplied a "commercial means for advance publicity"; they also showcased Whitefield's early awareness that even negative publicity in the press could be harnessed in the interests of revival.[27] In late 1739 he wrote:

> I have found the advantage of the things my adversaries have inserted in the public papers. They do but excite people's curiosity, and serve to raise their attention, while men of seriousness and candour naturally infer that some good must be doing where such stories and falsities are invented.[28]

22 Noll, *The Rise of Evangelicalism*, 107.
23 Sweeney, *The American Evangelical Story*, 29.
24 William Wordsworth, *The Poetical Works of William Wordsworth*, 8 vols. (Boston: Little, Brown, 1859), 7:265.
25 Thomas S. Kidd, *George Whitefield: America's Spiritual Founding Father* (New Haven, CT: Yale University Press, 2014), 260.
26 Sweeney, *The American Evangelical Story*, 29–30.
27 Frank Lambert, *"Pedlar in Divinity": George Whitefield and the Transatlantic Revivals* (Princeton, NJ: Princeton University Press, 1994), 7.
28 *Journals*, 373.

His "preach and print" strategy extended beyond newspapers to include the publication of his sermons and *Journals*. Vast numbers of people could lay claim to having heard him preach, but by printing his sermons Whitefield dramatically expanded the evangelistic scope of his ministry. Buying and reading his sermons "represented an opportunity to participate in the revivals when there was no chance to hear him preach. Indeed some people knew Whitefield only through his publications."[29] As for his *Journals*, he serialized their publication and, in the process, astutely "not only made purchasing easier" but also "created a heightened sense of anticipation as readers followed the evangelist's progress toward their own communities."[30] All told, if John Wesley "left a greater organizational legacy" and Jonathan Edwards "a more significant theological contribution," the entrepreneurial evangelist Whitefield "was the key figure in the first generation of evangelical Christianity; of the three, he linked, by far, the most pastors and leaders through his relentless travels, preaching, publishing and letter-writing networks."[31]

Evangelical Ecumenist

And yet Whitefield did not simply introduce a spirit of entrepreneurialism into his practice of evangelism. He was also willing to transcend traditional denominational boundaries. The "flexibility with respect to church forms and inherited religious traditions" that he pioneered in the eighteenth century have henceforth "always been important characteristics of evangelical movements."[32] Whitefield's evangelical ecumenism expressed itself in a variety of ways, ranging from his distinctly pragmatic ecclesiology to his far more principled theology.

When it came to his theology, as we have previously observed in chapter 2, Whitefield held his Calvinistic convictions tightly. As an ordained priest in the Church of England, he regularly appealed to the Thirty-Nine Articles to defend and commend this theological stream within the evangelical family. After reading Jonathan Warne's *The Church of England Turn'd Dissenter at Last* while crossing the Atlantic in 1739, he became convinced that "the Reformed faith was the true position of the Church of England

---

29 Lambert, *Pedlar in Divinity*, 126.
30 Lambert, *Pedlar in Divinity*, 80–81.
31 Kidd, *George Whitefield*, 260.
32 Noll, *The Rise of Evangelicalism*, 153.

expressed in her articles and Homilies."[33] Throughout his ministry, he was adept at establishing and nurturing ministry connections with theologically like-minded evangelicals across the transatlantic world. Indeed, "the critical importance of George Whitefield for the early history of evangelicalism is suggested by the fact that he was the only major figure as completely at home" in a "Calvinist internationale" that comprised Welsh Anglicans like William Williams, Scottish Presbyterians like Ralph and Ebenezer Erskine, and New England Congregationalists like Jonathan Edwards as he was "among the Church of England revivalists."[34]

By comparison, Whitefield's approach toward ecclesiology was decidedly more pragmatic. He viewed ecclesiastical governance structures primarily as means to evangelistic and disciple-making ends and evaluated their usefulness accordingly. Lamenting the way "Christ's seamless coat should be rent in pieces on account of things in themselves purely indifferent," Whitefield left to future evangelicals a laudable emphasis on matters of first importance, but often in a way that rendered ecclesiological convictions a matter of very little importance—other than as a help or hindrance to evangelism.[35] While he never disinherited his Church of England affiliation, he nonetheless often declared that "a catholic spirit is best."[36] In practice, this meant presenting himself first and foremost as an interdenominational evangelist, embodying in his person and wide-ranging relationships the early evangelical movement's character as a geographically, theologically, and denominationally diverse unity—an ecclesial coalition comprising a tradition of traditions.

These ecumenical intuitions began to solidify around the same time he committed himself to itinerant field preaching. As a budding ecclesiological role model for evangelicals to come, Whitefield had role models of his own, and none more influential than Howell Harris. The Welshman's evangelical ecumenicity, and not just his pioneering itinerant ministry, left a profound impact on the impressionable Whitefield. Reflecting on Harris's ministry in March 1739, Whitefield commented, "He is of a most catholic spirit." Aspiring to follow not just in his itinerant but also his interdenominational footsteps, Whitefield approvingly observed how, in Harris's ministry, "the partition wall of bigotry and party-zeal is broken

---

[33] Mark K. Olson, "Whitefield's Conversion and Early Theological Formation," in Hammond and Jones, *George Whitefield*, 43.
[34] Noll, *The Rise of Evangelicalism*, 128.
[35] *Journals*, 138.
[36] *Journals*, 458.

down, and ministers and teachers of different communions, join with one heart and one mind to carry on the Kingdom of Jesus Christ." He continued, "The Lord make all the Christian world thus minded!"[37] It would not be long before Whitefield had the opportunity to personally enact something of the catholicity he had admired in Harris's ministry. On April 18, 1739, he wrote: "Almost every day persons of all denominations come unto me, telling how they intercede in my behalf. And it shall now be my particular business, wherever I go, to bring all the children of God, notwithstanding their [denominational] differences, to rejoice together."[38]

Having begun to enact this panevangelical vision at home, he turned his thoughts to America's Eastern Seaboard and its untapped opportunities for his growing ministry brand. As he settled on an itinerary for his upcoming preaching tour, Philadelphia, with "its policy of religious toleration" and "heterogeneous population," was a propitious first port-of-call for Whitefield to introduce himself to the colonies.[39] Evangelical theological "soundness," rather than "denominational adherence," was his functional criterion for entering into ministry partnerships.[40] Less than a month into his precedent-establishing tour, he rejoiced with a theologically like-minded Presbyterian minister at how the evangelical doctrinal unity they shared overcame whatever denominational differences threatened to keep them apart: "Blessed be God that His love is so far shed abroad in our hearts as to cause us to love one another, though we a little differ as to externals. For my part, I hate to mention them. My one sole question is, *Are you a Christian*."[41]

At every opportunity, Whitefield cast himself as an interdenominational evangelical, refusing to be "pre-empted by local concerns and interests, whether Presbyterian, Methodist, Baptist or New World Separatist."[42] He regularly downplayed his Anglican credentials, yet without ever completely jettisoning them. For example, he distanced himself from Boston's Dr. Cutler, who took "it for granted that the Church of England was the only true apostolical Church." By contrast, Whitefield wore his Anglican affiliation lightly, advocating an evangelical-flavored ecumenism on the basis

---

[37] *Journals*, 230.
[38] *Journals*, 253.
[39] Harry S. Stout, *The Divine Dramatist: George Whitefield and the Rise of Modern Evangelicalism* (Grand Rapids, MI: Eerdmans, 1991), 89.
[40] Arnold A. Dallimore, *George Whitefield: The Life and Times of the Great Evangelist of the Eighteenth-Century Revival*, 2 vols. (London: Banner of Truth, 1970, 1980), 1:438.
[41] Whitefield to Mr. P—, November 28, 1739, in *Letters*, 126 (italics in the original).
[42] Stout, *The Divine Dramatist*, 139.

that, in his experience, no one denomination had a monopoly on the new birth. He contended, "I saw regenerate souls among the Baptists, among the Presbyterians, among the Independents, and among the Church folks,—all children of God and yet all born again in a different way of worship," before metaphorically tossing his ecclesiological hands in the air and concluding, "Who can tell which is the most evangelical?"[43]

Whether one was an admirer or a detractor of the breadth of White-field's ministry, it was impossible to ignore the way he "rejected captivity to any single denomination."[44] He faced criticism for his ecumenism on diverse fronts. For example, the *South Carolina Gazette* made much of his intentional catholicity, but interpreted it as part of a cynical project to exploit his audiences financially. The June 18, 1741, edition pejoratively cast Whitefield as "a staunch Churchman in Old England! A thorough Independent in new England! An Anabaptist among Anabaptists! A true-blue Kirkman in Scotland! And a Quaker among Quakers! Becoming all things to all men, not that he might gain some, but make some gain of all!"[45]

At the same time as the motivations for his catholicity were being slandered in the American South, Whitefield's promising ministry alliance with Scottish Presbyterians Ralph and Ebenezer Erskine was rapidly foundering because of his unwillingness to renounce his Church of England ordination, align himself exclusively with the Scottish Seceders, and forgo preaching in all but Associate Presbytery pulpits. Quickly recognizing that acceding to their demand threatened to drastically curtail the scope and very essence of his interdenominational ministry, Whitefield pleaded for ecclesiological forbearance in the interests of a higher evangelistic good. "I come only as an occasional preacher, to preach the simple gospel to all that are willing to hear me, of whatever denomination," he wrote to Ebenezer Erskine. Despite the strong Calvinistic alignment he shared with the Erskines, he contended, "It will be wrong in me to join in a reformation as to church government, any further than I have light given me from above."[46]

While his relationship with the Erskines survived the encounter bruised but intact, an irreparable breach emerged between Whitefield and the larger Associate Presbytery. He openly admitted that he had not given any consideration to the intricacies, let alone the worthiness, of the

---

[43] *Journals*, 458.
[44] Timothy D. Hall, *Contested Boundaries: Itinerancy and the Reshaping of the Colonial American Religious World* (Durham, NC: Duke University Press, 1994), 78.
[45] Quoted in Lambert, *Pedlar in Divinity*, 21.
[46] Whitefield to Mr. E— E—, May 16, 1741, in *Letters*, 262.

Scottish Seceder's cause on the grounds that he had "been too busy about matters . . . of greater importance."[47] Unsurprisingly, it appears some Scots interpreted this cavalier dismissal of their cherished distinctives as evidence of ecclesiological heresy. In fact, the following year, an incendiary essay appeared, entitled *A Warning against Countenancing the Ministrations of Mr. George Whitefield*, in which the author, Edinburgh minister Adam Gib, felt so provoked as to label him "one of those false Christs, of whom the Church is forewarned."[48]

Whitefield was taken aback by the vitriolic tone of Gib's lengthy denunciation, describing it as "the most virulent pamphlet I ever saw."[49] Lamenting being on the receiving end of (un)friendly fire from a fellow Calvinist, he never wavered in his commitment to advancing the evangelical cause across sectarian and provincial boundaries. If anything, efforts to limit the scope of his ministry only seemed to strengthen his resolve to maintain an interdenominational course that would leave a lasting impression on the evangelical movement. At a meeting with the Associate Presbytery in Edinburgh in August 1741—one that quickly seems to have taken on the flavor of an ecclesiastical trial—Whitefield doubled down on his panevangelical sensibilities, defiantly declaring, presumably to the horror of many of the staunch Scottish separatists in attendance, "If the Pope himself would lend me his pulpit, I would gladly proclaim the righteousness of Jesus Christ therein."[50]

Almost three decades later, as Whitefield prepared to embark on his seventh and final preaching tour of the American colonies, his evangelical ecumenism had not diminished in the slightest. In a parting sermon delivered on August 30, 1769—the last he would ever deliver in England—Whitefield reaffirmed the evangelical catholicity that had been a consistent feature of his ministry. Preaching from his chosen text, John 10:27–28, he observed:

> It is very remarkable, there are but two sorts of people. Christ does not say, Are you an Independent, or Baptist, or Presbyterian? Or are you a Church of England-man? Nor did he ask, Are you a Methodist? All these things are of our own silly invention. But the whole world the Lord divides into two classes of people, sheep and goats.[51]

---

47 Whitefield to Mr. Thomas N—, August 8, 1741, in *Letters*, 307.
48 Adam Gib, *A Warning against Countenancing the Ministrations of Mr. George Whitefield* (Edinburgh: David Duncan, 1742), iv.
49 Whitefield to Mr. D— A—, July 31, 1742, in *Letters*, 413.
50 Whitefield to Mr. Thomas N—, August 8, 1741, in *Letters*, 308.
51 George Whitefield, *A Sermon by the Reverend Mr. George Whitefield Being His Last Farewell to His Friends* (London: S. Bladon, 1769), 11.

The location of the sermon, London's Moorfields, affords an insight into a further dimension to Whitefield's evangelical ecumenicity: not simply the interdenominational nature of his ministry but its trans-denominational qualities. In practice, Whitefield was willing to bypass denominational structures altogether and appeal directly to individuals in the extra-ecclesial setting of massed outdoor gatherings—or, in this in-stance, his standing-room-only tabernacle, which, despite its considerable size, left many hoping to catch a glimpse of the famous itinerant on that late summer morning "disappointed on account of the place being filled so soon."[52]

Parachurch Minister and Celebrity Preacher

Indeed, throughout his ministry, Whitefield personally helped establish and cultivate two of evangelicalism's signature characteristics: a fond-ness for parachurch ministries and celebrity preachers. Before his inno-vative ministry, "aspiring religious leaders and reformers could think of nothing grander than reviving their own denominations and convinc-ing those in other denominations of the errors of their ways," suggests Stout. By contrast, "only Whitefield thought to transcend denomina-tional lines entirely and, in effect, ply a religious trade in the open air of the marketplace." In this way, Whitefield was not only energetic in establishing interdenominational connections with theological kindred spirits from a range of Protestant backgrounds; he was also instrumen-tal in pioneering the creation of a transdenominational "transatlantic parachurch" community.[53]

While his ecclesial innovation was celebrated by admirers who saw in Whitefield's ministry a return to apostolical times,[54] others viewed him as a self-promoting ecclesial law unto himself. For example, Adam Gib cen-sured Whitefield for engaging in a parachurch ministry that, to all intents, lacked any external accountability. He took exception to the way Whitefield went "through the World preaching, as some *notable* Person, or as a general *Quickener of Ministers* and People, while standing co-ordinate with none of them." Gib suspected that when the dust settled on Whitefield's preaching events that had set the world "a wondering after him," little would be left

52 Whitefield, *Last Farewell*, iv.
53 Stout, *The Divine Dramatist*, xviii, 205.
54 See Ian J. Maddock, "'Like One of the Old Apostles': The Acts of the Apostles and George Whitefield's Criteria for Describing Preaching Events," *Colloquium* 49, no. 2 (2017): 55–65.

"but a Throng of Individuals, unconnected with, and independent upon one another."[55]

Gib also charged him with being motivated by self-aggrandizement, contending that "the general scope of his *Journals* is to publish and celebrate himself."[56] Gib was neither the first nor the last to level accusations of this sort. Whitefield appears to have had an ambiguous attitude toward the fame that attended his ministry. On the one hand, he habitually espoused a self-effacing humility and overwhelming sense of his unworthiness that, at face value, was utterly sincere; quite possibly the last letter he wrote was signed, "Less than the least of all, George Whitefield."[57] On the other hand, "few great people," suggests Stout, "achieve fame without aspiring to it, and Whitefield was no exception."[58] Whether he actively sought out fame or it found him, the level of stardom he attained throughout his ministry prefigured evangelicalism's habit of elevating and feting superstar ministers and evangelists. For all their differences, D. L. Moody and Billy Graham—not to mention the plethora of modern-day platformed evangelical influencers—could trace their ministry lineage back to Whitefield as the original transdenominational parachurch celebrity.

Accidental Revolutionary—and Abolitionist

For someone who crammed so much life into relatively few years, it is not surprising that Whitefield left a wide-ranging legacy. While much of our focus has been on his impact on subsequent generations of evangelicals, Whitefield also left an imprint on the American political landscape. As "the first international celebrity," he was probably the most well-known and beloved "George" in the American colonies at the time of his death in 1770—decidedly more acclaimed, at that point, than even the thirty-eight-year-old former British Army colonel, and soon-to-be general of the American Continental Army, George Washington.[59]

As a unifying figure in the increasingly prorepublican American consciousness, Whitefield would be remembered as revolutionary in ways he may not have fully anticipated during his lifetime. Having spent three

---

55 Gib, *Warning*, 6, 31 (italics in the original).
56 Gib, *Warning*, v.
57 Whitefield to Mr. R— K—, September 23, 1770, in *Works*, 3:427.
58 Stout, *The Divine Dramatist*, xxi.
59 Jerome Mahaffey, *The Accidental Revolutionary: George Whitefield and the Creation of America* (Waco, TX: Baylor University Press, 2011), x.

decades sowing seeds of individual liberty in the spiritual realm—a liberty that, as we have observed, transcended and bypassed previously inviolable ecclesial authority structures—Whitefield arguably helped foster an appetite among Americans for liberty in the political realm. As an "accidental revolutionary," he "may have been reluctant to join a revolution," but "his ideas converted the colonies into a unified America from the diverse ethnic and religious-based communities all over the eastern seaboard."[60] Whether or not he intended for his gospel of spiritual freedom to translate into a quest for political freedom, much less revolution, he unwittingly helped establish the preconditions for American independence, contributing "as much to America's birth on the political front as many other . . . founders."[61]

Whitefield was undoubtedly sympathetic toward the colonists' plight. Just one week before his death, and with the Boston Massacre earlier that year still fresh in people's minds, he wrote on September 23, 1770: "Poor New-England is much to be pitied; Boston people most of all. How falsely misrepresented! What a mercy, that our Christian charter cannot be dissolved!"[62] This commiseration notwithstanding, it is difficult to discern whether Whitefield would have supported their quest for full-blown independence. John Wesley, who did live long enough to see the outbreak of armed hostilities, left no doubts as to where he stood, interpreting the colonists' quest for independence as nothing short of treason. While it is hard to imagine Whitefield straightforwardly echoing Wesley's politics, it is equally difficult to imagine him—as a loyal subject of the crown—rejoicing at the loss of such a substantial portion of the British Empire. It is also hard to imagine Whitefield allowing himself to be distracted from his core business of gospel proclamation, let alone becoming entangled in contentious political wrangling that would likely alienate a portion of his geographically and politically diverse audience.

In addition to casting Whitefield as an "accidental revolutionary," some have even suggested—surprisingly at first glance, given his status as a slave master—that Whitefield was also an "accidental abolitionist."[63] While acknowledging that he never came even remotely close to advocating abolition during his lifetime, those who argue for this facet of his legacy point

---

[60] Mahaffey, *Accidental Revolutionary*, xi, 189.
[61] Mahaffey, *Accidental Revolutionary*, 189.
[62] Whitefield to Mr. R— K—, September 23, 1770, in *Works*, 3:426.
[63] Jessica M. Parr, *Inventing George Whitefield: Race, Revivalism, and the Making of a Religious Icon* (Jackson: University Press of Mississippi, 2015), 154.

to the way Whitefield nonetheless "unwittingly helped to inspire several black evangelicals who, in turn, used his preaching to refute scriptural arguments for slavery." Undeniably and, indeed, "somewhat ironically, given Whitefield's proslavery sentiments in the last decades of his life, his preaching struck a chord with Black Americans."[64] While Phillis Wheatley's elegy stands out as one of the most famous celebrations of Whitefield's ministry by a Black slave, his legacy includes several individuals, either converted under his preaching or otherwise impacted by his ministry, who would go on to shape early Black evangelicalism.

One notable example was John Marrant, a Black man born free in 1755 who subsequently experienced the new birth in early 1770. After attending a revival gathering with the express intention of disrupting Whitefield's sermon, he instead departed having been converted. In a bestselling autobiography that went through fifteen editions in England, he recounted the way Whitefield declared to him, "Jesus Christ has got thee at last."[65] Marrant followed in Whitefield's footsteps as an evangelist, preaching especially to Black and Native Americans. He was also a prominent abolitionist voice. Alluding to Deuteronomy 32 and Revelation 7, he eagerly anticipated "black nations" becoming "white in the blood of the Lamb," together with "vast multitudes of hard tongues, and of strange speech," learning "the language of Canaan" and singing "the songs of Moses."[66] Crucially, the gospel of spiritual liberation that Marrant proclaimed was accompanied by calls for abolition absent in Whitefield's preaching.

Another African impacted by Whitefield's ministry was the former slave Olaudah Equiano. While not converted until 1774, he had heard Whitefield preach some years earlier. In Equiano's narrative, he recalled being struck not only by the content of the itinerant's sermon—the gospel would come to "underscore Equiano's abolitionist convictions"—but also by the energy with which he preached and the size of the crowd that had gathered.[67] Whitefield's reputation preceded him: Equiano wrote that he "had often heard of this gentleman, and wished to see and hear him" but had "never before had an opportunity." The "fervour and earnestness" with which Whitefield delivered his sermon, "sweating as much as I [Equiano] ever did while in slavery on Montserrat beach," left a lasting impression.

---

[64] Parr, *Inventing George Whitefield*, 148.
[65] John Marrant, *A Narrative of the Lord's Wonderful Dealing with John Marrant, a Black*, 6th ed. (London: Gilbert & Plummer, 1788), 10–11.
[66] Marrant, *A Narrative*, 39.
[67] Parr, *Inventing George Whitefield*, 148.

"I thought it strange I had never seen divines exert themselves in this manner before," he marveled.[68]

Equiano, in turn, would go on to encourage other prominent Black abolitionists, including the former Ghanaian slave Quobna Ottobah Cugoano. Like Equiano and Marrant before him, Cugoano published gospel-motivated abolitionist works. These included his 1787 *Thoughts and Sentiments on the Evil and Wicked Traffic of Slavery and Commerce of the Human Species* and, later that same year, an autobiographical narrative in which he recounted his deliverance from slavery in Grenada. Once a free man, Cugoano devoted himself to the cause of abolition, arguing that slavery is "contrary to all the genuine principles of Christianity."[69] Going further than Whitefield and challenging the very institution of slavery itself, Cugoano went on, "Can the slave-holders think that the Universal Father and Sovereign of Mankind will be pleased with them, for the brutal transgression of his law, in bowing down the necks of those to the yoke of their cruel bondage?"[70]

Collectively, examples like these point to the considerable impact Whitefield had on Black Christianity in America. This extended beyond the personal role he played in the conversion of many in the slave community and entailed his unwitting role in shaping those who would actively promote the cause of abolition in succeeding generations.

Preacher of the New Birth

For all their variety, these aspects of Whitefield's legacy have a common denominator: his vocation as a preacher of the new birth. He was, returning to John Greenleaf Whittier's poetic description,

> Called in his youth to sound and gauge
> The moral lapse of his race and age, . . .
> Up and down the world he went,
> A John the Baptist crying, Repent![71]

And yet as much as Whitefield sought to "preach up poverty of spirit, for that is the only foundation whereon to build solid abiding comfort," he

---

[68] Vincent Carretta, ed., *Olaudah Equiano, "The Interesting Narrative" and Other Writings* (New York: Penguin, 2003), 132.

[69] Vincent Carretta, ed., *Quobna Ottobah Cugoano: "Thoughts and Sentiments on the Evil of Slavery," and Other Writings* (New York: Penguin, 1999), 24.

[70] Carretta, *Cugoano*, 24.

[71] Whittier, *Poetical Works*, 71.

was much more than simply a preacher of God's law.[72] His reputation was founded on proclaiming the necessity of conversion, brought about through spiritual new birth: "a thorough, real, inward change of nature, wrought in us by the powerful operations of the Holy Ghost."[73] The purpose of this regeneration is relational in both a vertical and horizontal sense: it is a new birth to enjoy God. As a gift from above, regeneration results not simply in freedom from sin but also in freedom to enjoy a restored and renewed relationship with God.

Whereas the doctrine of the new birth was "much neglected and denied"[74] within his Anglican denomination in the 1730s—"seldom preached . . . hardly understood, and rarely felt"[75]—Whitefield's ministry established a precedent: henceforth, the personal experience of the new birth became a shibboleth of orthodoxy and authenticity among future generations of evangelicals. Indeed, Whitefield and the new birth were virtually synonymous: "The hard and basic core of the Whitefield personality was the fact that he had experienced the new birth."[76]

Not only did Whitefield experience what he preached, but he practiced it too. Those who knew him well testified to the way his Christian character complemented his unrivaled ability as a preacher. Unsurprisingly, however, given the jealousies and indignation that his ministry often aroused, Whitefield faced no shortage of detractors hoping to smear his name and, by association, the gospel that he preached. But in contrast to the scandals, moral failures, and glaring hypocrisy that have so often been the undoing of high-profile evangelical celebrities in years to come, Whitefield "remained undistracted by the allure of sex or wealth" and was arguably "his own finest convert to the Christian lifestyle he proclaimed."[77] Fending off the postmortem insinuation that Whitefield was less than upright in his financial dealings, longstanding ally Benjamin Franklin responded, "I knew him intimately upwards of 30 years: his integrity, disinterestedness, and indefatigable zeal in prosecuting every good work, I have never seen equalled, I shall never see excelled."[78]

---

[72] Whitefield to Mr. J— H—, June 25, 1740, in *Letters*, 190.
[73] Whitefield, "The Benefits of an Early Piety," in *Works*, 5:161.
[74] Dallimore, *George Whitefield*, 2:533.
[75] Luke Tyerman, *The Life of the Rev. George Whitefield*, 2 vols. (London: Hodder and Stoughton, 1876–1877), 1:79.
[76] Stuart Henry, *George Whitefield: Wayfaring Witness* (Nashville: Abingdon, 1957), 179.
[77] Stout, *The Divine Dramatist*, xxiv.
[78] William B. Willcox, ed., *The Papers of Benjamin Franklin: January 1 through December 31, 1771*, vol. 18 (New Haven, CT: Yale University Press, 1974), 53.

And yet, if Whitefield's integrity has been a resilient facet of his legacy, then all the more his preaching by which he became "a bona-fide
sensation."[79] Not only was he "the most influential Anglo-American
evangelical leader of the eighteenth century"; he was "perhaps the greatest evangelical preacher the world has ever seen."[80] Indeed, there was an
awareness in the immediate wake of his death that Whitefield's ministry was unique. On November 11, 1770, the evangelical abolitionist John
Newton delivered a funeral sermon at Olney that attempted to encapsulate Whitefield's hyperbole-inducing ministry. He stated, "I have had
some opportunities of looking over the History of the Church in past ages,
and I am not backward to say, that I have not read or heard of any person
since the Apostle's days, of whom it may more emphatically be said, he
was a burning and shining light, than the late Mr. Whitefield." Most of
all, Newton drew mourners' attention to Whitefield's preaching with all
its dramatic, extemporaneous, evangelistic, and itinerant qualities: "The
Lord gave him a manner of preaching, which was peculiarly his own. He
copied from none, and I never met anyone who could imitate him with
success." While "other ministers could, perhaps, preach the Gospel as
clearly, and in general say the same things . . . no man living could say
them in his way. Here I always thought him unequalled, and I hardly expect to see his equal while I live."[81]

By the nineteenth and twentieth centuries, Whitefield's legacy as a
preacher had lost none of its luster. Admitting a sense of palpable inad-
equacy when he compared himself with Whitefield, no less than Charles
Haddon Spurgeon held him in the highest esteem:

> Often I have read his life, I am conscious of distinct quickening whenever
> I turn to it. He lived. Other men seem to be only half alive; but Whitefield
> was all life, fire, wing, force. My own model, if I may have such a thing
> in due subordination to my Lord, is George Whitefield; but with unequal
> footsteps must I follow in his glorious track.[82]

Indeed, in J. I. Packer's assessment, only Spurgeon "ever came close" to
Whitefield, who "was and remains in a class by himself among British
evangelists." Packer continued, "Both were pastoral Calvinists of genius,

---

79 Noll, *The Rise of Evangelicalism*, 102.
80 Kidd, *George Whitefield*, 263.
81 *Memoirs*, 342, 344–46.
82 Dallimore, *George Whitefield*, 2:534.

marked by tremendous inner intensity, vividness of imagination, freshness of vision and sublimity of rhetoric. . . . Spurgeon neither roared nor soared in the pulpit as Whitefield did. As a preacher, Whitefield was supreme."[83]

But perhaps the most poignant testimony, especially since their relationship was as complex as it was enduring, came from none other than Whitefield's fellow Methodist pioneer John Wesley. In the memorial sermon he delivered at Whitefield's Tottenham Court Road Chapel on November 18, 1770, Wesley asked rhetorically:

> Have we ever read or heard of any person since the apostles, who testified the gospel of the grace of God through so widely extended a space, through so large a part of the habitable world? Have we read or heard of any person, who called so many thousands, so many myriads of sinners to repentance? Above all, have we read or heard of any, who has been a blessed instrument in his hand of bringing so many sinners, "from darkness to light, and from the power of Satan unto God"?[84]

In Wesley's estimation, the answer was self-evident: as a preacher of the new birth, no one compared to George Whitefield.

Whitefield's profound delight in God motivated his passionate proclamation of the gospel. He longed for others to enjoy God too, urging his listeners to reject the "almost Christian" lifestyle and instead come to know the liberating truths that had so transformed his own life. All told, his experience of the new birth was central to both his theology and his preaching. Indeed, it was central to his Christian life.

---

[83] J. I. Packer, "Great George," Christianity Today 30, no. 13 (1986): 12.

[84] John Wesley, "On the Death of George Whitefield," in The Works of John Wesley: Bicentennial Edition, vols. 1–4, Sermons, ed. Albert C. Outler (Nashville: Abingdon, 1984–1987), 2:340–41.

A TIMELINE OF GEORGE WHITEFIELD'S LIFE

1714	Is born in Gloucester, England, December 16
1732	Enrolls at Pembroke College, Oxford University
1733–1734	Meets the Wesleys and becomes part of the Oxford Methodists, late fall or early spring
1735	Is converted at age twenty, spring
1736	Is ordained as a deacon in the Church of England, June 20; preaches his first sermon, on the importance of religious societies, in his home church in Gloucester, June 27
1737	Third edition of his signature sermon on the new birth, "On Regeneration," published; preaches for the first time without notes
1738	First visit to America
1739	Is ordained a priest in the Church of England, January 14; begins open-air preaching, February 17; sees tensions develop with John Wesley, who attacks Calvinism in his initial preaching on "Free Grace"
1739–1741	Second visit to America
1741	Marries Elizabeth James, November 14
1744	Buries his four-month-old son, John, February 8
1744–1748	Third visit to America

1745	Discontinues keeping his journal
1751–1752	Fourth visit to America
1754–1755	Fifth visit to America
1756	Revises his *Journals*, deleting sections regarding the felt presence of the Holy Spirit and other controversial themes
1763–1765	Sixth visit to America
1768	Death of Elizabeth, his wife, August 9
1769	Departs for seventh and final visit to America
1770	Preaches his final sermon, September 29; dies, September 30 (age fifty-five); is buried in Newburyport, Massachusetts, in the church he was instrumental in founding*

---

*For the most extensive timeline, see Stuart C. Henry, *George Whitefield: Wayfaring Witness* (Nashville: Abingdon, 1957), 200–210.

GENERAL INDEX

SCRIPTURE INDEX

WISDOM FROM THE PAST FOR LIFE IN THE PRESENT

Theologians on the Christian Life

AUGUSTINE by GERALD BRAY

BAVINCK by JOHN BOLT

BONHOEFFER by STEPHEN J. NICHOLS

CALVIN by MICHAEL HORTON

EDWARDS by DANE C. ORTLUND

GRIMKÉ by ANDREW J. MARTIN

LEWIS by JOE RIGNEY

LLOYD-JONES by JASON MEYER

LUTHER by CARL R. TRUEMAN

NEWTON by TONY REINKE

OWEN by MATTHEW BARRETT & MICHAEL A. G. HAYKIN

PACKER by SAM STORMS

RYLE by ANDREW ATHERSTONE

SCHAEFFER by WILLIAM EDGAR

SPURGEON by MICHAEL REEVES

STOTT by TIM CHESTER

WARFIELD by FRED G. ZASPEL

WESLEY by FRED SANDERS

WHITEFIELD by TOM SCHWANDA & IAN MADDOCK

The Theologians on the Christian Life series provides accessible introductions to the great teachers on the Christian life, exploring their personal lives and writings, especially as they pertain to the walk of faith.

For more information, visit **crossway.org.**